# Go Cookbook

Build modular, readable, and testable applications in Go

**Aaron Torres**

BIRMINGHAM - MUMBAI

# Go Cookbook

Copyright © 2017 Packt Publishing

All rights reserved. No part of this book may be reproduced, stored in a retrieval system, or transmitted in any form or by any means, without the prior written permission of the publisher, except in the case of brief quotations embedded in critical articles or reviews.

Every effort has been made in the preparation of this book to ensure the accuracy of the information presented. However, the information contained in this book is sold without warranty, either express or implied. Neither the author, nor Packt Publishing, and its dealers and distributors will be held liable for any damages caused or alleged to be caused directly or indirectly by this book.

Packt Publishing has endeavored to provide trademark information about all of the companies and products mentioned in this book by the appropriate use of capitals. However, Packt Publishing cannot guarantee the accuracy of this information.

First published: June 2017

Production reference: 1240617

Published by Packt Publishing Ltd.
Livery Place
35 Livery Street
Birmingham
B3 2PB, UK.

ISBN 978-1-78328-683-6

www.packtpub.com

# Credits

**Author**
Aaron Torres

**Reviewer**
Julien Da Silva

**Commissioning Editor**
Kunal Parikh

**Acquisition Editor**
Karan Sadawana

**Content Development Editor**
Rohit Kumar Singh

**Technical Editor**
Vivek Pala

**Copy Editor**
Pranjali Chury

**Project Coordinator**
Vaidehi Sawant

**Proofreader**
Safis Editing

**Indexer**
Tejal Daruwale Soni

**Graphics**
Jason Monteiro

**Production Coordinator**
Nilesh Mohite

# About the Author

**Aaron Torres** received his master's of science degree in computer science from New Mexico Institute of Mining and Technology. He has worked on distributed systems in high performance computing and in large-scale web and microservices applications. He currently leads a team of Go developers that refines and focuses on Go best practices with an emphasis on continuous delivery and automated testing.

Aaron has published a number of papers and has several patents in the area of storage and I/O. He is passionate about sharing his knowledge and ideas with others. He is also a huge fan of the Go language and open source for backend systems and development.

# About the Reviewer

**Julien Da Silva** is a software engineer and architect specializing in scalable, distributed systems. Previously at Hailo, he was a part of the team that built its Golang platform, which is widely recognized as one of the early successful implementations of microservices. Hailo was later acquired by MyTaxi in 2016. He is currently working as a core architect at LastMileLink, part of CitySprint group, UK leader in same day courier services.

# www.PacktPub.com

For support files and downloads related to your book, please visit www.PacktPub.com.

Did you know that Packt offers eBook versions of every book published, with PDF and ePub files available? You can upgrade to the eBook version at www.PacktPub.com and as a print book customer, you are entitled to a discount on the eBook copy. Get in touch with us at service@packtpub.com for more details.

At www.PacktPub.com, you can also read a collection of free technical articles, sign up for a range of free newsletters and receive exclusive discounts and offers on Packt books and eBooks.

https://www.packtpub.com/mapt

Get the most in-demand software skills with Mapt. Mapt gives you full access to all Packt books and video courses, as well as industry-leading tools to help you plan your personal development and advance your career.

## Why subscribe?

- Fully searchable across every book published by Packt
- Copy and paste, print, and bookmark content
- On demand and accessible via a web browser

# Customer Feedback

Thanks for purchasing this Packt book. At Packt, quality is at the heart of our editorial process. To help us improve, please leave us an honest review on this book's Amazon page at `https://www.amazon.com/Go-Cookbook-Aaron-Torres-ebook/dp/B01MS2MOFP/ref=sr_1_16?ie=UTF8&qid=1497940919&sr=8-16&keywords=go+cookbook`.

If you'd like to join our team of regular reviewers, you can e-mail us at `customerreviews@packtpub.com`. We award our regular reviewers with free eBooks and videos in exchange for their valuable feedback. Help us be relentless in improving our products!

# Table of Contents

# Preface

Thank you for choosing this book! I hope it will be a handy reference for developers to quickly look up Go development patterns. It is meant to be a companion to other resources and a reference that will hopefully be useful long after reading it once. Each recipe in this book includes working, simple, and tested code that can be used as a reference or foundation for your own applications. The book covers a range of content from basic to advanced topics.

# What this book covers

Chapter 1, *I/O and File Systems*, covers common Go I/O interfaces and explores working with filesystems. This includes temporary files, templates, and CSV files.

Chapter 2, *Command-Line Tools*, looks at taking in user input via a command line and explores processing common datatypes such as TOML, YAML, and JSON.

Chapter 3, *Data Conversion and Composition*, demonstrates methods for casting and converting between Go interfaces and data types. It also showcases encoding strategies and some functional design patterns for Go.

Chapter 4, *Error Handling in Go*, showcases strategies to handle errors in Go. It explores how to pass errors, handle them, and log them.

Chapter 5, *All about Databases and Storage*, deals with various storage libraries for accessing data storage systems such as MySQL. It also demonstrates the use of interfaces to decouple your library from your application logic.

Chapter 6, *Web Clients and APIs*, implements Go HTTP client interfaces, REST clients, OAuth2 clients, decorating and extending clients, and GRPC.

Chapter 7, *Microservices for Applications in Go*, explores web handlers, passing in a state to a handler, validation of user input, and middleware.

Chapter 8, *Testing*, focuses on mocking, test coverage, fuzzing, behavior testing, and helpful testing tools.

Chapter 9, *Parallelism and Concurrency*, provides a reference for channels and async operations, atomic values, Go context objects, and channel state management.

Chapter 10, *Distributed Systems*, implements service discovery, Docker containerization, metrics and monitoring, and orchestration. It mostly deals with deployment and productionisation of Go applications.

Chapter 11, *Reactive Programming and Data Streams*, explores reactive and dataflow applications, Kafka and distributed message queues, and GraphQL servers.

Chapter 12, *Serverless Programming*, deals with deploying Go applications without maintaining a server. This includes using Google App Engine, Firebase, Lambda, and logging in these serverless environment.

Chapter 13, *Performance Improvements, Tips, and Tricks*, is the final chapter and deals with benchmarking, identifying bottlenecks, optimizing, and improving the HTTP performance for Go applications.

# What you need for this book

To use this book, you'll need the following:

- A Unix programming environment
- The latest version of the Go 1.x series
- An Internet connection
- Permission to install additional packages as described in each chapter

# Who this book is for

JIRA 7 Cookbook is intended for administrators that will be customizing, supporting and maintaining JIRA for their organizations. You will need to be familiar and have a good understanding of JIRA's core concepts. For some recipes, basic understanding in HTML, CSS, JavaScript, and basic programming knowledge will also be helpful.

# Sections

In this book, you will find several headings that appear frequently (Getting ready, How to do it..., How it works..., There's more..., and See also). To give clear instructions on how to complete a recipe, we use these sections as follows:

# Getting ready

This section tells you what to expect in the recipe, and describes how to set up any software or any preliminary settings required for the recipe.

# How to do it…

This section contains the steps required to follow the recipe.

# How it works…

This section usually consists of a detailed explanation of what happened in the previous section.

# There's more…

This section consists of additional information about the recipe in order to make the reader more knowledgeable about the recipe.

# See also

This section provides helpful links to other useful information for the recipe.

# Conventions

In this book, you will find a number of text styles that distinguish between different kinds of information. Here are some examples of these styles and an explanation of their meaning. Code words in text, database table names, folder names, filenames, file extensions, pathnames, dummy URLs, user input, and Twitter handles are shown as follows: "The Copy() function copies between interfaces and treats them like streams."

A block of code is set as follows:

```
package main
import "github.com/agtorre/go-cookbook/chapter1/tempfiles"
func main() {
        if err := tempfiles.WorkWithTemp(); err != nil {
                panic(err)
        }
}
```

Any command-line input or output is written as follows:

```
$ go run main.go
/var/folders/kd/ygq5l_0d1xq1lzk_c7htft900000gn/T
/tmp764135258/tmp588787953
```

**New terms** and **important words** are shown in bold.

Warnings or important notes appear in a box like this.

Tips and tricks appear like this.

# Reader feedback

Feedback from our readers is always welcome. Let us know what you think about this book-what you liked or disliked. Reader feedback is important for us as it helps us develop titles that you will really get the most out of. To send us general feedback, simply e-mail feedback@packtpub.com, and mention the book's title in the subject of your message. If there is a topic that you have expertise in and you are interested in either writing or contributing to a book, see our author guide at www.packtpub.com/authors .

# Customer support

Now that you are the proud owner of a Packt book, we have a number of things to help you to get the most from your purchase.

# Downloading the example code

You can download the example code files for this book from your account at http://www.packtpub.com. If you purchased this book elsewhere, you can visit http://www.packtpub.com/support and register to have the files e-mailed directly to you. You can download the code files by following these steps:

1. Log in or register to our website using your e-mail address and password.
2. Hover the mouse pointer on the **SUPPORT** tab at the top.

3. Click on **Code Downloads & Errata**.
4. Enter the name of the book in the **Search** box.
5. Select the book for which you're looking to download the code files.
6. Choose from the drop-down menu where you purchased this book from.
7. Click on **Code Download**.

You can also download the code files by clicking on the **Code Files** button on the book's webpage at the Packt Publishing website. This page can be accessed by entering the book's name in the **Search** box. Please note that you need to be logged in to your Packt account. Once the file is downloaded, please make sure that you unzip or extract the folder using the latest version of:

- WinRAR / 7-Zip for Windows
- Zipeg / iZip / UnRarX for Mac
- 7-Zip / PeaZip for Linux

The code bundle for the book is also hosted on GitHub at `https://github.com/PacktPubl ishing/Go-Cookbook`. We also have other code bundles from our rich catalog of books and videos available at `https://github.com/PacktPublishing/`. Check them out!

# Errata

Although we have taken every care to ensure the accuracy of our content, mistakes do happen. If you find a mistake in one of our books-maybe a mistake in the text or the code-we would be grateful if you could report this to us. By doing so, you can save other readers from frustration and help us improve subsequent versions of this book. If you find any errata, please report them by visiting `http://www.packtpub.com/submit-errata`, selecting your book, clicking on the **Errata Submission Form** link, and entering the details of your errata. Once your errata are verified, your submission will be accepted and the errata will be uploaded to our website or added to any list of existing errata under the Errata section of that title. To view the previously submitted errata, go to `https://www.packtpub.com/book s/content/support`and enter the name of the book in the search field. The required information will appear under the **Errata** section.

# Piracy

Piracy of copyrighted material on the Internet is an ongoing problem across all media. At Packt, we take the protection of our copyright and licenses very seriously. If you come across any illegal copies of our works in any form on the Internet, please provide us with the location address or website name immediately so that we can pursue a remedy. Please contact us at `copyright@packtpub.com` with a link to the suspected pirated material. We appreciate your help in protecting our authors and our ability to bring you valuable content.

# Questions

If you have a problem with any aspect of this book, you can contact us at `questions@packtpub.com`, and we will do our best to address the problem.

# 1
# I/O and File Systems

In this chapter, the following recipes will be covered:

- Using the common I/O interfaces
- Using the bytes and strings packages
- Working with directories and files
- Working with the CSV format
- Working with temporary files
- Working with text/template and HTML/templates

## Introduction

Go provides excellent support for both basic and complex I/O. The recipes in this chapter will explore common Go interfaces to deal with I/O and show how to make use of them. The Go standard library frequently uses these interfaces, and these interfaces will be used by recipes throughout the book.

You'll learn how to work with data in memory and in the form of streams. You'll see examples of working with files and directories and of working with the CSV format. The temporary files recipe discusses a mechanism to work with files without the overhead of dealing with name collision and more. Lastly, we'll explore Go standard templates for both plain text and HTML.

These recipes should lay the foundation for the use of interfaces to represent and modify data and should help you think about data in an abstract and flexible way.

# Using the common I/O interfaces

Go provides a number of I/O interfaces used throughout the standard library. It is a best practice to make use of these interfaces wherever possible rather than passing structs or other types directly. Two powerful interfaces we explore in this recipe are the io.Reader and io.Writer interfaces. These interfaces are used throughout the standard library and understanding how to use them will make you a better Go developer.

The Reader and Writer interfaces look like this:

```
type Reader interface {
        Read(p []byte) (n int, err error)
}

type Writer interface {
        Write(p []byte) (n int, err error)
}
```

Go also makes it easy to combine interfaces. For example, take a look at the following code:

```
type Seeker interface {
        Seek(offset int64, whence int) (int64, error)
}

type ReadSeeker interface {
        Reader
        Seeker
}
```

The recipe will also explore an io function called Pipe():

```
func Pipe() (*PipeReader, *PipeWriter)
```

The remainder of this book will make use of these interfaces.

# Getting ready

Configure your environment according to these steps:

1.  Download and install Go on your operating system at https://golang.org/doc/install and configure your GOPATH environment variable.

2.  Open a terminal/console application, navigate to your GOPATH/src directory, and create a project directory such as $GOPATH/src/github.com/yourusername/customrepo.

    All code will be run and modified from this directory.

3.  Optionally, install the latest tested version of the code using the following command:

    **go get github.com/agtorre/go-cookbook/**

# How to do it...

These steps cover writing and running your application:

1.  From your terminal/console application, create a new directory called chapter1/interfaces.
2.  Navigate to that directory.

Copy tests from https://github.com/agtorre/go-cookbook/tree/master/chapter1/interfaces, or use this as an exercise to write some of your own code.

1.  Create a file called interfaces.go with the following contents:

```go
package interfaces

import (
        "fmt"
        "io"
        "os"
)

// Copy copies data from in to out first directly,
// then using a buffer. It also writes to stdout
func Copy(in io.ReadSeeker, out io.Writer) error {
        // we write to out, but also Stdout
        w := io.MultiWriter(out, os.Stdout)
        // a standard copy, this can be dangerous if there's a
        // lot of data in in
        if _, err := io.Copy(w, in); err != nil {
            return err
        }
        in.Seek(0, 0)
```

```
        // buffered write using 64 byte chunks
        buf := make([]byte, 64)
        if _, err := io.CopyBuffer(w, in, buf); err != nil {
            return err
        }

        // lets print a new line
        fmt.Println()
        return nil
    }
}
```

5. Create a file called `pipes.go` with the following contents:

```
package interfaces

import (
        "io"
        "os"
)
// PipeExample helps give some more examples of using io
//interfaces
func PipeExample() error {
        // the pipe reader and pipe writer implement
        // io.Reader and io.Writer
        r, w := io.Pipe()

        // this needs to be run in a separate go routine
        // as it will block waiting for the reader
        // close at the end for cleanup
        go func() {
            // for now we'll write something basic,
            // this could also be used to encode json
            // base64 encode, etc.
            w.Write([]byte("testn"))
            w.Close()
        }()
        if _, err := io.Copy(os.Stdout, r); err != nil {
            return err
        }
        return nil
    }
}
```

6. Create a new directory named `example`.

7. Navigate to `example`.

8. Create a `main.go` file with the following contents and ensure that you modify the interfaces imported to use the path you set up in step 2:

```
package main

import (
        "bytes"
        "fmt"
        "github.com/agtorre/go-cookbook/chapter1/interfaces"
)
func main() {
        in := bytes.NewReader([]byte("example"))
        out := &bytes.Buffer{}
        fmt.Print("stdout on Copy = ")
        if err := interfaces.Copy(in, out); err != nil {
                panic(err)
        }
        fmt.Println("out bytes buffer =", out.String())
        fmt.Print("stdout on PipeExample = ")
        if err := interfaces.PipeExample(); err != nil {
                panic(err)
        }
}
```

9. Run `go run main.go`.
10. You may also run these:

```
go build
./example
```

You should see the following output:

```
$ go run main.go
stdout on Copy = exampleexample
out bytes buffer = exampleexample
stdout on PipeExample = test
```

11. If you copied or wrote your own tests, go up one directory and run `go test`, and ensure all tests pass.

# How it works...

The `Copy()` function copies between interfaces and treats them like streams. Thinking of data as streams has a lot of practical uses, especially when working with network traffic or filesystems. The `Copy()` function also creates a multi-writer that combines two writer streams and writes to them twice using `ReadSeeker`. If a `Reader` interface were used instead rather than seeing `exampleexample`, you would only see `example` despite copying to the `MultiWriter` interface twice. There's also an example of a buffered write that you might use if your stream is not fit into the memory.

The `PipeReader` and `PipeWriter` structs implement `io.Reader` and `io.Writer` interfaces. They're connected, creating an in-memory pipe. The primary purpose of a pipe is to read from a stream while simultaneously writing from the same stream to a different source. In essence, it combines the two streams into a pipe.

Go interfaces are a clean abstraction to wrap data that performs common operations. This is made apparent when doing I/O operations, and so the `io` package is a great resource for learning about interface composition. The `pipe` package is often underused but provides great flexibility with thread-safety when linking input and output streams.

# Using the bytes and strings packages

The `bytes` and `string` packages have a number of useful helpers to work with and convert between strings and byte types. They allow the creation of buffers that work with a number of common I/O interfaces.

# Getting ready

Refer to the *Getting ready* section's steps in the *Using the common I/O interfaces* recipe.

# How to do it...

These steps cover writing and running your application:

1. From your terminal/console application, create a new directory called `chapter1/bytestrings`.
2. Navigate to this directory.

3. Copy tests from `https://github.com/agtorre/go-cookbook/tree/master/chapter1/bytesstrings`, or use this as an exercise to write some of your own code!

4. Create a file called `buffer.go` with the following contents:

```go
package bytestrings
import (
        "bytes"
        "io"
        "io/ioutil"
)
// Buffer demonstrates some tricks for initializing bytes
//Buffers
// These buffers implement an io.Reader interface
func Buffer(rawString string) *bytes.Buffer {
        // we'll start with a string encoded into raw bytes
        rawBytes := []byte(rawString)
        // there are a number of ways to create a buffer from
        // the raw bytes or from the original string
        var b = new(bytes.Buffer)
        b.Write(rawBytes)
        // alternatively
        b = bytes.NewBuffer(rawBytes)
        // and avoiding the intial byte array altogether
        b = bytes.NewBufferString(rawString)
        return b
}
// ToString is an example of taking an io.Reader and consuming
// it all, then returning a string
func toString(r io.Reader) (string, error) {
        b, err := ioutil.ReadAll(r)
        if err != nil {
            return "", err
        }
        return string(b), nil
}
```

5. Create a file called `bytes.go` with the following contents:

```go
package bytestrings
import (
        "bufio"
        "bytes"
        "fmt"
)
// WorkWithBuffer will make use of the buffer created by the
// Buffer function
func WorkWithBuffer() error {
```

```
                    rawString := "it's easy to encode unicode into a byte
                                  array"

                    b := Buffer(rawString)

                    // we can quickly convert a buffer back into byes with
                    // b.Bytes() or a string with b.String()
                    fmt.Println(b.String())
                    // because this is an io Reader we can make use of
                    // generic io reader functions such as
                    s, err := toString(b)
                    if err != nil {
                        return err
                    }
                    fmt.Println(s)

                    // we can also take our bytes and create a bytes reader
                    // these readers implement io.Reader, io.ReaderAt,
                    // io.WriterTo, io.Seeker, io.ByteScanner, and
                    // io.RuneScanner interfaces
                    reader := bytes.NewReader([]byte(rawString))
                    // we can also plug it into a scanner that allows
                    // buffered reading and tokenzation
                    scanner := bufio.NewScanner(reader)
                    scanner.Split(bufio.ScanWords)
                    // iterate over all of the scan events
                    for scanner.Scan() {
                        fmt.Print(scanner.Text())
                    }
                    return nil
      }
```

6.  Create a file called `string.go` with the following contents:

```
package bytestrings
import (
        "fmt"
        "io"
        "os"
        "strings"
)
// SearchString shows a number of methods
// for searching a string
func SearchString() {
        s := "this is a test"
        // returns true because s contains
        // the word this
        fmt.Println(strings.Contains(s, "this"))
```

```
        // returns true because s contains the letter a
        // would also match if it contained b or c
        fmt.Println(strings.ContainsAny(s, "abc"))
        // returns true because s starts with this
        fmt.Println(strings.HasPrefix(s, "this"))
        // returns true because s ends with this
        fmt.Println(strings.HasSuffix(s, "test"))
        }
// ModifyString modifies a string in a number of ways
func ModifyString() {
        s := "simple string"
        // prints [simple string]
        fmt.Println(strings.Split(s, " "))
        // prints "Simple String"
        fmt.Println(strings.Title(s))
        // prints "simple string"; all trailing and
        // leading white space is removed
        s = " simple string "
        fmt.Println(strings.TrimSpace(s))
}
// StringReader demonstrates how to create
// an io.Reader interface quickly with a string
func StringReader() {
        s := "simple stringn"
        r := strings.NewReader(s)
        // prints s on Stdout
        io.Copy(os.Stdout, r)
}
```

7. Create a new directory named `example`.

8. Navigate to `example`.

9. Create a `main.go` file with the following contents and ensure that you modify the interfaces imported to use the path you set up in step 2:

```
package main
import "github.com/agtorre/go-cookbook/chapter1/bytestrings"
func main() {
        err := bytestrings.WorkWithBuffer()
        if err != nil {
                panic(err)
        }
        // each of these print to stdout
        bytestrings.SearchString()
        bytestrings.ModifyString()
        bytestrings.StringReader()
}
```

10. Run `go run main.go`.

11. You may also run these:

    ```
    go build
    ./example
    ```

    You should see the following output:

    ```
    $ go run main.go
    it's easy to encode unicode into a byte array ??
    it's easy to encode unicode into a byte array ??
    it'seasytoencodeunicodeintoabytearray??true
    true
    true
    true
    [simple string]
    Simple String
    simple string
    simple string
    ```

12. If you copied or wrote your own tests, go up one directory and run `go test`, and ensure all tests pass.

# How it works...

The bytes library provides a number of convenience functions when working with data. A buffer, for example, is far more flexible than an array of bytes when working with stream processing libraries or methods. Once you've created a buffer, it can be used to satisfy an `io.Reader` interface so you can take advantage of `ioutil` functions to manipulate the data. For steaming applications, you'd probably want to use a buffer and a scanner. The `bufio` package comes in handy for these cases. Sometimes, using an array or slice is more appropriate for smaller datasets or when you have a lot of memory on your machine.

Go provides a lot of flexibility in converting between interfaces with these basic types--it's relatively simple to convert between strings and bytes. When working with strings, the `strings` package provides a number of convenience functions to work with, search, and manipulate strings. In some cases, a good regular expression may be appropriate, but most of the time, the `strings` and `strconv` packages are sufficient. The `strings` package allows you to make a string look like a title, split it into an array, or trim whitespace. It also provides a `Reader` interface of its own that can be used instead of the `bytes` package reader type.

# Working with directories and files

Working with directories and files can be difficult when you switch between platforms (Windows and Linux, for example). Go provides cross-platform support to work with files and directories in the os and ioutils packages. We've already seen examples of ioutils, but now we'll explore how to use them in another way!

## Getting ready

Refer to the *Getting ready* section's steps in the *Using the common I/O interfaces* recipe.

## How to do it...

These steps cover writing and running your application:

1. From your terminal/console application, create a new directory called chapter1/filedirs.
2. Navigate to this directory.
3. Copy tests from https://github.com/agtorre/go-cookbook/tree/master/chapter1/filedirs, or use this as an exercise to write some of your own code!
4. Create a file called dirs.go with the following contents:

```go
package filedirs
import (
        "errors"
        "io"
        "os"
)
// Operate manipulates files and directories
func Operate() error {
        // this 0777 is similar to what you'd see with chown
        // on a command line this will create a director
        // /tmp/example, you may also use an absolute path
        // instead of a relative one
        if err := os.Mkdir("example_dir", os.FileMode(0755));
        err != nil {
                return err
        }

        // go to the /tmp directory
        if err := os.Chdir("example_dir"); err != nil {
                return err
```

```go
        }

        // f is a generic file object
        // it also implements multiple interfaces
        // and can be used as a reader or writer
        // if the correct bits are set when opening
        f, err := os.Create("test.txt")
        if err != nil {
                return err
        }

        // we write a known-length value to the file and
        // validate that it wrote correctly
        value := []byte("hellon")
        count, err := f.Write(value)
        if err != nil {
                return err
        }
        if count != len(value) {
                return errors.New("incorrect length returned
                from write")
        }

        if err := f.Close(); err != nil {
                return err
        }

        // read the file
        f, err = os.Open("test.txt")
        if err != nil {
                return err
        }
        io.Copy(os.Stdout, f)
        if err := f.Close(); err != nil {
                return err
        }
        // go to the /tmp directory
        if err := os.Chdir(".."); err != nil {
                return err
        }
        // cleanup, os.RemoveAll can be dangerous if you
        // point at the wrong directory, use user input,
        // and especially if you run as root
        if err := os.RemoveAll("example_dir"); err != nil {
                return err
        }
        return nil
}
```

5. Create a file called `bytes.go` with the following contents:

```go
package filedirs
import (
        "bytes"
        "io"
        "os"
        "strings"
)
// Capitalizer opens a file, reads the contents,
// then writes those contents to a second file
        func Capitalizer(f1 *os.File, f2 *os.File) error {
        if _, err := f1.Seek(0, 0); err != nil {
                return err
        }
        var tmp = new(bytes.Buffer)
        if _, err := io.Copy(tmp, f1); err != nil {
                return err
        }

        s := strings.ToUpper(tmp.String())
        if _, err := io.Copy(f2, strings.NewReader(s)); err !=
        nil {
                return err
        }
        return nil
}
// CapitalizerExample creates two files, writes to one
//then calls Capitalizer() on both
func CapitalizerExample() error {
        f1, err := os.Create("file1.txt")
        if err != nil {
                return err
        }
        if _, err := f1.Write([]byte(`this file contains a
        number of words and new lines`)); err != nil {
                return err
        }
        f2, err := os.Create("file2.txt")
        if err != nil {
                return err
        }
        if err := Capitalizer(f1, f2); err != nil {
                return err
        }
        if err := os.Remove("file1.txt"); err != nil {
                return err
        }
```

```
        if err := os.Remove("file2.txt"); err != nil {
                return err
        }
        return nil
}
```

6. Create a new directory named `example`.

7. Navigate to `example`.

8. Create a `main.go` file with the following contents and ensure that you modify the `filedirs` package import to use the path you set up in step 2:

```
package main
import "github.com/agtorre/go-cookbook/chapter1/filedirs"
func main() {
        if err := filedirs.Operate(); err != nil {
                panic(err)
        }
        if err := filedirs.CapitalizerExample(); err != nil {
                panic(err)
        }
}
```

9. Run `go run main.go`.

10. You may also run these:

```
go build
./example
```

You should see the following output:

```
$ go run main.go
hello
```

11. If you copied or wrote your own tests, go up one directory and run `go test`, and ensure all tests pass.

# How it works...

If you're familiar with files in Unix, the Go `os` library should feel very familiar. You can do basically all common operations--stat a file to collect attributes, collect a file with different permissions, and create and modify directories and files. We performed a number of manipulations to directories and files and then cleaned up after ourselves.

Working with file objects is very similar to in-memory streams. Files also provide a number of convenience functions directly, such as `Chown`, `Stat`, and `Truncate`. The easiest way to get comfortable with files is to make use of them. In all the previous recipes, we have to be careful to clean up after our programs.

Working with files is a very common operation when building backend applications. Files can be used for configuration, secret keys, as temporary storage, and more. Go wraps OS system calls using the `os` package and allows the same functions to operate regardless of whether you're using Windows or Unix.

Once your file is opened and stored in a `File` struct, it can easily be passed into a number of interfaces discussed earlier. All the earlier examples of working with buffers and in-memory data streams can be replaced directly with file objects. This may be useful for things such as writing all logs to `stderr` and the file at the same time with a single write call.

# Working with the CSV format

CSV is a common format to manipulate data. It's common, for example, to import or export a CSV file into Excel. The Go `csv` package operates on data interfaces, and as a result, it's easy to write data to a buffer, stdout, a file, or to a socket. The examples in this section will show some common ways to get data into and out of the CSV format.

## Getting ready

Refer to the *Getting ready* section's steps in the *Using the common I/O interfaces* recipe.

## How to do it...

These steps cover writing and running your application:

1. From your terminal/console application, create a new directory called `chapter1/csvformat`.
2. Navigate to this directory.
3. Copy tests from `https://github.com/agtorre/go-cookbook/tree/master/chapter1/csvformat`, or use this as an exercise to write some of your own code!

4. Create a file called `read_csv.go` with the following contents:

```go
package csvformat
import (
        "bytes"
        "encoding/csv"
        "fmt"
        "io"
        "strconv"
)
// Movie will hold our parsed CSV
type Movie struct {
        Title string
        Director string
        Year int
}
// ReadCSV gives shows some examples of processing CSV
// that is passed in as an io.Reader
func ReadCSV(b io.Reader) ([]Movie, error) {
        r := csv.NewReader(b)
        // These are some optional configuration options
        r.Comma = ';'
        r.Comment = '-'
        var movies []Movie
        // grab and ignore the header for now
        // we may also wanna use this for a dictionary key or
        // some other form of lookup
        _, err := r.Read()
        if err != nil && err != io.EOF {
                return nil, err
        }
        // loop until it's all processed
        for {
                record, err := r.Read()
                if err == io.EOF {
                        break
                } else if err != nil {
                        return nil, err
                }
                year, err := strconv.ParseInt(record[2], 10,
                64)
                if err != nil {
                        return nil, err
                }

                m := Movie{record[0], record[1], int(year)}
                movies = append(movies, m)
        }
```

```
        return movies, nil
}

// AddMoviesFromText uses the CSV parser with a string
func AddMoviesFromText() error {
        // this is an example of us taking a string, converting
        // it into a buffer, and reading it
        // with the csv package
        in := `
        - first our headers
        movie title;director;year released
        - then some data
        Guardians of the Galaxy Vol. 2;James Gunn;2017
        Star Wars: Episode VIII;Rian Johnson;2017
        `

        b := bytes.NewBufferString(in)
        m, err := ReadCSV(b)
        if err != nil {
                return err
        }
        fmt.Printf("%#vn", m)
        return nil
}
```

5. Create a file called `write_csv.go` with the following contents:

```
package csvformat
import (
        "bytes"
        "encoding/csv"
        "io"
        "os"
)
// A Book has an Author and Title
type Book struct {
        Author string
        Title string
}
// Books is a named type for an array of books
type Books []Book
// ToCSV takes a set of Books and writes to an io.Writer
// it returns any errors
func (books *Books) ToCSV(w io.Writer) error {
        n := csv.NewWriter(w)
        err := n.Write([]string{"Author", "Title"})
        if err != nil {
                return err
        }
```

```
        for _, book := range *books {
                err := n.Write([]string{book.Author,
                book.Title})
                if err != nil {
                        return err
                }
        }
        n.Flush()
        return n.Error()
}

// WriteCSVOutput initializes a set of books
// and writes the to os.Stdout
func WriteCSVOutput() error {
        b := Books{
                Book{
                        Author: "F Scott Fitzgerald",
                        Title: "The Great Gatsby",
                },
                Book{
                        Author: "J D Salinger",
                        Title: "The Catcher in the Rye",
                },
        }
        return b.ToCSV(os.Stdout)
}

// WriteCSVBuffer returns a buffer csv for
// a set of books
func WriteCSVBuffer() (*bytes.Buffer, error) {
        b := Books{
                Book{
                        Author: "F Scott Fitzgerald",
                        Title: "The Great Gatsby",
                },
                Book{
                        Author: "J D Salinger",
                        Title: "The Catcher in the Rye",
                },
        }
        w := &bytes.Buffer{}
        err := b.ToCSV(w)
        return w, err
}
```

6. Create a new directory named example.

7. Navigate to `example`.

8. Create a `main.go` file with the following contents and ensure that you modify the `csvformat` import to use the path you set up in step 2:

```
package main
import (
        "fmt"
        "github.com/agtorre/go-cookbook/chapter1/csvformat"
)
func main() {
        if err := csvformat.AddMoviesFromText(); err != nil {
                panic(err)
        }
        if err := csvformat.WriteCSVOutput(); err != nil {
                panic(err)
        }
        buffer, err := csvformat.WriteCSVBuffer()
        if err != nil {
                panic(err)
        }
        fmt.Println("Buffer = ", buffer.String())
}
```

9. Run go `run main.go`.

10. You may also run these:

```
go build
./example
```

You should see the following output:

```
$ go run main.go
[]csvformat.Movie{csvformat.Movie{Title:"Guardians of the
Galaxy Vol. 2", Director:"James Gunn", Year:2017},
csvformat.Movie{Title:"Star Wars: Episode VIII", Director:"Rian
Johnson", Year:2017}}
Author,Title
F Scott Fitzgerald,The Great Gatsby
J D Salinger,The Catcher in the Rye
Buffer = Author,Title
F Scott Fitzgerald,The Great Gatsby
J D Salinger,The Catcher in the Rye
```

11. If you copied or wrote your own tests, go up one directory and run go `test`, and ensure all tests pass.

# How it works...

In order to explore reading a CSV format, we first represent our data as a struct. It's very useful in Go to format data as a struct, as it makes things such as marshaling and encoding relatively simple. Our read example uses movies as our data type. The function takes an `io.Reader` interface that holds our CSV data as an input. This could be a file or a buffer. We then use that data to create and populate a `Movie` struct, including converting the year into an integer. We also add options to the CSV parser to use ; as the separator and – as a comment line.

Next, we explore the same idea, but in reverse. Novels are represented with a title and an author. We initialize an array of novels and then write specific novels in the CSV format to an `io.Writer` interface. Once again, this can be a file, stdout, or a buffer.

The CSV package is an excellent example of why you'd want to think of data flows in Go as implementing common interfaces. It's easy to change the source and destination of our data with small one-line tweaks, and we can easily manipulate CSV data without using an excessive amount of memory or time. For example, it would be possible to read from a stream of data one record at a time and write to a separate stream in a modified format one record at a time. Doing this would not incur significant memory or processor usage.

Later, when we explore data pipelines and worker pools, you'll see how these ideas can be combined and how to handle these streams in parallel.

# Working with temporary files

We've created and made use of files for a number of examples so far. We've also had to manually deal with cleanup, name collision, and more. Temporary files and directories are a quicker, simpler way to handle these cases.

# Getting ready

Refer to the *Getting ready* section's steps in the *Using the common I/O interfaces* recipe.

# How to do it...

These steps cover writing and running your application:

1. From your terminal/console application, create a new directory called `chapter1/tempfiles`.
2. Navigate to this directory.
3. Copy tests from `https://github.com/agtorre/go-cookbook/tree/master/chapter1/tempfiles`, or use this as an exercise to write some of your own code!
4. Create a file called `temp_files.go` with the following contents:

```go
package tempfiles
import (
        "fmt"
        "io/ioutil"
        "os"
)
// WorkWithTemp will give some basic patterns for working
// with temporary files and directories
func WorkWithTemp() error {
        // If you need a temporary place to store files with
        // the same name ie. template1-10.html a temp directory
        //  is a good way to approach it, the first argument
        // being blank means it will use create the directory
        // in the location returned by
        // os.TempDir()
        t, err := ioutil.TempDir("", "tmp")
        if err != nil {
                return err
        }
        // This will delete everything inside the temp file
        // when this function exits if you want to do this
        //  later, be sure to return the directory name to the
        // calling function
        defer os.RemoveAll(t)
        // the directory must exist to create the tempfile
        // created. t is an *os.File object.
        tf, err := ioutil.TempFile(t, "tmp")
        if err != nil {
                return err
        }
        fmt.Println(tf.Name())
        // normally we'd delete the temporary file here, but
        // because we're placing it in a temp directory, it
        // gets cleaned up by the earlier defer
```

```
                    return nil
     }
```

5. Create a new directory named `example`.

6. Navigate to `example`.

7. Create a `main.go` file with the following contents and ensure that you modify the tempfiles imported to use the path you set up in step 2:

```
package main
import "github.com/agtorre/go-cookbook/chapter1/tempfiles"
func main() {
        if err := tempfiles.WorkWithTemp(); err != nil {
                panic(err)
        }
}
```

9. Run `go run main.go`.

10. You may also run these:

```
go build
./example
```

You should see (with a different path) the following output:

```
$ go run main.go
/var/folders/kd/ygq5l_0d1xq1lzk_c7htft900000gn/T
/tmp764135258/tmp588787953
```

11. If you copied or wrote your own tests, go up one directory and run `go test`, and ensure all tests pass.

# How it works...

Creating temporary files and directories can be done using the `ioutil` package. Although you must still delete the files yourself, `RemoveAll` is the convention, and it will do that for you with only one extra line of code.

When writing tests, the use of temporary files is highly recommended. It's also useful for things such as build artifacts and more. The Go `ioutil` package will try and honor the OS preferences by default, but it allows you to fall back to other directories if required.

# Working with text/template and HTML/templates

Go provides rich support for templates. It is simple to nest templates, import functions, represent variables, iterate over data, and so on. If you need something more sophisticated than a CSV writer, templates may be a great solution.

Another application for templates is for websites. When we want to render server-side data to the client, templates fit the bill nicely. At first, Go templates can appear confusing. This chapter will explore working with templates, collecting templates inside of a directory, and working with HTML templates.

## Getting ready

Refer to the *Getting ready* section's steps in the *Using the common I/O interfaces* recipe.

## How to do it...

These steps cover writing and running your application:

1. From your terminal/console application, create a new directory called `chapter1/templates`.
2. Navigate to this directory.
3. Copy tests from `https://github.com/agtorre/go-cookbook/tree/master/chapter1/templates`, or use this as an exercise to write some of your own!
4. Create a file called `templates.go` with the following contents:

```
package templates
import (
        "os"
        "strings"
        "text/template"
)
const sampleTemplate = `
        This template demonstrates printing a {{ .Variable |
        printf "%#v" }}.
        {{if .Condition}}
        If condition is set, we'll print this
        {{else}}
        Otherwise, we'll print this instead
```

```
        {{end}}
        Next we'll iterate over an array of strings:
        {{range $index, $item := .Items}}
        {{$index}}: {{$item}}
        {{end}}

        We can also easily import other functions like
        strings.Split
        then immediately used the array created as a result:
        {{ range $index, $item := split .Words ","}}
        {{$index}}: {{$item}}
        {{end}}
        Blocks are a way to embed templates into one another
        {{ block "block_example" .}}
        No Block defined!
        {{end}}
        {{/*
        This is a way
        to insert a multi-line comment
        */}}
`

const secondTemplate = `
        {{ define "block_example" }}
        {{.OtherVariable}}
        {{end}}
`

// RunTemplate initializes a template and demonstrates a
// variety of template helper functions
func RunTemplate() error {
        data := struct {
                Condition bool
                Variable string
                Items []string
                Words string
                OtherVariable string
        }{
                Condition: true,
                Variable: "variable",
                Items: []string{"item1", "item2", "item3"},
                Words:
                "another_item1,another_item2,another_item3",
                OtherVariable: "I'm defined in a second
                template!",
        }
        funcmap := template.FuncMap{
                "split": strings.Split,
        }
        // these can also be chained
```

```
t := template.New("example")
t = t.Funcs(funcmap)
// We could use Must instead to panic on error
// template.Must(t.Parse(sampleTemplate))
t, err := t.Parse(sampleTemplate)
if err != nil {
        return err
}
// to demonstrate blocks we'll create another template
// by cloning the first template, then parsing a second
t2, err := t.Clone()
if err != nil {
        return err
}
t2, err = t2.Parse(secondTemplate)
if err != nil {
        return err
}
// write the template to stdout and populate it
// with data
err = t2.Execute(os.Stdout, &data)
if err != nil {
        return err
}
return nil
}
```

5. Create a file called `template_files.go` with the following contents:

```
package templates
import (
        "io/ioutil"
        "os"
        "path/filepath"
        "text/template"
)
//CreateTemplate will create a template file that contains data
func CreateTemplate(path string, data string) error {
        return ioutil.WriteFile(path, []byte(data),
        os.FileMode(0755))
}

// InitTemplates sets up templates from a directory
func InitTemplates() error {
        tempdir, err := ioutil.TempDir("", "temp")
        if err != nil {
                return err
        }
```

```
                    defer os.RemoveAll(tempdir)
                    err = CreateTemplate(filepath.Join(tempdir, "t1.tmpl"),
                    `Template 1! {{ .Var1 }}
                    {{ block "template2" .}} {{end}}
                    {{ block "template3" .}} {{end}}
                    `)
                    if err != nil {
                            return err
                    }
                    err = CreateTemplate(filepath.Join(tempdir, "t2.tmpl"),
                    `{{ define "template2"}}Template 2! {{ .Var2 }}{{end}}
                    `)
                    if err != nil {
                            return err
                    }

                    err = CreateTemplate(filepath.Join(tempdir, "t3.tmpl"),
                    `{{ define "template3"}}Template 3! {{ .Var3 }}{{end}}
                    `)
                    if err != nil {
                            return err
                    }
                    pattern := filepath.Join(tempdir, "*.tmpl")

                    // Parse glob will combine all the files that match
                    // glob and combine them into a single template
                    tmpl, err := template.ParseGlob(pattern)
                    if err != nil {
                            return err
                    }
                    // Execute can also work with a map instead
                    // of a struct
                    tmpl.Execute(os.Stdout, map[string]string{
                            "Var1": "Var1!!",
                            "Var2": "Var2!!",
                            "Var3": "Var3!!",
                     })

                     return nil
            }
```

6. Create a file called `html_templates.go` with the following content:

```
package templates
import (
        "fmt"
        "html/template"
        "os"
```

```go
)
// HTMLDifferences highlights some of the differences
// between html/template and text/template
func HTMLDifferences() error {
        t := template.New("html")
        t, err := t.Parse("<h1>Hello! {{.Name}}</h1>n")
        if err != nil {
                return err
}

        // html/template auto-escapes unsafe operations like
        // javascript injection this is contextually aware and
        // will behave differently
        // depending on where a variable is rendered
        err = t.Execute(os.Stdout, map[string]string{"Name": "
<script>alert('Can you see me?')</script>"})
        if err != nil {
                return err
        }
        // you can also manually call the escapers
        fmt.Println(template.JSEscaper(`example
        <example@example.com>`))
        fmt.Println(template.HTMLEscaper(`example
        <example@example.com>`))
        fmt.Println(template.URLQueryEscaper(`example
        <example@example.com>`))
        return nil
}
```

7. Create a new directory named `example`.

8. Navigate to `example`.

9. Create a `main.go` file with the following contents and ensure that you modify the tempfiles imported to use the path you set up in step 2:

```go
package main
import "github.com/agtorre/go-cookbook/chapter1/templates"
func main() {
        if err := templates.RunTemplate(); err != nil {
                panic(err)
        }
        if err := templates.InitTemplates(); err != nil {
                panic(err)
        }
        if err := templates.HTMLDifferences(); err != nil {
                panic(err)
        }
}
```

10. Run `go run main.go`.

11. You may also run these:

```
go build
./example
```

You should see (with a different path) the following output:

```
$ go run main.go

This template demonstrates printing a "variable".


If condition is set, we'll print this


Next we'll iterate over an array of strings:

0: item1

1: item2

2: item3


We can also easily import other functions like strings.Split
then immediately used the array created as a result:

0: another_item1

1: another_item2

2: another_item3


Blocks are a way to embed templates into one another

I'm defined in a second template!




Template 1! Var1!!
Template 2! Var2!!
Template 3! Var3!!
<h1>Hello! &lt;script&gt;alert('Can you see
me?')&lt;/script&gt;</h1>
```

```
example  x3Cexample@example.comx3E
example  &lt;example@example.com&gt;
example+%3Cexample%40example.com%3E
```

12. If you copied or wrote your own tests, go up one directory and run `go test`, and ensure all tests pass.

# How it works...

Go has two template packages--`text/template` and `html/template`. These share functionality and a variety of functions. In general, use `html/template` to render websites and text/html for everything else. Templates are plain text, but variables and functions can be used inside of curly brace blocks.

The template packages also provide convenience methods to work with files. The example creates a number of templates in a temporary directory and then reads them all with a single line of code.

The `html/template` package is a wrapper around the `text/template` package. All of the template examples work with the `html/template` package directly, using no modification and only changing the import statement. HTML templates provide the added benefit of context-aware safety. This prevents things such as JavaScript injection.

The template packages provide what you'd expect out of a modern template library. It's easy to combine templates, add application logic, and ensure safety when emitting results to HTML and JavaScript.

# 2
# Command-Line Tools

In this chapter, the following recipes will be covered:

- Using command-line flags
- Using command-line arguments
- Reading and setting environment variables
- Configuration using TOML, YAML, and JSON
- Working with Unix pipes
- Catching and handling signals
- An ANSI coloring application

# Introduction

Command-line applications are among the easiest ways to handle user input and output. This chapter will focus on command-line-based interactions, such as command-line arguments, configuration, and environment variables. It'll conclude with a library for coloring text output in Unix and Bash for Windows.

With the recipes in this chapter, you should be equipped to handle expected and unexpected user input. The signal recipe is an example of cases where users may send unexpected signals to your application, and the pipes recipe is a good alternative to taking user inputs compared to flags or command-line arguments.

The ANSI color recipe will hopefully provide some examples of cleaning up output to users. For example, in logging, being able to color text based on its purpose can sometimes make large blocks of text significantly more clear.

# Using command-line flags

The `flag` package makes it simple to add command-line flag arguments to a Go application. It has a few shortcomings--you tend to duplicate a lot of code in order to add shorthand versions of flags, and they're ordered alphabetically from the help prompt. There are a number of third-party libraries that attempt to address these shortcomings, but this chapter will focus on the standard library version and not on those libraries.

## Getting ready

Configure your environment according to these steps:

1. Download and install Go on your operating system from `https://golang.org/doc/install`, and configure your `GOPATH` environment variable:

2. Open a terminal/console application, and navigate to your `GOPATH/src` and create a project directory, for example, `$GOPATH/src/github.com/yourusername/customrepo`.

   All code will be run and modified from this directory.

3. Optionally, install the latest tested version of the code using the `go get github.com/agtorre/go-cookbook/` command.

## How to do it...

These steps cover writing and running your application:

1. From your terminal/console application, create and navigate to the `chapter2/flags` directory.

2. Copy tests from `https://github.com/agtorre/go-cookbook/tree/master/chapter2/flags`, or use this as an exercise to write some of your own code!

3. Create a file called `flags.go` with the following contents:

```go
package main

import (
    "flag"
    "fmt"
)

// Config will be the holder for our flags
type Config struct {
    subject string
    isAwesome bool
    howAwesome int
    countTheWays CountTheWays
}

// Setup initializes a config from flags that
// are passed in
func (c *Config) Setup() {
    // you can set a flag directly like so:
    // var someVar = flag.String("flag_name", "default_val",
    // "description")
    // but in practice putting it in a struct is generally
    // better longhand
    flag.StringVar(&c.subject, "subject", "", "subject is a
    string, it defaults to empty")
    // shorthand
    flag.StringVar(&c.subject, "s", "", "subject is a string,
    it defaults to empty (shorthand)")

    flag.BoolVar(&c.isAwesome, "isawesome", false, "is it
    awesome or what?")
    flag.IntVar(&c.howAwesome, "howawesome", 10, "how awesome
    out of 10?")

    // custom variable type
    flag.Var(&c.countTheWays, "c", "comma separated list of
    integers")
}

// GetMessage uses all of the internal
// config vars and returns a sentence
func (c *Config) GetMessage() string {
    msg := c.subject
    if c.isAwesome {
        msg += " is awesome"
    } else {
```

```
            msg += " is NOT awesome"
        }

        msg = fmt.Sprintf("%s with a certainty of %d out of 10. Let
        me count the ways %s", msg, c.howAwesome,
        c.countTheWays.String())
        return msg
    }
```

4. Create a file called `custom.go` with the following contents:

```
package main

import (
    "fmt"
    "strconv"
    "strings"
)

// CountTheWays is a custom type that
// we'll read a flag into
type CountTheWays []int

func (c *CountTheWays) String() string {
    result := ""
    for _, v := range *c {
        if len(result) > 0 {
            result += " ... "
        }
        result += fmt.Sprint(v)
    }
    return result
}

// Set will be used by the flag package
func (c *CountTheWays) Set(value string) error {
    values := strings.Split(value, ",")

    for _, v := range values {
        i, err := strconv.Atoi(v)
        if err != nil {
            return err
        }
        *c = append(*c, i)
    }

    return nil
}
```

5. Create a file called `main.go` with the following contents:

```go
package main

import (
    "flag"
    "fmt"
)

func main() {
    // initialize our setup
    c := Config{}
    c.Setup()

    // generally call this from main
    flag.Parse()

    fmt.Println(c.GetMessage())
}
```

6. Run the following commands on the command line:

```
go build
./flags -h
```

7. Try these and some other arguments, and you should see the following output:

```
$ go build
$ ./flags -h
Usage of ./flags:
 -c value
 comma separated list of integers
 -howawesome int
 how awesome out of 10? (default 10)
 -isawesome
 is it awesome or what? (default false)
 -s string
 subject is a string, it defaults to empty (shorthand)
 -subject string
 subject is a string, it defaults to empty
$ ./flags -s Go -isawesome -howawesome 10 -c 1,2,3
Go is awesome with a certainty of 10 out of 10. Let me count
the ways 1 ... 2 ... 3
```

8. If you copied or wrote your own tests, go up one directory and run `go test`, and ensure all tests pass.

# How it works...

This recipe attempts to demonstrate most of the common usages of the `flag` package. It shows custom variable types, a variety of built-in variables, shorthand flags, and writing all flags to a common struct. This is the first recipe to require a main function, as the main usage of flag (`flag.Parse()`) should be called from main. As a result, the normal example directory is omitted.

The example usage of this application shows that you get `-h` automatically to get a list of flags that are included. Some other things to note are Boolean flags that are invoked without arguments, and the flag order doesn't matter.

The `flag` package is a quick way to structure input for command-line applications and provide a flexible means of specifying upfront user input for things such as setting up log levels or verbosity of an application. In the command-line arguments recipe, we'll explore flag sets and switch between them using arguments.

# Using command-line arguments

The flags from the previous recipe are a type of command-line argument. This chapter will expand on other uses for these arguments by constructing a command that supports nested subcommands. This will demonstrate Flagsets and also use positional arguments passed into your application.

Like the previous recipe, this one requires a main function to run. There are a number of third-party packages to deal with complex nested arguments and flags, but we'll investigate how to do that using only the standard library.

# Getting ready

Refer to the *Getting ready* section's steps in the *Using command-line flags* recipe.

# How to do it...

These steps cover writing and running your application:

1.  From your terminal/console application, create a new directory called `chapter2/cmdargs` and navigate to that directory.

2. Copy tests from `https://github.com/agtorre/go-cookbook/tree/master/chapter2/cmdargs`, or use this as an exercise to write some of your own code!

3. Create a file called `cmdargs.go` with the following contents:

```go
package main
import (
    "flag"
    "fmt"
    "os"
)
const version = "1.0.0"
const usage = `Usage:
%s [command]
Commands:
    Greet
    Version
`

const greetUsage = `Usage:
%s greet name [flag]
Positional Arguments:
    name
        the name to greet
Flags:
`
// MenuConf holds all the levels
// for a nested cmd line argument
type MenuConf struct {
    Goodbye bool
}
// SetupMenu initializes the base flags
func (m *MenuConf) SetupMenu() *flag.FlagSet {
    menu := flag.NewFlagSet("menu", flag.ExitOnError)
    menu.Usage = func() {
        fmt.Printf(usage, os.Args[0])
        menu.PrintDefaults()
    }
    return menu
}
// GetSubMenu return a flag set for a submenu
func (m *MenuConf) GetSubMenu() *flag.FlagSet {
    submenu := flag.NewFlagSet("submenu", flag.ExitOnError)
    submenu.BoolVar(&m.Goodbye, "goodbye", false, "Say goodbye
    instead of hello")
    submenu.Usage = func() {
        fmt.Printf(greetUsage, os.Args[0])
        submenu.PrintDefaults()
    }
```

```
        return submenu
}
// Greet will be invoked by the greet command
func (m *MenuConf) Greet(name string) {
    if m.Goodbye {
        fmt.Println("Goodbye " + name + "!")
    } else {
        fmt.Println("Hello " + name + "!")
    }
}
// Version prints the current version that is
// stored as a const
func (m *MenuConf) Version() {
    fmt.Println("Version: " + version)
}
```

4. Create a file called `main.go` with the following contents:

```
package main

import (
    "fmt"
    "os"
    "strings"
)

func main() {
    c := MenuConf{}
    menu := c.SetupMenu()
    menu.Parse(os.Args[1:])

  // we use arguments to switch between commands
  // flags are also an argument
  if len(os.Args) > 1 {
      // we don't care about case
      switch strings.ToLower(os.Args[1]) {
      case "version":
          c.Version()
      case "greet":
          f := c.GetSubMenu()
          if len(os.Args) < 3 {
              f.Usage()
              return
          }
          if len(os.Args) > 3 {
          if.Parse(os.Args[3:])
          }
          c.Greet(os.Args[2])
```

```
        default:
            fmt.Println("Invalid command")
            menu.Usage()
            return
        }
    } else {
        menu.Usage()
        return
    }
}
```

5. Run `go build`.

6. Run the following commands and try a few other combinations of arguments:

```
$./cmdargs -h
Usage:

./cmdargs [command]

Commands:
 Greet
 Version

$./cmdargs version
Version: 1.0.0

$./cmdargs greet
Usage:

./cmdargs greet name [flag]

Positional Arguments:
 name
 the name to greet

Flags:
 -goodbye
 Say goodbye instead of hello

$./cmdargs greet reader
Hello reader!

$./cmdargs greet reader -goodbye
Goodbye reader!
```

7. If you copied or wrote your own tests, go up one directory and run `go test`, and ensure all tests pass.

# How it works...

Flagsets can be used to set up independent lists of expected arguments, usage strings, and more. The developer is required to do validation on a number of arguments, parsing in the right subset of arguments to commands and defining usage strings. This can be error-prone and requires a lot of iteration to get it completely right.

The `flag` package makes parsing arguments much easier and includes convenience methods to get the number of flags, arguments, and more. This recipe demonstrates basic ways to construct a complex command-line application using arguments including a package-level config, required positional arguments, multi-level command usage, and how to split these things into multiple files or packages if required.

# Reading and setting environment variables

Environment variables are another way to pass state into an application beyond reading data in from a file or passing it explicitly over the command line. This recipe will explore some very basic getting and setting of environment variables and then work with the highly useful third-party library `https://github.com/kelseyhightower/envconfig`.

We'll build an application that can read a config via JSON or through environment variables. The next recipe will further explore alternative formats, including TOML and YAML.

# Getting ready

Configure your environment according to these steps:

1. Refer to the *Getting ready* section's steps in the *Using command-line flags* recipe.
2. Run the `go get github.com/kelseyhightower/envconfig/` command.
3. Run the `go get github.com/pkg/errors/` command.

# How to do it...

These steps cover writing and running your application:

1. From your terminal/console application, create a new directory called `chapter2/envvar` and navigate to that directory.

2. Copy tests from `https://github.com/agtorre/go-cookbook/tree/master/cha pter2/envvar`, or use this as an exercise to write some of your own code!

3. Create a file called `config.go` with the following contents:

```
package envvar

import (
    "encoding/json"
    "os"

    "github.com/kelseyhightower/envconfig"
    "github.com/pkg/errors"
)

// LoadConfig will load files optionally from the json file
// stored at path, then will override those values based on the
// envconfig struct tags. The envPrefix is how we prefix our
// environment variables.
func LoadConfig(path, envPrefix string, config interface{})
error {
    if path != "" {
        err := LoadFile(path, config)
        if err != nil {
            return errors.Wrap(err, "error loading config from
            file")
        }
    }
    err := envconfig.Process(envPrefix, config)
    return errors.Wrap(err, "error loading config from env")
}

// LoadFile unmarshalls a json file into a config struct
func LoadFile(path string, config interface{}) error {
    configFile, err := os.Open(path)
    if err != nil {
        return errors.Wrap(err, "failed to read config file")
    }
    defer configFile.Close()

    decoder := json.NewDecoder(configFile)
    if err = decoder.Decode(config); err != nil {
        return errors.Wrap(err, "failed to decode config file")
    }
    return nil
}
```

4. Create a new directory named `example`.

5. Navigate to `example`.

6. Create a file, `main.go`, with the following contents and ensure that you modify the `envvar` import to use the path you set up in step 1:

```
package main

import (
    "bytes"
    "fmt"
    "io/ioutil"
    "os"

    "github.com/agtorre/go-cookbook/chapter2/envvar"
)

// Config will hold the config we
// capture from a json file and env vars
type Config struct {
    Version string `json:"version" required:"true"`
    IsSafe bool `json:"is_safe" default:"true"`
    Secret string `json:"secret"`
}

func main() {
    var err error

    // create a temporary file to hold
    // an example json file
    tf, err := ioutil.TempFile("", "tmp")
    if err != nil {
        panic(err)
    }
    defer tf.Close()
    defer os.Remove(tf.Name())

    // create a json file to hold
    // our secrets
    secrets := `{
        "secret": "so so secret"
    }`

    if _, err =
    tf.Write(bytes.NewBufferString(secrets).Bytes());
    err != nil {
        panic(err)
    }
```

```go
    // We can easily set environment variables
    // as needed
    if err = os.Setenv("EXAMPLE_VERSION", "1.0.0"); err != nil
    {
        panic(err)
    }
    if err = os.Setenv("EXAMPLE_ISSAFE", "false"); err != nil {
        panic(err)
    }

    c := Config{}
    if err = envvar.LoadConfig(tf.Name(), "EXAMPLE", &c);
    err != nil {
        panic(err)
    }

    fmt.Println("secrets file contains =", secrets)

    // We can also read them
    fmt.Println("EXAMPLE_VERSION =",
    os.Getenv("EXAMPLE_VERSION"))
    fmt.Println("EXAMPLE_ISSAFE =",
    os.Getenv("EXAMPLE_ISSAFE"))

    // The final config is a mix of json and environment
    // variables
    fmt.Printf("Final Config: %#v\n", c)
}
```

7. Run `go run main.go`.

8. You may also run these commands:

```
go build
./example
```

9. You should see the following output:

```
$ go run main.go
secrets file contains = {
  "secret": "so so secret"
  }
EXAMPLE_VERSION = 1.0.0
EXAMPLE_ISSAFE = false
Final Config: main.Config{Version:"1.0.0", IsSafe:false,
Secret:"so so secret"}
```

10. If you copied or wrote your own tests, go up one directory and run `go test`, and ensure all tests pass.

# How it works...

Reading and writing environment variables is pretty simple with the `os` package. The `envconfig` third-party library this recipe uses is a clever way to capture environment variables and specify certain requirements using struct tags.

The `LoadConfig` function is a flexible way to pull in configuration information from a variety of sources without a lot of overhead or too many extra dependencies. It would be simple to convert the primary config into another format aside from JSON or just always use environment variables as well.

Also, note the use of errors. We wrap errors throughout the code in this recipe so that we can annotate errors without losing the original error information. There will be more details on this in `Chapter 4`, *Error Handling in Go*.

# Configuration using TOML, YAML, and JSON

There are many configuration formats that Go, with the use of third-party libraries, has support for. Three of the most popular data formats are TOML, YAML, and JSON. Go can support JSON out of the box, and the others have clues on how to marshal/unmarshal or encode/decode data for these formats. The formats have many benefits beyond configuration, but this chapter will largely focus on converting a Go struct in the form of a configuration struct. This recipe will explore basic input and output using these formats.

These formats also provide an interface by which Go and applications written in other languages can share the same configuration. There are also a number of tools that deal with these formats and simplify working with them.

# Getting ready

Configure your environment according to these steps:

1. Refer to the *Getting ready* section's steps in the *Using command-line flags* recipe.
2. Run the `go get github.com/BurntSushi/toml` command.
3. Run the `go get github.com/go-yaml/yaml` command.

# How to do it...

These steps cover writing and running your application:

1. From your terminal/console application, create a new directory called `chapter2/confformat` and navigate to that directory.

2. Copy tests from `https://github.com/agtorre/go-cookbook/tree/master/chapter2/confformat`, or use this as an exercise to write some of your own code!

3. Create a file called `toml.go` with the following contents:

```
package confformat

import (
    "bytes"

    "github.com/BurntSushi/toml"
)

// TOMLData is our common data struct
// with TOML struct tags
type TOMLData struct {
    Name string `toml:"name"`
    Age int `toml:"age"`
}

// ToTOML dumps the TOMLData struct to
// a TOML format bytes.Buffer
func (t *TOMLData) ToTOML() (*bytes.Buffer, error) {
    b := &bytes.Buffer{}
    encoder := toml.NewEncoder(b)
    if err := encoder.Encode(t); err != nil {
        return nil, err
    }
    return b, nil
}

// Decode will decode into TOMLData
func (t *TOMLData) Decode(data []byte) (toml.MetaData, error) {
    return toml.Decode(string(data), t)
}
```

4. Create a file called `yaml.go` with the following contents:

```
package confformat

import (
```

```
    "bytes"

    "github.com/go-yaml/yaml"
)

// YAMLData is our common data struct
// with YAML struct tags
type YAMLData struct {
    Name string `yaml:"name"`
    Age int `yaml:"age"`
}

// ToYAML dumps the YAMLData struct to
// a YAML format bytes.Buffer
func (t *YAMLData) ToYAML() (*bytes.Buffer, error) {
    d, err := yaml.Marshal(t)
    if err != nil {
        return nil, err
    }

    b := bytes.NewBuffer(d)

    return b, nil
}

// Decode will decode into TOMLData
func (t *YAMLData) Decode(data []byte) error {
    return yaml.Unmarshal(data, t)
}
```

5. Create a file called `json.go` with the following contents:

```
package confformat

import (
    "bytes"
    "encoding/json"
    "fmt"
)

// JSONData is our common data struct
// with JSON struct tags
type JSONData struct {
    Name string `json:"name"`
    Age int `json:"age"`
}

// ToJSON dumps the JSONData struct to
```

```go
// a JSON format bytes.Buffer
func (t *JSONData) ToJSON() (*bytes.Buffer, error) {
    d, err := json.Marshal(t)
    if err != nil {
        return nil, err
    }

    b := bytes.NewBuffer(d)

    return b, nil
}

// Decode will decode into JSONData
func (t *JSONData) Decode(data []byte) error {
    return json.Unmarshal(data, t)
}

// OtherJSONExamples shows ways to use types
// beyond structs and other useful functions
func OtherJSONExamples() error {
    res := make(map[string]string)
    err := json.Unmarshal([]byte(`{"key": "value"}`), &res)
    if err != nil {
        return err
    }

    fmt.Println("We can unmarshal into a map instead of a
    struct:", res)

    b := bytes.NewReader([]byte(`{"key2": "value2"}`))
    decoder := json.NewDecoder(b)

    if err := decoder.Decode(&res); err != nil {
        return err
    }

    fmt.Println("we can also use decoders/encoders to work with
    streams:", res)

    return nil
}
```

6.  Create a file called `marshal.go` with the following contents:

```go
package confformat

import "fmt"
```

```go
// MarshalAll takes some data stored in structs
// and converts them to the various data formats
func MarshalAll() error {
    t := TOMLData{
        Name: "Name1",
        Age: 20,
    }

    j := JSONData{
        Name: "Name2",
        Age: 30,
    }

    y := YAMLData{
        Name: "Name3",
        Age: 40,
    }

    tomlRes, err := t.ToTOML()
    if err != nil {
        return err
    }

    fmt.Println("TOML Marshal =", tomlRes.String())

    jsonRes, err := j.ToJSON()
    if err != nil {
        return err
    }

    fmt.Println("JSON Marshal=", jsonRes.String())

    yamlRes, err := y.ToYAML()
    if err != nil {
        return err
    }

    fmt.Println("YAML Marshal =", yamlRes.String())
        return nil
}
```

7. Create a file called `unmarshal.go` with the following contents:

```go
package confformat

import "fmt"

const (
```

```
        exampleTOML = `name="Example1"
age=99
        `

        exampleJSON = `{"name":"Example2","age":98}`

        exampleYAML = `name: Example3
age: 97
        `

)

// UnmarshalAll takes data in various formats
// and converts them into structs
func UnmarshalAll() error {
    t := TOMLData{}
    j := JSONData{}
    y := YAMLData{}

    if _, err := t.Decode([]byte(exampleTOML)); err != nil {
        return err
    }
    fmt.Println("TOML Unmarshal =", t)

    if err := j.Decode([]byte(exampleJSON)); err != nil {
        return err
    }
    fmt.Println("JSON Unmarshal =", j)

    if err := y.Decode([]byte(exampleYAML)); err != nil {
        return err
    }
    fmt.Println("Yaml Unmarshal =", y)
        return nil
    }
```

8. Create a new directory named `example`.
9. Navigate to `example`.
10. Create a `main.go` file with the following contents and ensure that you modify the `confformat` import to use the path you set up in step 1:

```
package main

import "github.com/agtorre/go-cookbook/chapter2/confformat"

func main() {
    if err := confformat.MarshalAll(); err != nil {
        panic(err)
```

```
        }

        if err := confformat.UnmarshalAll(); err != nil {
            panic(err)
        }

        if err := confformat.OtherJSONExamples(); err != nil {
            panic(err)
        }
    }
```

11. Run `go run main.go`.

12. You may also run these commands:

```
go build
./example
```

13. You should see the following:

```
$ go run main.go
TOML Marshal = name = "Name1"
age = 20

JSON Marshal= {"name":"Name2","age":30}
YAML Marshal = name: Name3
age: 40

TOML Unmarshal = {Example1 99}
JSON Unmarshal = {Example2 98}
Yaml Unmarshal = {Example3 97}
We can unmarshal into a map instead of a struct: map[key:value]
we can also use decoders/encoders to work with streams:
map[key:value key2:value2]
```

14. If you copied or wrote your own tests, go up one directory and run `go test`. Ensure all tests pass.

# How it works...

This recipe gave examples of using a TOML, YAML, and JSON parser to both write raw data to a go struct and read data out of it and into the corresponding format. Like with the recipes in Chapter 1, *I/O and File Systems*, we see how common it is to quickly switch between `[]byte`, `string`, `bytes.Buffer`, and other I/O interfaces.

The `encoding/json` package is the most comprehensive in providing encoding, marshaling, and other methods to work with the JSON format. We abstracted these away with our `ToFormat` functions, and it would be very simple to attach multiple methods such as this to use a single struct that can quickly be converted to or from any of these types.

This section also used and touched upon struct tags and their use. The previous chapter also made use of these, and they're a common way in Go to give hints to packages and libraries about how to treat data contained within a struct.

# Working with Unix pipes

Unix pipes are useful when passing the output of one program to the input of another. For example, take a look at this:

```
$ echo "test case" | wc -l
    1
```

In a Go application, the left-hand side of the pipe can be read in using `os.Stdin` and acts like a file descriptor. To demonstrate this, this recipe will take an input on the left-hand side of a pipe and return a list of words and their number of occurrences. These words will be tokenized on white space.

# Getting ready

Refer to the *Getting ready* section's steps in the *Using command-line flags* recipe.

# How to do it...

These steps cover writing and running your application:

1. From your terminal/console application, create a new directory called `chapter2/pipes` and navigate to that directory.
2. Copy tests from `https://github.com/agtorre/go-cookbook/tree/master/chapter2/pipes`, or use this as an exercise to write some of your own code!

3. Create a file called `pipes.go` with the following contents:

```go
package main

import (
    "bufio"
    "fmt"
    "io"
    "os"
)

// WordCount takes a file and returns a map
// with each word as a key and it's number of
// appearances as a value
func WordCount(f io.Reader) map[string]int {
    result := make(map[string]int)

    // make a scanner to work on the file
    // io.Reader interface
    scanner := bufio.NewScanner(f)
    scanner.Split(bufio.ScanWords)

    for scanner.Scan() {
        result[scanner.Text()]++
    }

    if err := scanner.Err(); err != nil {
        fmt.Fprintln(os.Stderr, "reading input:", err)
    }

    return result
}

func main() {
    fmt.Printf("string: number_of_occurrences\n\n")
    for key, value := range WordCount(os.Stdin) {
        fmt.Printf("%s: %d\n", key, value)
    }
}
```

4. Run `echo "some string" | go run pipes.go`.

5. You may also run these:

```
go build
echo "some string" | ./pipes
```

You should see the following output:

```
$ echo "test case" | go run pipes.go
string: number_of_occurrences

test: 1
case: 1

$ echo "test case test" | go run pipes.go
string: number_of_occurrences

test: 2
case: 1
```

6. If you copied or wrote your own tests, go up one directory and run `go test`. Ensure all tests pass.

# How it works...

Working with pipes in go is pretty simple, especially if you're familiar with working with files. For example, you could use the pipe recipe from `Chapter 1`, *I/O and File Systems*, to create a **tee** application (`https://en.wikipedia.org/wiki/Tee_(command)`) where everything piped in is immediately written to stdout and to a file.

This recipe uses a scanner to tokenize the `io.Reader` interface of the `os.Stdin` file object. You can see how you must check for errors after completing all of the reads.

# Catching and handling signals

Signals are a useful way for the user or the OS to kill your running application. Sometimes, it makes sense to handle these signals in a more graceful way than the default behavior. Go provides a mechanism to catch and handle signals. In this recipe, we'll explore the handling of signals through the use of a signal handling the Go routine.

# Getting ready

Refer to the *Getting ready* section's steps in the *Using command-line flags* recipe.

# How to do it...

These steps cover writing and running your application:

1. From your terminal/console application, create a new directory called `chapter2/signals`, and navigate to that directory.

2. Copy tests from `https://github.com/agtorre/go-cookbook/tree/master/chapter2/signals`, or use this as an exercise to write some of your own code!

3. Create a file called `signals.go` with the following contents:

```go
package main

import (
    "fmt"
    "os"
    "os/signal"
    "syscall"
)

// CatchSig sets up a listener for
// SIGINT interrupts
func CatchSig(ch chan os.Signal, done chan bool) {
    // block on waiting for a signal
    sig := <-ch
    // print it when it's received
    fmt.Println("nsig received:", sig)

    // we can set up handlers for all types of
    // sigs here
    switch sig {
    case syscall.SIGINT:
        fmt.Println("handling a SIGINT now!")
    case syscall.SIGTERM:
        fmt.Println("handling a SIGTERM in an entirely
        different way!")
    default:
        fmt.Println("unexpected signal received")
    }

    // terminate
    done <- true
}

func main() {
    // initialize our channels
    signals := make(chan os.Signal)
```

```
done := make(chan bool)

// hook them up to the signals lib
signal.Notify(signals, syscall.SIGINT, syscall.SIGTERM)

// if a signal is caught by this go routine
// it will write to done
go CatchSig(signals, done)

fmt.Println("Press ctrl-c to terminate...")
// the program blogs until someone writes to done
<-done
fmt.Println("Done!")

}
```

4. Run these commands:

```
go build
./signals
```

5. Try running and pressing *Ctrl + C*, and you should see this:

```
$./signals
Press ctrl-c to terminate...
^C
sig received: interrupt
handling a SIGINT now!
Done!
```

6. Try running it again and from a separate terminal, determine the PID, and kill the application:

```
$./signals
Press ctrl-c to terminate...

# in a separate terminal
$ ps -ef | grep signals
  501 30777 26360 0 5:00PM ttys000 0:00.00 ./signals

$ kill -SIGTERM 30777

# in the original terminal

sig received: terminated
handling a SIGTERM in an entirely different way!
Done!
```

7. If you copied or wrote your own tests, go up one directory and run `go test`. Ensure all tests pass.

## How it works...

This recipe makes use of channels, which are covered more extensively in `Chapter 9`, *Parallelism and Concurrency*. This is because signals. The `Notify` function requires a channel to send signal notifications to. The `kill` command is a good way to test passing signals to the applications. We register the types of signal we care about with the signal. The `Notify` function. Then, we set up a function in a Go routine to handle any activity on the channel we passed to that function. Once we receive the signal, we can handle it however we want. We can terminate the application, respond with a message, and have different behavior for different signals.

We also use a `done` channel to block the application from terminating until a signal is received. Otherwise, the program would terminate immediately. This is unnecessary for long-running applications such as web applications. It can be very useful to create appropriate signal handling routines to do cleanup, especially in applications with large amounts of Go routines that are holding a significant amount of state. A practical example of a graceful shutdown might be to allow current handlers to complete their HTTP requests without terminating them midway.

# An ANSI coloring application

Coloring an ANSI terminal application is handled by a variety of code before and after a section of text you want colored. This chapter will explore a basic coloring mechanism to color text red or plain. For a complete application, take a look at `https://github.com/agtorre/gocolorize`, which supports many more colors and text types and also implements the `fmt.Formatter` interface for ease of printing.

# Getting ready

Refer to the *Getting ready* section's steps in the *Using command-line flags* recipe.

# How to do it...

These steps cover writing and running your application:

1. From your terminal/console application, create and navigate to the `chapter2/ansicolor` directory.

2. Copy tests from `https://github.com/agtorre/go-cookbook/tree/master/chapter2/ansicolor`, or use this as an exercise to write some of your own code!

3. Create a file called `color.go` with the following contents:

```go
package ansicolor

import "fmt"

//Color of text
type Color int

const (
    // ColorNone is default
    ColorNone = iota
    // Red colored text
    Red
    // Green colored text
    Green
    // Yellow colored text
    Yellow
    // Blue colored text
    Blue
    // Magenta colored text
    Magenta
    // Cyan colored text
    Cyan
    // White colored text
    White
    // Black colored text
    Black Color = -1
)

// ColorText holds a string and its color
type ColorText struct {
    TextColor Color
    Text      string
}

func (r *ColorText) String() string {
    if r.TextColor == ColorNone {
```

```
            return r.Text
    }

    value := 30
    if r.TextColor != Black {
        value += int(r.TextColor)
    }
    return fmt.Sprintf("33[0;%dm%s33[0m", value, r.Text)
}
```

4. Create a new directory named `example`.

5. Navigate to `example`.

6. Create a `main.go` file with the following contents and ensure that you modify the `ansicolor` import to use the path you set up in step 1:

```
package main

import (
    "fmt"

    "github.com/agtorre/go-cookbook/chapter2/ansicolor"
)

func main() {
    r := ansicolor.ColorText{
        TextColor: ansicolor.Red,
        Text:      "I'm red!",
    }

    fmt.Println(r.String())

    r.TextColor = ansicolor.Green
    r.Text = "Now I'm green!"

    fmt.Println(r.String())

    r.TextColor = ansicolor.ColorNone
    r.Text = "Back to normal..."

    fmt.Println(r.String())
}
```

7. Run `go run main.go`.

8. You may also run these commands:

   ```
   go build
   ./example
   ```

9. You should see the following output with the text colored if your terminal supports the ANSI coloring format:

   ```
   $ go run main.go
   I'm red!
   Now I'm green!
   Back to normal...
   ```

10. If you copied or wrote your own tests, go up one directory and run `go test`. Ensure all tests pass.

# How it works...

This application makes use of a struct to maintain the state of the colored text. In this case, it stores the color of the text and the value of the text. The final string is rendered when you call the `String()` method, which will return either the colored text or plain text depending on the values stored in the struct. By default, the text will be plain.

# 3
# Data Conversion and Composition

In this chapter, the following recipes will be covered:

- Converting data types and interface casting
- Working with numeric data types using math and math/big
- Currency conversions and float64 considerations
- Using pointers and SQL NullTypes for encoding and decoding
- Encoding and decoding Go data
- Struct tags and basic reflection in Go
- Implementing collections via closures

## Introduction

Reasoning about Go's typing system is a critical step to all levels of Go development. This chapter will show examples of converting between data types, working with very big numbers, working with currency, types of encoding and decoding, including base64 and gob, and creating custom collections using closures.

# Converting data types and interface casting

Go is typically very flexible in conversion between data. A type may inherit another type as follows:

```
type A int
```

Then, we can always cast back to the type we inherited as follows:

```
var a A = 1
fmt.Println(int(a))
```

There are also convenience functions for converting between numbers with casting, between strings and other types using `fmt.Sprint` and with `strconv`, and between interfaces and types using reflection. This recipe will explore some of these basic conversions that will be used throughout the book.

## Getting ready

Configure your environment according to these steps:

1. Download and install Go on your operating system from `https://golang.org/doc/install` and configure your `GOPATH` environment variable.
2. Open a terminal/console application, and navigate to your `GOPATH/src` and create a project directory such as `$GOPATH/src/github.com/yourusername/customrepo`.

   All the code will be run and modified from this directory.

3. Optionally, install the latest tested version of the code using the `go get github.com/agtorre/go-cookbook/` command.

## How to do it...

These steps cover writing and running your application:

1. From your terminal/console application, create and navigate to the `chapter3/dataconv` directory.

2. Copy tests from `https://github.com/agtorre/go-cookbook/tree/master/cha` `pter3/dataconv`or use this as an exercise to write some of your own code.

3. Create a file called `dataconv.go` with the following contents:

```go
package dataconv

import "fmt"

// ShowConv demonstrates some type conversion
func ShowConv() {
    // int
    var a = 24

    // float 64
    var b = 2.0

    // convert the int to a float64 for this calculation
    c := float64(a) * b
    fmt.Println(c)
    // fmt.Sprintf is a good way to convert to strings
    precision := fmt.Sprintf("%.2f", b)

    // print the value and the type
    fmt.Printf("%s - %T\n", precision, precision)
}
```

4. Create a file called `strconv.go` with the following contents:

```go
package dataconv

import (
    "fmt"
    "strconv"
)

// Strconv demonstrates some strconv
// functions
func Strconv() error {
    //strconv is a good way to convert to and from strings
    s := "1234"
    // we can specify the base (10) and precision
    // 64 bit
    res, err := strconv.ParseInt(s, 10, 64)
    if err != nil {
        return err
    }
```

```
        fmt.Println(res)

        // lets try hex
        res, err = strconv.ParseInt("FF", 16, 64)
        if err != nil {
            return err
        }

        fmt.Println(res)

        // we can do other useful things like:
        val, err := strconv.ParseBool("true")
        if err != nil {
            return err
        }

        fmt.Println(val)

        return nil
    }
```

5. Create a file called `interfaces.go` with the following contents:

```
    package dataconv

    import "fmt"

    // CheckType will print based on the
    // interface type
    func CheckType(s interface{}) {
        switch s.(type) {
        case string:
            fmt.Println("It's a string!")
        case int:
            fmt.Println("It's an int!")
        default:
            fmt.Println("not sure what it is...")
        }
    }

    // Interfaces demonstrates casting
    // from anonymous interfaces to types
    func Interfaces() {
        CheckType("test")
        CheckType(1)
        CheckType(false)

        var i interface{}
```

```
        i = "test"

        // manually check an interface
        if val, ok := i.(string); ok {
            fmt.Println("val is", val)
        }

        // this one should fail
        if _, ok := i.(int); !ok {
            fmt.Println("uh oh! glad we handled this")
        }
    }
```

6. Create a new directory named `example`.
7. Navigate to `example`.
8. Create a file `main.go` with the following contents. Be sure to modify the `dataconv` import to use the path you set up in step 2:

```
package main

import "github.com/agtorre/go-cookbook/chapter3/dataconv"

func main() {
    dataconv.ShowConv()
    if err := dataconv.Strconv(); err != nil {
        panic(err)
    }
    dataconv.Interfaces()
}
```

9. Run `go run main.go`.
10. You could also run:

```
go build
./example
```

You should see the following output:

```
$ go run main.go
48
2.00 – string
1234
255
true
It's a string!
It's an int!
not sure what it is...
```

```
val is test
uh oh! glad we handled this
```

11. If you copied or wrote your own tests, go up one directory and run `go test`. Ensure that all tests pass.

## How it works...

This recipe demonstrates casting between types by wrapping them in a new type, using the `strconv` package, and by using interface reflection. These methods allow Go developer to quickly convert between various abstract Go types. will both reveal errors during compilation, but reflection can be more tricky. If you reflect incorrectly to an unsupported type, you'll cause a panic. Switching on type is a way to generalize and is also demonstrated in this recipe.

Conversion becomes important for packages such as `math`, which operate on float64 exclusively.

# Working with numeric data types using math and math/big

The `math` and `math/big` packages focus on exposing more complex mathematical operations to the Go language, such as `Pow`, `Sqrt`, and `Cos`. The `math` package itself operates predominately on float64 unless a function says otherwise. The `math/big` package is for numbers that are too large to represent in a 64-bit value. This recipe will show some basic usage of the `math` package and demonstrate `math/big` for fibonacci.

## Getting ready

Refer to the steps given in the *Getting ready* section of the *Converting data types and interface casting* recipe.

# How to do it...

These steps cover writing and running your application:

1. From your terminal/console application, create and navigate to the `chapter3/math` directory.

2. Copy tests from `https://github.com/agtorre/go-cookbook/tree/master/chapter3/math` or use this as an exercise to write some of your own code.

3. Create a file called `math.go` with the following contents:

```go
package math

import (
  "fmt"
  "math"
)

// Examples demonstrates some of the functions
// in the math package
func Examples() {
    //sqrt Examples
    i := 25

    // i is an int, so convert
    result := math.Sqrt(float64(i))

    // sqrt of 25 == 5
    fmt.Println(result)

    // ceil rounds up
    result = math.Ceil(9.5)
    fmt.Println(result)

    // floor rounds down
    result = math.Floor(9.5)
    fmt.Println(result)

    // math also stores some consts:
    fmt.Println("Pi:", math.Pi, "E:", math.E)
}
```

4. Create a file called `fib.go` with the following contents:

```go
package math

import "math/big"

// global to memoize fib
var memoize map[int]*big.Int

func init() {
    // initialize the map
    memoize = make(map[int]*big.Int)
}

// Fib prints the nth digit of the fibonacci sequence
// it will return 1 for anything < 0 as well...
// it's calculated recursively and use big.Int since
// int64 will quickly overflow
func Fib(n int) *big.Int {
    if n < 0 {
        return nil
    }

    // base case
    if n < 2 {
        memoize[n] = big.NewInt(1)
    }

    // check if we stored it before
    // if so return with no calculation
    if val, ok := memoize[n]; ok {
        return val
    }

    // initialize map then add previous 2 fib values
    memoize[n] = big.NewInt(0)
    memoize[n].Add(memoize[n], Fib(n-1))
    memoize[n].Add(memoize[n], Fib(n-2))

    // return result
    return memoize[n]
}
```

5. Create a new directory named `example`.

6. Navigate to `example`.

7. Create a file `main.go` with the following contents; be sure to modify the `math` import to use the path you set up in step 2:

```
package main

import (
    "fmt"

    "github.com/agtorre/go-cookbook/chapter3/math"
)

func main() {
    math.Examples()

    for i := 0; i < 10; i++ {
        fmt.Printf("%v ", math.Fib(i))
    }
    fmt.Println()
}
```

8. Run `go run main.go`.

9. You could also run:

```
go build
./example
```

You should see the following output:

```
$ go run main.go
5
10
9
Pi: 3.141592653589793 E: 2.718281828459045
1 1 2 3 5 8 13 21 34 55
```

10. If you copied or wrote your own tests, go up one directory and run `go test`. Ensure that all tests pass.

# How it works...

The `math` package makes it possible to do complex mathematical operations in Go. This recipe should be used in conjunction with this package for doing complex floating point operations and converting between types as needed. It's worth noting that even with float64, there may still be rounding errors for certain floating point numbers, and the following recipe demonstrates some techniques for dealing with this.

The `math/big` section showcases a recursive Fibonacci sequence. If you modify `main.go` to loop well beyond 10, you'll quickly overflow int64 if it was used instead of `big.Int`. This package also has helper methods to convert between the big types to other types.

# Currency conversions and float64 considerations

Working with currency is always a tricky process. It can be tempting to represent money as a float64, but this can result in some pretty tricky (and wrong) rounding errors when doing calculations. For this reason, it's preferable to think of money in terms of cents and store it as an Int64.

When collecting user input from forms, the command line, or other sources, money is usually represented in dollar form. For this reason, it's best to treat it as a string and convert that string directly to pennies without floating point conversions. This recipe will present ways to convert a string representation of currency into an int64 (pennies) and back again.

# Getting ready

Refer to the steps given in the *Getting ready* section of the *Converting data types and interface casting* recipe.

# How to do it...

These steps cover writing and running your application:

1. From your terminal/console application, create and navigate to the `chapter3/currency` directory.
2. Copy tests from `https://github.com/agtorre/go-cookbook/tree/master/chapter3/currency` or use this as an exercise to write some of your own.

3. Create a file called `dollars.go` with the following contents:

```go
package currency

import (
    "errors"
    "strconv"
    "strings"
)

// ConvertStringDollarsToPennies takes a dollar amount
// as a string, i.e. 1.00, 55.12 etc and converts it
// into an int64
func ConvertStringDollarsToPennies(amount string) (int64,
error) {
    // check if amount can convert to a valid float
    _, err := strconv.ParseFloat(amount, 64)
    if err != nil {
        return 0, err
    }

    // split the value on "."
    groups := strings.Split(amount, ".")

    // if there is no . result will still be
    // captured here
    result := groups[0]

    // base string
    r := ""

    // handle the data after the "."
    if len(groups) == 2 {
        if len(groups[1]) != 2 {
            return 0, errors.New("invalid cents")
        }
        r = groups[1]
        if len(r) > 2 {
            r = r[:2]
        }
    }

    // pad with 0, this will be
    // 2 0's if there was no .
    for len(r) < 2 {
        r += "0"
    }
```

```
        result += r

        // convert it to an int
        return strconv.ParseInt(result, 10, 64)
    }
```

4.  Create a file called `pennies.go` with the following contents:

```
package currency

import (
    "strconv"
)

// ConvertPenniesToDollarString takes a penny amount as
// an int64 and returns a dollar string representation
func ConvertPenniesToDollarString(amount int64) string {
    // parse the pennies as a base 10 int
    result := strconv.FormatInt(amount, 10)

    // check if negative, will set it back later
    negative := false
    if result[0] == '-' {
        result = result[1:]
        negative = true
    }

    // left pad with 0 if we're passed in value < 100
    for len(result) < 3 {
        result = "0" + result
    }
    length := len(result)

    // add in the decimal
    result = result[0:length-2] + "." + result[length-2:]

    // from the negative we stored earlier!
    if negative {
        result = "-" + result
    }

    return result
}
```

5. Create a new directory named `example`.

6. Navigate to `example`.

7. Create a file called `main.go` with the following contents; be sure to modify the `currency` import to use the path you set up in step 2:

```go
package main

import (
    "fmt"

    "github.com/agtorre/go-cookbook/chapter3/currency"
)

func main() {
    // start with our user input
    // of fifteen dollars and 93 cents
    userInput := "15.93"

    pennies, err :=
    currency.ConvertStringDollarsToPennies(userInput)
    if err != nil {
        panic(err)
    }

    fmt.Printf("User input converted to %d pennies\n", pennies)

    // adding 15 cents
    pennies += 15

    dollars := currency.ConvertPenniesToDollarString(pennies)

    fmt.Printf("Added 15 cents, new values is %s dollars\n",
    dollars)
}
```

8. Run `go run main.go`.

9. You could also run this:

```
go build
./example
```

You should see the following output:

```
$ go run main.go
User input converted to 1593 pennies
Added 15 cents, new values is 16.08 dollars
```

10. If you copied or wrote your own tests, go up one directory and run `go test`. Ensure that all tests pass.

## How it works...

This recipe makes use of the `strconv` and `strings` packages to convert currency between dollars in string format and pennies in int64. It does this without even converting to a float64 other than as validation.

The `strconv.ParseInt` and `strconv.FormatInt` functions are very useful for converting to and from int64 and strings. We also made use of the fact that Go strings can easily be appended and sliced as needed.

# Using pointers and SQL NullTypes for encoding and decoding

When you encode or decode into an object in Go, types that are not explicitly set will be set to their default values. Strings will default to empty string "", and integers will default to 0 as an example. Normally, this is fine, unless 0 means something for your API or service that is consuming the user input or returning it.

In addition, if you use struct tags such as `json omitempty`, 0 values will be ignored even if they're valid. Another example of this is `Null` that returns from SQL. What value best represents `Null` for an `Int`? This recipe will explore some of the ways Go developers deal with this issue.

## Getting ready

Refer to the steps given in the *Getting ready* section of the *Converting data types and interface casting* recipe.

# How to do it...

These steps cover writing and running your application:

1. From your terminal/console application, create and navigate to the `chapter3/nulls` directory.

2. Copy tests from `https://github.com/agtorre/go-cookbook/tree/master/chapter3/nulls` or use this as an exercise to write some of your own code.

3. Create a file called `base.go` with the following contents:

```go
package nulls

import (
    "encoding/json"
    "fmt"
)

// json that has name but not age
const (
    jsonBlob = `{"name": "Aaron"}`
    fulljsonBlob = `{"name":"Aaron", "age":0}`
)

// Example is a basic struct with age
// and name fields
type Example struct {
    Age int `json:"age,omitempty"`
    Name string `json:"name"`
}

// BaseEncoding shows encoding and
// decoding with normal types
func BaseEncoding() error {
    e := Example{}

    // note that no age = 0 age
    if err := json.Unmarshal([]byte(jsonBlob), &e); err != nil
    {
        return err
    }
    fmt.Printf("Regular Unmarshal, no age: %+v\n", e)
    value, err := json.Marshal(&e)
    if err != nil {
        return err
    }
    fmt.Println("Regular Marshal, with no age:", string(value))
```

```
        if err := json.Unmarshal([]byte(fulljsonBlob), &e);
        err != nil {
            return err
        }
        fmt.Printf("Regular Unmarshal, with age = 0: %+v\n", e)

        value, err = json.Marshal(&e)
        if err != nil {
            return err
        }
        fmt.Println("Regular Marshal, with age = 0:",
        string(value))

        return nil
    }
```

4. Create a file called `pointer.go` with the following contents:

```
package nulls

import (
    "encoding/json"
    "fmt"
)

// ExamplePointer is the same, but
// uses a *Int
type ExamplePointer struct {
    Age *int `json:"age,omitempty"`
    Name string `json:"name"`
}

// PointerEncoding shows methods for
// dealing with nil/omitted values
func PointerEncoding() error {

    // note that no age = nil age
    e := ExamplePointer{}
    if err := json.Unmarshal([]byte(jsonBlob), &e); err != nil
    {
        return err
    }
    fmt.Printf("Pointer Unmarshal, no age: %+v\n", e)

    value, err := json.Marshal(&e)
    if err != nil {
        return err
    }
```

```
fmt.Println("Pointer Marshal, with no age:", string(value))

if err := json.Unmarshal([]byte(fulljsonBlob), &e);
err != nil {
    return err
}
fmt.Printf("Pointer Unmarshal, with age = 0: %+v\n", e)

value, err = json.Marshal(&e)
if err != nil {
    return err
}
fmt.Println("Pointer Marshal, with age = 0:",
string(value))

return nil
}
```

5. Create a file called `nullencoding.go` with the following contents:

```
package nulls

import (
    "database/sql"
    "encoding/json"
    "fmt"
)

type nullInt64 sql.NullInt64

// ExampleNullInt is the same, but
// uses a sql.NullInt64
type ExampleNullInt struct {
    Age *nullInt64 `json:"age,omitempty"`
    Name string `json:"name"`
}

func (v *nullInt64) MarshalJSON() ([]byte, error) {
    if v.Valid {
        return json.Marshal(v.Int64)
    }
    return json.Marshal(nil)
}

func (v *nullInt64) UnmarshalJSON(b []byte) error {
    v.Valid = false
    if b != nil {
        v.Valid = true
```

```
        return json.Unmarshal(b, &v.Int64)
    }
    return nil
}

// NullEncoding shows an alternative method
// for dealing with nil/omitted values
func NullEncoding() error {
    e := ExampleNullInt{}

    // note that no means an invalid value
    if err := json.Unmarshal([]byte(jsonBlob), &e); err != nil
    {
        return err
    }
    fmt.Printf("nullInt64 Unmarshal, no age: %+v\n", e)

    value, err := json.Marshal(&e)
    if err != nil {
        return err
    }
    fmt.Println("nullInt64 Marshal, with no age:",
    string(value))

    if err := json.Unmarshal([]byte(fulljsonBlob), &e);
    err != nil {
        return err
    }
    fmt.Printf("nullInt64 Unmarshal, with age = 0: %+v\n", e)

    value, err = json.Marshal(&e)
    if err != nil {
        return err
    }
    fmt.Println("nullInt64 Marshal, with age = 0:",
    string(value))

    return nil
}
```

6. Create a new directory named `example`.
7. Navigate to `example`.
8. Create a file called `main.go` with the following contents; be sure to modify the `nulls` import to use the path you set up in step 2:

```
package main
```

```
import (
    "fmt"

    "github.com/agtorre/go-cookbook/chapter3/nulls"
)

func main() {
    if err := nulls.BaseEncoding(); err != nil {
        panic(err)
    }
    fmt.Println()

    if err := nulls.PointerEncoding(); err != nil {
        panic(err)
    }
    fmt.Println()

    if err := nulls.NullEncoding(); err != nil {
        panic(err)
    }
}
```

9. Run `go run main.go`.

10. You could also run this:

    **go build**
    **./example**

    You should see the following output:

    **$ go run main.go**
    **Regular Unmarshal, no age: {Age:0 Name:Aaron}**
    **Regular Marshal, with no age: {"name":"Aaron"}**
    **Regular Unmarshal, with age = 0: {Age:0 Name:Aaron}**
    **Regular Marshal, with age = 0: {"name":"Aaron"}**

    **Pointer Unmarshal, no age: {Age:<nil> Name:Aaron}**
    **Pointer Marshal, with no age: {"name":"Aaron"}**
    **Pointer Unmarshal, with age = 0: {Age:0xc42000a610 Name:Aaron}**
    **Pointer Marshal, with age = 0: {"age":0,"name":"Aaron"}**

    **nullInt64 Unmarshal, no age: {Age:<nil> Name:Aaron}**
    **nullInt64 Marshal, with no age: {"name":"Aaron"}**
    **nullInt64 Unmarshal, with age = 0: {Age:0xc42000a750**
    **Name:Aaron}**
    **nullInt64 Marshal, with age = 0: {"age":0,"name":"Aaron"}**

11. If you copied or wrote your own tests, go up one directory and run `go test`. Ensure that all tests pass.

# How it works...

Switching from a value to a pointer is a quick way to express null values when marshaling and unmarshaling. It can be a bit unclear on setting these values as you can't assign them directly to a pointer -- `*a := 1`, but otherwise it's a flexible way of dealing with it.

This recipe also demonstrated an alternative method using the `sql.NullInt64` type. This is normally used with SQL and valid is set if anything other than `Null` is returned, otherwise it sets `Null`. We added a `MarshalJSON` and `UnmarshallJSON` method to allow this type to interact with the `JSON` package and we chose to use a pointer so that `omitempty` would continue to work as expected.

# Encoding and decoding Go data

Go features a number of alternative encoding types aside from JSON, TOML, and YAML. These are largely meant for transporting data between Go processes with things such as wire protocols and RPC or in cases where some character formats are restricted.

This recipe will explore encoding and decoding gob format and base64. The later chapters will explore protocols such as GRPC.

# Getting ready

Refer to the steps given in the *Getting ready* section of the *Converting Data Types and Interface Casting* recipe.

# How to do it...

These steps cover writing and running your application:

1. From your terminal/console application, create and navigate to a the `chapter3/encoding` directory.
2. Copy tests from `https://github.com/agtorre/go-cookbook/tree/master/chapter3/encoding` or use this as an exercise to write some of your own.

3. Create a file called gob.go with the following contents:

```go
package encoding

import (
    "bytes"
    "encoding/gob"
    "fmt"
)

// pos stores the x, y position
// for Object
type pos struct {
    X       int
    Y       int
    Object string
}

// GobExample demonstrates using
// the gob package
func GobExample() error {
    buffer := bytes.Buffer{}

    p := pos{
        X:       10,
        Y:       15,
        Object: "wrench",
    }

    // note that if p was an interface
    // we'd have to call gob.Register first

    e := gob.NewEncoder(&buffer)
    if err := e.Encode(&p); err != nil {
        return err
    }

    // note this is a binary format so it wont print well
    fmt.Println("Gob Encoded valued length: ",
    len(buffer.Bytes()))

    p2 := pos{}
    d := gob.NewDecoder(&buffer)
    if err := d.Decode(&p2); err != nil {
        return err
    }

    fmt.Println("Gob Decode value: ", p2)
```

```
        return nil
    }
```

4.  Create a file called `base64.go` with the following contents:

```go
package encoding

import (
    "bytes"
    "encoding/base64"
    "fmt"
    "io/ioutil"
)

// Base64Example demonstrates using
// the base64 package
func Base64Example() error {
    // base64 is useful for cases where
    // you can't support binary formats
    // it operates on bytes/strings

    // using helper functions and URL encoding
    value := base64.URLEncoding.EncodeToString([]byte("encoding
    some data!"))
    fmt.Println("With EncodeToString and URLEncoding: ", value)

    // decode the first value
    decoded, err := base64.URLEncoding.DecodeString(value)
    if err != nil {
        return err
    }
    fmt.Println("With DecodeToString and URLEncoding: ",
    string(decoded))

    return nil
}

// Base64ExampleEncoder shows similar examples
// with encoders/decoders
func Base64ExampleEncoder() error {
    // using encoder/ decoder
    buffer := bytes.Buffer{}

    // encode into the buffer
    encoder := base64.NewEncoder(base64.StdEncoding, &buffer)

    // be sure to close
    if err := encoder.Close(); err != nil {
```

```
            return err
        }
        if _, err := encoder.Write([]byte("encoding some other
        data")); err != nil {
            return err
        }

        fmt.Println("Using encoder and StdEncoding: ",
        buffer.String())

        decoder := base64.NewDecoder(base64.StdEncoding, &buffer)
        results, err := ioutil.ReadAll(decoder)
        if err != nil {
            return err
        }

        fmt.Println("Using decoder and StdEncoding: ",
        string(results))

        return nil
    }
```

5. Create a new directory named `example`.
6. Navigate to `example`.
7. Create a file called `main.go` with the following contents; be sure to modify the `encoding` import to use the path you set up in step 2:

```
package main

import (
    "github.com/agtorre/go-cookbook/chapter3/encoding"
)

func main() {
    if err := encoding.Base64Example(); err != nil {
        panic(err)
    }

    if err := encoding.Base64ExampleEncoder(); err != nil {
        panic(err)
    }

    if err := encoding.GobExample(); err != nil {
        panic(err)
    }
}
```

8. Run `go run main.go`.

9. You could also run this:

```
go build
./example
```

You should see the following output:

```
$ go run main.go
With EncodeToString and URLEncoding:
ZW5jb2Rpbmcgc29tZSBkYXRhIQ==
With DecodeToString and URLEncoding: encoding some data!
Using encoder and StdEncoding: ZW5jb2Rpbmcgc29tZSBvdGhlciBkYXRh
Using decoder and StdEncoding: encoding some other data
Gob Encoded valued length: 57
Gob Decode value: {10 15 wrench}
```

10. If you copied or wrote your own tests, go up one directory and run `go test`. Ensure that all tests pass.

## How it works...

Gob encoding is a streaming format built with Go data types in mind. It is most efficient when sending and encoding many consecutive items. For a single item, other encoding formats such as JSON are potentially more efficient and portable. Despite this, gob encoding makes it simple to marshal large complex structs and reconstruct them in a separate process. Although it wasn't shown here, gob can also operate on custom types or unexported types with custom `MarshalBinary` and `UnmarshalBinary` methods.

Base64 encoding is useful for communicating via URLs in GET requests or for generating a string representation encoding of binary data. Most languages can support this format and unmarshal the data on the other end. As a result, it's common to encode things such as JSON payloads in cases where the JSON format is not supported.

## Struct tags and basic reflection in Go

Reflection is a complicated topic that can't really be covered in a single recipe. However, a practical application of reflection is dealing with struct tags. At their core, struct tags are just key-value strings. You lookup the key, then deal with the value. As you can imagine, for something like JSON marshal and unmarshal, there's a lot of complexity for dealing with these values.

The `reflect` package is designed for interrogating and understanding interface objects. It has helper methods to look at kind of structs, values, struct tags, and more. If you need something beyond the basic interface conversion like at the beginning of this chapter, this is the package you should look at.

# Getting ready

Refer to the steps given in the *Getting ready* section of the *Converting Data Types and Interface Casting* recipe.

# How to do it...

These steps cover writing and running your application:

1. From your terminal/console application, create and navigate to the `chapter3/tags` directory .
2. Copy tests from `https://github.com/agtorre/go-cookbook/tree/master/chapter3/tags`or use this as an exercise to write some of your own code.
3. Create a file called `serialize.go` with the following contents:

```
package tags

import "reflect"

// SerializeStructStrings converts a struct
// to our custom serialization format
// it honors serialize struct tags for string types
func SerializeStructStrings(s interface{}) (string, error) {
    result := ""

    // reflect the interface into
    // a type
    r := reflect.TypeOf(s)
    value := reflect.ValueOf(s)
    // if a pointer to a struct is passed
    // in, handle it appropriately
    if r.Kind() == reflect.Ptr {
        r = r.Elem()
        value = value.Elem()
    }

    // loop over all of the fields
```

```
        for i := 0; i < r.NumField(); i++ {
            field := r.Field(i)
            // struct tag found
            key := field.Name
            if serialize, ok := field.Tag.Lookup("serialize"); ok {
                // ignore "-" otherwise that whole value
                // becomes the serialize 'key'
                if serialize == "-" {
                    continue
                }
                key = serialize
            }

            switch value.Field(i).Kind() {
            // this recipe only supports strings!
            case reflect.String:
                result += key + ":" + value.Field(i).String() + ";"
                // by default skip it
            default:
                continue
            }
        }
    }
    return result, nil
}
```

4. Create a file called `deserialize.go` with the following contents:

```
package tags

import (
    "errors"
    "reflect"
    "strings"
)

// DeSerializeStructStrings converts a serialized
// string using our custom serialization format
// to a struct
func DeSerializeStructStrings(s string, res interface{}) error
{
    r := reflect.TypeOf(res)

    // we're setting using a pointer so
    // it must always be a pointer passed
    // in
    if r.Kind() != reflect.Ptr {
        return errors.New("res must be a pointer")
    }
```

```go
    // dereference the pointer
    r = r.Elem()
    value := reflect.ValueOf(res).Elem()

    // split our serialization string into
    // a map
    vals := strings.Split(s, ";")
    valMap := make(map[string]string)
    for _, v := range vals {
        keyval := strings.Split(v, ":")
        if len(keyval) != 2 {
            continue
        }
        valMap[keyval[0]] = keyval[1]
    }

    // iterate over fields
    for i := 0; i < r.NumField(); i++ {
        field := r.Field(i)

        // check if in the serialize set
        if serialize, ok := field.Tag.Lookup("serialize"); ok {
            // ignore "-" otherwise that whole value
            // becomes the serialize 'key'
            if serialize == "-" {
                continue
            }
            // is it in the map
            if val, ok := valMap[serialize]; ok {
                value.Field(i).SetString(val)
            }
        } else if val, ok := valMap[field.Name]; ok {
            // is our field name in the map instead?
            value.Field(i).SetString(val)
        }
    }
    return nil
}
```

5. Create a file called `tags.go` with the following contents:

```go
package tags

import "fmt"

// Person is a struct that stores a persons
// name, city, state, and a misc attribute
type Person struct {
```

```
        Name string `serialize:"name"`
        City string `serialize:"city"`
        State string
         Misc string `serialize:"-"`
         Year int `serialize:"year"`
}

// EmptyStruct demonstrates serialize
// and deserialize for an Empty struct
// with tags
func EmptyStruct() error {
    p := Person{}

    res, err := SerializeStructStrings(&p)
    if err != nil {
        return err
    }
    fmt.Printf("Empty struct: %#v\n", p)
    fmt.Println("Serialize Results:", res)

    newP := Person{}
    if err := DeSerializeStructStrings(res, &newP); err != nil
    {
        return err
    }
    fmt.Printf("Deserialize results: %#v\n", newP)
        return nil
    }

    // FullStruct demonstrates serialize
    // and deserialize for an Full struct
    // with tags
    func FullStruct() error {
        p := Person{
            Name: "Aaron",
            City: "Seattle",
            State: "WA",
            Misc: "some fact",
            Year: 2017,
        }
        res, err := SerializeStructStrings(&p)
        if err != nil {
            return err
        }
        fmt.Printf("Full struct: %#v\n", p)
        fmt.Println("Serialize Results:", res)

        newP := Person{}
```

```
            if err := DeSerializeStructStrings(res, &newP);
            err != nil {
                return err
            }
            fmt.Printf("Deserialize results: %#v\n", newP)
            return nil
    }
```

6. Create a new directory named `example`.

7. Navigate to `example`.

8. Create a file called `main.go` with the following contents; be sure to modify the `tags` import to use the path you set up in step 2:

```
package main

import (
    "fmt"

    "github.com/agtorre/go-cookbook/chapter3/tags"
)

func main() {

    if err := tags.EmptyStruct(); err != nil {
        panic(err)
    }

    fmt.Println()

    if err := tags.FullStruct(); err != nil {
        panic(err)
    }
}
```

9. Run `go run main.go`.

10. You could also run this:

```
go build
./example
```

You should see the following output:

```
$ go run main.go
Empty struct: tags.Person{Name:"", City:"", State:"", Misc:"",
Year:0}
Serialize Results: name:;city:;State:;
Deserialize results: tags.Person{Name:"", City:"", State:"",
```

```
    Misc:"", Year:0}

    Full struct: tags.Person{Name:"Aaron", City:"Seattle",
    State:"WA", Misc:"some fact", Year:2017}
    Serialize Results: name:Aaron;city:Seattle;State:WA;
    Deserialize results: tags.Person{Name:"Aaron", City:"Seattle",
State:"WA", Misc:"", Year:0}
```

11. If you copied or wrote your own tests, go up one directory and run `go test`. Ensure that all tests pass.

# How it works...

This recipe makes a string serialization format that takes a struct, and serializes all the string fields into a parseable format. This recipe doesn't deal with certain edge cases; in particular, strings must not contain : or ; characters. Here is a summary of its behavior:

1. If a field is a string, it will be serialized/deserialized.
2. If a field is not a string, it will be ignored.
3. If the struct tag of the field contains the serialize"key", then key will be the returned serialized/deserialized environment.
4. Duplicates are not handled.
5. If a struct tag is not specified, the field name is used instead.
6. If serialize – is specified, the field is ignored even if it's a string.

Some other things to note are that reflection does not work entirely with non-exported values.

# Implementing collections via closures

If you've been working with functional or dynamic programming languages, you may feel that `for` loops and `if` statements produce verbose code. Functional constructs such as `map` and `filter` for processing lists can be useful and make code appear more readable. However, in Go, these types are not in the standard library and can be difficult to generalize without generics or very complex reflection and use of empty interfaces. This recipe will provide you with some basic examples of implementing collections using Go closures.

# Getting ready

Refer to the steps given in the *Getting ready* section of the *Converting Data Types and Interface Casting* recipe.

# How to do it...

These steps cover writing and running your application:

1. From your terminal/console application, create and navigate to the `chapter3/collections` directory.

2. Copy tests from `https://github.com/agtorre/go-cookbook/tree/master/chapter3/collections`or use this as an exercise to write some of your own code.

3. Create a file called `collections.go` with the following contents:

```
package collections

// WorkWith is the struct we'll
// be implementing collections for
type WorkWith struct {
    Data     string
    Version int
}

// Filter is a functional filter. It takes a list of
// WorkWith and a WorkWith Function that returns a bool
// for each "true" element we return it to the resultant
// list
func Filter(ws []WorkWith, f func(w WorkWith) bool) []WorkWith
{
    // depending on results, smalles size for result
    // is len == 0
    result := make([]WorkWith, 0)
    for _, w := range ws {
        if f(w) {
            result = append(result, w)
        }
    }
    return result
}

// Map is a functional map. It takes a list of
// WorkWith and a WorkWith Function that takes a WorkWith
// and returns a modified WorkWith. The end result is
```

```
    // a list of modified WorkWiths
    func Map(ws []WorkWith, f func(w WorkWith) WorkWith) []WorkWith
    {
        // the result should always be the same
        // length
        result := make([]WorkWith, len(ws))

        for pos, w := range ws {
            newW := f(w)
            result[pos] = newW
        }
        return result
    }
```

4.  Create a file called `functions.go` with the following contents:

```
    package collections

    import "strings"

    // LowerCaseData does a ToLower to the
    // Data string of a WorkWith
    func LowerCaseData(w WorkWith) WorkWith {
        w.Data = strings.ToLower(w.Data)
        return w
    }

    // IncrementVersion increments a WorkWiths
    // Version
    func IncrementVersion(w WorkWith) WorkWith {
        w.Version++
        return w
    }

    // OldVersion returns a closures
    // that validates the version is greater than
    // the specified amount
    func OldVersion(v int) func(w WorkWith) bool {
        return func(w WorkWith) bool {
            return w.Version >= v
        }
    }
```

5.  Create a new directory named `example`.
6.  Navigate to `example`.

7. Create a file called `main.go` with the following contents; be sure to modify the `collections` import to use the path you set up in step 2:

```
package main

import (
    "fmt"

    "github.com/agtorre/go-cookbook/chapter3/collections"
)

func main() {
    ws := []collections.WorkWith{
        collections.WorkWith{"Example", 1},
        collections.WorkWith{"Example 2", 2},
    }

    fmt.Printf("Initial list: %#v\n", ws)

    // first lower case the list
    ws = collections.Map(ws, collections.LowerCaseData)
    fmt.Printf("After LowerCaseData Map: %#v\n", ws)

    // next increment all versions
    ws = collections.Map(ws, collections.IncrementVersion)
    fmt.Printf("After IncrementVersion Map: %#v\n", ws)

    // lastly remove all versions older than 3
    ws = collections.Filter(ws, collections.OldVersion(3))
    fmt.Printf("After OldVersion Filter: %#v\n", ws)
}
```

8. Run `go run main.go`.

9. You could also run this:

```
go build
./example
```

You should see the following output:

```
$ go run main.go
Initial list:
[]collections.WorkWith{collections.WorkWith{Data:"Example",
Version:1}, collections.WorkWith{Data:"Example 2", Version:2}}
After LowerCaseData Map:
[]collections.WorkWith{collections.WorkWith{Data:"example",
Version:1}, collections.WorkWith{Data:"example 2", Version:2}}
```

```
After IncrementVersion Map:
[]collections.WorkWith{collections.WorkWith{Data:"example",
Version:2}, collections.WorkWith{Data:"example 2", Version:3}}
After OldVersion Filter:
[]collections.WorkWith{collections.WorkWith{Data:"example 2",
Version:3}}
```

10. If you copied or wrote your own tests, go up one directory and run `go test`. Ensure that all tests pass.

## How it works...

Closures in Go are very powerful. Although our collections functions are not generic, they're relatively small and easily applied with a variety of functions to our `WorkWith` struct. You may notice from looking at this that we're not returning errors anywhere. The idea of these functions are that they're pure. There are no side effects to the original list, except that we choose to write over it after each call.

If you need to apply layers of modification to a list or struct of lists, this pattern can save you a lot of confusion and makes testing very straightforward. It is also possible to chain maps and filters together for a very expressive coding style.

# 4
# Error Handling in Go

In this chapter, the following recipes will be covered:

- Handling errors and the Error interface
- Using the pkg/errors package and wrapping errors
- Using the log package and understanding when to log errors
- Structured logging with the apex and logrus packages
- Logging with the context package
- Using package-level global variables
- Catching panics for long running processes

## Introduction

Error handling is important for even the most basic Go program. Errors in Go implement the Error interface and must be dealt with at every layer of the code. Go errors do not work like exceptions, and unhandled errors can cause enormous problems. You should strive to handle and consider errors whenever they occur.

This chapter also covers logging since it's common to log whenever an actual error occurs. We'll also investigate wrapping errors so that a given error has the appropriate amount of context for the calling function.

# Handling errors and the Error interface

The `Error` interface is a pretty small and simple interface:

```
type Error interface{
  Error() string
}
```

This interface is elegant because it's simple to make anything to satisfy it. Unfortunately, this also creates confusion for packages that need to take certain actions depending on the error received.

There are a number of ways to create errors in Go, this recipe will explore the creation of basic errors, errors that have assigned values or types, and of a custom error using a struct.

## Getting ready

Configure your environment according to these steps:

1. Download and install Go on your operating system from `https://golang.org/d oc/install`, and configure your `GOPATH` environment variable.
2. Open a terminal/console application.
3. Navigate to your `GOPATH/src` and create a project directory, for example, `$GOPATH/src/github.com/yourusername/customrepo`.

   All code will be run and modified from this directory.

4. Optionally, install the latest tested version of the code using the `go get` `github.com/agtorre/go-cookbook/` command.

## How to do it...

These steps cover writing and running your application:

1. From your terminal/console application, create the `chapter4/basicerrors` directory and navigate to it.
2. Copy tests from `https://github.com/agtorre/go-cookbook/tree/master/cha pter4/basicerrors`or use this as an exercise to write some of your own code.

3. Create a file called `basicerrors.go` with the following content:

```go
package basicerrors

import (
    "errors"
    "fmt"
)

// ErrorTyped is a way to make a package level
// error to check against. I.e. if err == TypedError
var ErrorTyped = errors.New("this is a typed error")

//BasicErrors demonstrates some ways to create errors
func BasicErrors() {
    err := errors.New("this is a quick and easy way to create
    an error")
    fmt.Println("errors.New: ", err)

    err = fmt.Errorf("an error occurred: %s", "something")
    fmt.Println("fmt.Errorf: ", err)

    err = ErrorTyped
    fmt.Println("typed error: ", err)
}
```

4. Create a file called `custom.go` with the following content:

```go
package basicerrors

import (
    "errors"
    "fmt"
)

// ErrorValue is a way to make a package level
// error to check against. I.e. if err == ErrorValue
var ErrorValue = errors.New("this is a typed error")

// TypedError is a way to make an error type
// you can do err.(type) == ErrorValue
type TypedError struct{
    error
}

//BasicErrors demonstrates some ways to create errors
func BasicErrors() {
    err := errors.New("this is a quick and easy way to create
```

```
            an error")
        fmt.Println("errors.New: ", err)

        err = fmt.Errorf("an error occurred: %s", "something")
        fmt.Println("fmt.Errorf: ", err)

        err = ErrorValue
        fmt.Println("value error: ", err)
        err = TypedError{errors.New("typed error")}
        fmt.Println("typed error: ", err)
    }
```

5. Create a new directory named `example` and navigate to it.

6. Create a `main.go` file with the following content. Ensure that you modify the `basicerrors` import to use the path you set up in step 2:

```
package main

import (
    "fmt"

    "github.com/agtorre/go-cookbook/chapter4/basicerrors"
)

func main() {
    basicerrors.BasicErrors()

    err := basicerrors.SomeFunc()
    fmt.Println("custom error: ", err)
}
```

7. Run `go run main.go`.

8. You may also run:

```
go build
./example
```

You should now see the following output:

```
$ go run main.go
errors.New: this is a quick and easy way to create an error
fmt.Errorf: an error occurred: something
typed error: this is a typed error
custom error: there was an error; this was the result
```

9. If you copied or wrote your own tests, go up one directory and run `go test`. Ensure that all the tests pass.

# How it works...

Whether you use `errors.New`, `fmt.Errorf`, or a custom error, the most important thing is that you should never leave errors unhandled in your code. These different methods of defining errors give a lot of flexibility. You can, for example, put extra functions in your struct to further interrogate an error and cast the interface to your error type in the calling function to get some added functionality.

The interface itself is very simple and the only requirement is that you return a valid string. Connecting this to a struct may be useful for some high-level applications that have consistent error handling throughout but want to work nicely with other applications.

# Using the pkg/errors package and wrapping errors

The `errors` package located at `github.com/pkg/errors` is a drop in replacement for the standard Go `errors` package. In addition, it provides some very useful functionality for wrapping and handling errors. The typed and declared errors in the preceding recipe are a good example--they can be useful to add additional information to an error, but wrapping it in the standard way will change its type and break type assertion:

```
// this wont work if you wrapped it
// in a standard way. i.e.
// fmt.Errorf("custom error: %s", err.Error())
if err == Package.ErrorNamed{
  //handle this error in a specific way
}
```

This recipe will demonstrate how to use the `pkg/errors` package to add annotation to errors throughout your code.

# Getting ready

Configure your environment according to these steps:

1. Refer to the *Getting ready* section of the *Handling errors and the Error interface* recipe in this chapter.
2. Run the `go get github.com/pkg/errors/` command.

# How to do it...

These steps cover writing and running your application:

1. From your terminal/console application, create the `chapter4/errwrap` directory and navigate to it.

2. Copy tests from `https://github.com/agtorre/go-cookbook/tree/master/chapter4/errwrap`or use this as an exercise to write some of your own code.

3. Create a file called `errwrap.go` with the following content:

```go
package errwrap

import (
    "fmt"

    "github.com/pkg/errors"
)
// WrappedError demonstrates error wrapping and
// annotating an error
func WrappedError(e error) error {
    return errors.Wrap(e, "An error occurred in WrappedError")
}

// ErrorTyped is a error we can check against
type ErrorTyped struct{
    error
}

// Wrap shows what happens when we wrap an error
func Wrap() {
    e := errors.New("standard error")

    fmt.Println("Regular Error - ", WrappedError(e))

    fmt.Println("Typed Error - ",
    WrappedError(ErrorTyped{errors.New("typed error")}))

    fmt.Println("Nil -", WrappedError(nil))

}
```

4. Create a file called `unwrap.go` with the following content:

```go
package errwrap

import (
```

```
    "fmt"

    "github.com/pkg/errors"
)

// Unwrap will unwrap an error and do
// type assertion to it
func Unwrap() {

    err := error(ErrorTyped{errors.New("an error occurred")})
    err = errors.Wrap(err, "wrapped")
    fmt.Println("wrapped error: ", err)

    // we can handle many error types
    switch errors.Cause(err).(type) {
    case ErrorTyped:
        fmt.Println("a typed error occurred: ", err)
    default:
        fmt.Println("an unknown error occurred")
    }
}

// StackTrace will print all the stack for
// the error
func StackTrace() {
    err := error(ErrorTyped{errors.New("an error occurred")})
    err = errors.Wrap(err, "wrapped")

    fmt.Printf("%+v\n", err)
}
```

5. Create a new directory named `example` and navigate to it.

6. Create a `main.go` file with the following content. Ensure that you modify the `errwrap` import to use the path you set up in step 2:

```
package main

import (
    "fmt"

    "github.com/agtorre/go-cookbook/chapter4/errwrap"
)

func main() {
    errwrap.Wrap()
    fmt.Println()
    errwrap.Unwrap()
```

```
            fmt.Println()
            errwrap.StackTrace()
    }
```

7. Run `go run main.go`.

8. You may also run the following:

    **go build
    ./example**

    You should now see the following output:

    **$ go run main.go
    Regular Error - An error occurred in WrappedError: standard
    error
    Typed Error - An error occurred in WrappedError: typed error
    Nil - <nil>

    wrapped error: wrapped: an error occurred
    a typed error occurred: wrapped: an error occurred

    an error occurred
    github.com/agtorre/go-cookbook/chapter4/errwrap.StackTrace
    /Users/lothamer/go/src/github.com/agtorre/go-
    cookbook/chapter4/errwrap/unwrap.go:30
    main.main
    /tmp/go/src/github.com/agtorre/go-
    cookbook/chapter4/errwrap/example/main.go:14**

9. If you copied or wrote your own tests, go up one directory and run `go test`. Ensure that all the tests pass.

# How it works...

The `pkg/errors` package is a very useful tool. It makes sense to wrap basically every returned error using this package to provide extra context in logging and error debugging. It's flexible enough to print the entire stack traces when an error occurs or to just add a prefix to your errors when printing them. It can also clean up code since a wrapped nil returns a `nil` value. For example:

```
func RetError() error{
 err := ThisReturnsAnError()
 return errors.Wrap(err, "This only does something if err != nil")
}
```

In some cases, this can save you from having to check if an error is `nil` first before simply returning it. This recipe demonstrated how to use the package to wrap and unwrap errors, as well as basic stack trace functionality. The documentation for the package also provides some other useful examples such as printing partial stacks. Dave Cheney, the author of this library, has also written a number of helpful blogs and given talks on the subject, go to `http s://dave.cheney.net/2016/04/27/dont-just-check-errors-handle-them-gracefully` to know more.

# Using the log package and understanding when to log errors

Logging should typically occur when an error is the final result. In other words, it's useful to log when something exceptional or unexpected occurs. It might also be appropriate, if you use a log that provides log levels, to sprinkle debug or info statements at key parts of your code to quickly debug issues during development. Too much logging will make it difficult to find anything useful, but not enough logging can result in broken systems with no insight into the root cause. This recipe will demonstrate the use of the default Go `log` package and some useful options and showcase when a log should probably occur.

## Getting ready

Configure your environment according to these steps:

1. Refer to the *Getting ready* section of the *Handling errors and the Error interface* recipe in this chapter.
2. Run the `go get github.com/pkg/errors/` command.

## How to do it...

These steps cover writing and running your application:

1. From your terminal/console application, create the `chapter4/log` directory and navigate to it.
2. Copy tests from `https://github.com/agtorre/go-cookbook/tree/master/cha pter4/log`or use this as an exercise to write some of your own code.

3. Create a file called `log.go` with the following content:

```go
package log

import (
    "bytes"
    "fmt"
    "log"
)

// Log uses the setup logger
func Log() {
    // we'll configure the logger to write
    // to a bytes.Buffer
    buf := bytes.Buffer{}

    // second argument is the prefix last argument is about
    // options you combine them with a logical or.
    logger := log.New(&buf, "logger: ",
    log.Lshortfile|log.Ldate)

    logger.Println("test")

    logger.SetPrefix("new logger: ")

    logger.Printf("you can also add args(%v) and use Fataln to
    log and crash", true)

    fmt.Println(buf.String())
}
```

4. Create a file called `error.go` with the following content:

```go
package log

import "github.com/pkg/errors"
import "log"

// OriginalError returns the error original error
func OriginalError() error {
    return errors.New("error occurred")
}

// PassThroughError calls OriginalError and
// forwards the error along after wrapping.
func PassThroughError() error {
    err := OriginalError()
    // no need to check error
```

```
        // since this works with nil
        return errors.Wrap(err, "in passthrougherror")
    }

    // FinalDestination deals with the error
    // and doesn't forward it
    func FinalDestination() {
        err := PassThroughError()
        if err != nil {
            // we log because an unexpected error occurred!
            log.Printf("an error occurred: %s\n", err.Error())
            return
        }
    }
```

5. Create a new directory named `example` and navigate to it.

6. Create a `main.go` file with the following content. Ensure that you modify the `log` import to use the path you set up in step 2:

```
package main

import (
    "fmt"

    "github.com/agtorre/go-cookbook/chapter4/log"
)

func main() {
    fmt.Println("basic logging and modification of logger:")
    log.Log()
    fmt.Println("logging 'handled' errors:")
    log.FinalDestination()
}
```

7. Run `go run main.go`.

8. You may also run:

```
go build
./example
```

You should see the following output:

```
$ go run main.go
basic logging and modification of logger:
logger: 2017/02/05 log.go:19: test
new logger: 2017/02/05 log.go:23: you can also add args(true)
and use Fataln to log and crash
```

```
logging 'handled' errors:
2017/02/05 18:36:11 an error occurred: in passthrougherror:
error occurred
```

9. If you copied or wrote your own tests, go up one directory and run `go test`. Ensure that all the tests pass.

## How it works...

You can either initialize a logger and pass it around using `log.NewLogger()`, or use the `log` package level logger to log messages. The log file in this recipe does the former and error does the latter. It also shows when logging might make sense after an error has reached its final destination, otherwise it's likely that you'll log multiple times for one event.

There are a few issues with this approach. For one, you may have additional context in one of the intermediate functions, such as variables you'd like to log. Next, logging a bunch of variables can get messy and is confusing and difficult to read. The next recipe explores structured logging that provides flexibility in logging variables, and a later recipe will explore implementing a global package-level logger as well.

# Structured logging with the apex and logrus packages

The primary reason to log information is to examine the state of the system when events occur or occurred in the past. Basic log messages are tricky to comb over when you have a large number of microservices that are logging.

There's a variety of third-party packages for combing over logs if you can get the logs into a data format they understand. These packages provide indexing functionality, searchability, and more. The `sirupsen/logrus` and `apex/log` packages provide a way to do structured logging where you can log a number of fields that can be reformatted to fit these third-party log readers. For example, it's simple to emit logs in the JSON format to be parsed by a variety of services.

# Getting ready

Configure your environment according to these steps:

1. Refer to the *Getting ready* section of the *Handling errors and the Error interface* recipe.
2. Run the `go get github.com/sirupsen/logrus` command.
3. Run the `go get github.com/apex/log` command.

# How to do it...

These steps cover writing and running your application:

1. From your terminal/console application, create the `chapter4/structured` directory and navigate to it.
2. Copy tests from `https://github.com/agtorre/go-cookbook/tree/master/chapter4/structured`or use this as an exercise to write some of your own code.
3. Create a file called `logrus.go` with the following content:

```
package structured

import "github.com/sirupsen/logrus"

// Hook will implement the logrus
// hook interface
type Hook struct {
    id string
}

// Fire will trigger whenever you log
func (hook *Hook) Fire(entry *logrus.Entry) error {
    entry.Data["id"] = hook.id
    return nil
}

// Levels is what levels this hook will fire on
func (hook *Hook) Levels() []logrus.Level {
    return logrus.AllLevels
}

// Logrus demonstrates some basic logrus functionality
func Logrus() {
    // we're emitting in json format
```

```
        logrus.SetFormatter(&logrus.TextFormatter{})
        logrus.SetLevel(logrus.InfoLevel)
        logrus.AddHook(&Hook{"123"})

        fields := logrus.Fields{}
        fields["success"] = true
        fields["complex_struct"] = struct {
            Event string
            When string
        }{"Something happened", "Just now"}

        x := logrus.WithFields(fields)
        x.Warn("warning!")
        x.Error("error!")
    }
```

4. Create a file called `apex.go` with the following content:

```go
package structured

import (
    "errors"
    "os"

    "github.com/apex/log"
    "github.com/apex/log/handlers/text"
)

// ThrowError throws an error that we'll trace
func ThrowError() error {
    err := errors.New("a crazy failure")
    log.WithField("id", "123").Trace("ThrowError").Stop(&err)
    return err
}

// CustomHandler splits to two streams
type CustomHandler struct {
    id string
    handler log.Handler
}

// HandleLog adds a hook and does the emitting
func (h *CustomHandler) HandleLog(e *log.Entry) error {
    e.WithField("id", h.id)
    return h.handler.HandleLog(e)
}

// Apex has a number of useful tricks
```

```
func Apex() {
    log.SetHandler(&CustomHandler{"123", text.New(os.Stdout)})
    err := ThrowError()

    //With error convenience function
    log.WithError(err).Error("an error occurred")
}
```

5. Create a new directory named `example` and navigate to it.

6. Create a `main.go` file with the following content. Ensure that you modify the `structured` import to use the path you set up in step 2:

```
package main

import (
    "fmt"

    "github.com/agtorre/go-cookbook/chapter4/structured"
)

func main() {
    fmt.Println("Logrus:")
    structured.Logrus()

    fmt.Println()
    fmt.Println("Apex:")
    structured.Apex()
}
```

7. Run `go run main.go`.

8. You may also run:

```
go build
./example
```

You should now see the following output:

```
$ go run main.go
Logrus:
WARN[0000] warning! complex_struct={Something happened Just now}
id=123 success=true
ERRO[0000] error! complex_struct={Something happened Just now}
id=123 success=true

Apex:
INFO[0000] ThrowError id=123
ERROR[0000] ThrowError duration=133ns error=a crazy failure
```

```
id=123
ERROR[0000] an error occurred error=a crazy failure
```

9. If you copied or wrote your own tests, go up one directory and run `go test`. Ensure all tests pass.

# How it works...

The `sirupsen/logrus` and `apex/log` packages are both excellent structured loggers. Both provide hooks for either emitting to multiple events or to add extra fields to a log entry. It would be relatively simple, for example, to use the `logrus` hook or the `apex` custom handler to add line numbers to all of your logs as well as service names. Another use for a hook might include `traceID` to trace a request across different services.

While `logrus` splits the hook and the formatter, `apex` combines them. In addition, `apex` adds some convenience functions such as `WithError` to add an `error` field as well as tracing, both of which are demonstrated in the recipe. It's also relatively simple to adapt hooks from `logrus` into the `apex` handlers. For both solutions, it would be a simple change to convert to JSON formatting instead of ANSI colored text.

# Logging with the context package

This recipe will demonstrate a way to pass log fields between various functions. The Go `pkg/context` package is an excellent way to pass additional variables and cancelation between functions. This recipe will explore using this functionality to distribute variables between functions for logging purposes.

This style can be adapted to `logrus` or `apex` from the previous recipe. We'll use `apex` for this recipe.

# Getting ready

Configure your environment according to these steps:

1. Refer to the *Getting ready* section of the *Handling errors and the Error interface* recipe.
2. Run the `go get github.com/apex/log` command.

# How to do it...

These steps cover writing and running your application:

1. From your terminal/console application create and navigate to the chapter4/context directory.

2. Copy tests from https://github.com/agtorre/go-cookbook/tree/master/chapter4/context or use this as an exercise to write some of your own code.

3. Create a file called log.go with the following content:

```go
package context

import (
    "context"

    "github.com/apex/log"
)

type key int

// logFields is a key we use
// for our context logging
const logFields key = 0
func getFields(ctx context.Context) *log.Fields {
    fields, ok := ctx.Value(logFields).(*log.Fields)
    if !ok {
        f := make(log.Fields)
        fields = &f
    }
    return fields
}

// FromContext takes an entry and a context
// then returns an entry populated from the context object
func FromContext(ctx context.Context, l log.Interface)
(context.Context, *log.Entry) {
    fields := getFields(ctx)
    e := l.WithFields(fields)
    ctx = context.WithValue(ctx, logFields, fields)
    return ctx, e
}

// WithField adds a log field to the context
func WithField(ctx context.Context, key string, value
    interface{}) context.Context {
        return WithFields(ctx, log.Fields{key: value})
```

```
    }

    // WithFields adds many log fields to the context
    func WithFields(ctx context.Context, fields log.Fielder)
    context.Context {
        f := getFields(ctx)
        for key, val := range fields.Fields() {
            (*f)[key] = val
        }
        ctx = context.WithValue(ctx, logFields, f)
        return ctx
    }
```

4. Create a file called `collect.go` with the following content:

```
    package context

    import (
        "context"
        "os"

        "github.com/apex/log"
        "github.com/apex/log/handlers/text"
    )

    // Initialize calls 3 functions to set up, then
    // logs before terminating
    func Initialize() {
        // set basic log up
        log.SetHandler(text.New(os.Stdout))
        // initialize our context
        ctx := context.Background()
        // create a logger and link it to
        // the context
        ctx, e := FromContext(ctx, log.Log)

        // set a field
        ctx = WithField(ctx, "id", "123")
        e.Info("starting")
        gatherName(ctx)
        e.Info("after gatherName")
        gatherLocation(ctx)
        e.Info("after gatherLocation")
    }

    func gatherName(ctx context.Context) {
        ctx = WithField(ctx, "name", "Go Cookbook")
    }
```

```
func gatherLocation(ctx context.Context) {
    ctx = WithFields(ctx, log.Fields{"city": "Seattle",
    "state": "WA"})
}
```

5. Create a new directory named `example` and navigate to it.

6. Create a `main.go` file with the following content. Ensure that you modify the `context` import to use the path you set up in step 2:

```
package main

import "github.com/agtorre/go-cookbook/chapter4/context"

func main() {
    context.Initialize()
}
```

7. Run `go run main.go`.

8. You may also run the following:

```
go build
./example
```

You should see the following output:

```
$ go run main.go
 INFO[0000] starting id=123
 INFO[0000] after gatherName id=123 name=Go Cookbook
 INFO[0000] after gatherLocation city=Seattle id=123 name=Go
 Cookbook state=WA
```

9. If you copied or wrote your own tests, go up one directory and run `go test`. Ensure that all the tests pass.

# How it works...

The `context` package now appears in a variety of packages, including the databases and HTTP packages. This recipe will allow you to attach log fields to a context and use them for logging purposes. The idea is that separate methods can attach more fields onto a context as it is passed around, then the final call-site can perform logging and aggregate variables.

This recipe mimics the `WithField` and `WithFields` methods found in the logging packages in the previous recipe. These modify a single value stored in the context and also provide the other benefits of using a context: cancellation, timeouts, and thread safety.

# Using package-level global variables

The `apex` and `logrus` packages in the earlier examples both used a package-level global variable. Sometimes, it's useful to structure your libraries to support both structs with a variety of methods and top-level functions so that you can use them directly without passing them around.

This recipe also demonstrates using `sync.Once` to ensure that the global logger will only be initialized once. It can also be bypassed by the `Set` method. The recipe only exports `WithField` and `Debug`, but one can imagine exporting every method attached to a `log` object.

## Getting ready

Configure your environment according to these steps:

1. Refer to the *Getting ready* section of the *Handling errors and the Error interface* recipe.
2. Run the `go get github.com/sirupsen/logrus` command.

## How to do it...

These steps cover writing and running your application:

1. From your terminal/console application, create the `chapter4/global` directory and navigate to it.
2. Copy tests from `https://github.com/agtorre/go-cookbook/tree/master/chapter4/global`or use this as an exercise to write some of your own code.
3. Create a file called `global.go` with the following content:

```
package global

import (
    "errors"
    "os"
    "sync"

    "github.com/sirupsen/logrus"
)

// we make our global package level
```

```
// variable lower case
var (
    log *logrus.Logger
    initLog sync.Once
)

// Init sets up the logger intially
// if run multiple times, it returns
// an error
func Init() error {
    err := errors.New("already initialized")
    initLog.Do(func() {
        err = nil
        log = logrus.New()
        log.Formatter = &logrus.JSONFormatter{}
        log.Out = os.Stdout
        log.Level = logrus.DebugLevel
    })
    return err
}

// SetLog sets the log
func SetLog(l *logrus.Logger) {
    log = l
}

// WithField exports the logs withfield connected
// to our global log
func WithField(key string, value interface{}) *logrus.Entry {
    return log.WithField(key, value)
}

// Debug exports the logs Debug connected
// to our global log
func Debug(args ...interface{}) {
    log.Debug(args...)
}
```

4. Create a file called `log.go` with the following content:

```
package global

// UseLog demonstrates using our global
// log
func UseLog() error {
    if err := Init(); err != nil {
        return err
    }
```

```
// if we were in another package these would be
// global.WithField and
// global.Debug
WithField("key", "value").Debug("hello")
Debug("test")

return nil
}
```

5. Create a new directory named `example` and navigate to `example`.

6. Create a `main.go` file with the following content. Ensure that you modify the `global` import to use the path you set up in step 2:

```
package main

import "github.com/agtorre/go-cookbook/chapter4/global"

func main() {
    if err := global.UseLog(); err != nil {
        panic(err)
    }
}
```

7. Run `go run main.go`.

8. You may also run:

```
go build
./example
```

You should see the following output:

```
$ go run main.go
{"key":"value","level":"debug","msg":"hello","time":"2017-02-
12T19:22:50-08:00"}
{"level":"debug","msg":"test","time":"2017-02-12T19:22:50-
08:00"}
```

9. If you copied or wrote your own tests, go up one directory and run `go test`. Ensure that all the tests pass.

# How it works...

A common pattern for these global package-level objects is to keep the global unexported and expose only the functionality desired via methods. Typically, you could also include a method to return a copy of the global logger for packages that want a logger object.

The `sync.Once` type is a newly introduced structure. This structure, in conjunction with the `Do` method, will only execute in the code once. We use this in our initialization code, and the `Init` function will throw an error if `Init` is called more than once.

Although this example uses a log, you can also imagine cases where this might be useful with a database connection, data streams, and a number of other use cases.

# Catching panics for long running processes

When implementing long running processes, it's possible that certain code paths will result in a panic. This is usually common for things uninitialized maps and pointers, as well as division by zero problems in the case of poorly validated user input.

Having a program crash completely in these cases is frequently much worse than the panic itself, and so it can be helpful to catch and handle panics.

# Getting ready

Refer to the *Getting ready* section of the *Handling errors and the Error interface* recipe in this chapter.

# How to do it...

These steps cover writing and running your application:

1. From your terminal/console application, create the `chapter4/panic` directory and navigate to it.
2. Copy tests from `https://github.com/agtorre/go-cookbook/tree/master/chapter4/panic` or use this as an exercise to write some of your own code.

3. Create a file called `panic.go` with the following content:

```
package panic

import (
    "fmt"
    "strconv"
)

// Panic panics with a divide by zero
func Panic() {
    zero, err := strconv.ParseInt("0", 10, 64)
    if err != nil {
        panic(err)
    }
    a := 1 / zero
    fmt.Println("we'll never get here", a)
}

// Catcher calls Panic
func Catcher() {
    defer func() {
        if r := recover(); r != nil {
            fmt.Println("panic occurred:", r)
        }
    }()
    Panic()
}
```

4. Create a new directory named `example` and navigate to `example`.
5. Create a `main.go` file with the following content. Ensure that you modify the `panic` import to use the path you set up in step 2:

```
package main

import (
    "fmt"

    "github.com/agtorre/go-cookbook/chapter4/panic"
)

func main() {
    fmt.Println("before panic")
    panic.Catcher()
    fmt.Println("after panic")
}
```

6. Run `go run main.go`.

7. You may also run:

   ```
   go build
   ./example
   ```

   You should see the following output:

   ```
   $ go run main.go
   before panic
   panic occurred: runtime error: integer divide by zero
   after panic
   ```

8. If you copied or wrote your own tests, go up one directory and run `go test`. Ensure that all the tests pass.

# How it works...

This recipe is a very basic example of how to catch panics. You can imagine with more complex middleware how you can defer a recover and catch it after running many nested functions. Within the recover, you can do basically anything you want, although emitting a log is common.

In most web applications, it's common to catch panics and emit an `http.InternalServerError` message when a panic occurs.

# 5
# All about Databases and Storage

In this chapter, the following recipes will be covered:

- The database/sql package with MySQL
- Executing a database transaction interface
- Connection pooling, rate limiting, and timeouts for SQL
- Working with Redis
- Using NoSQL with MongoDB and mgo
- Creating storage interfaces for data portability

## Introduction

Go applications frequently need to make use of long-term storage. This is usually in the form of relational and non-relational databases, as well as key-value stores and more. When working with these storage applications, it helps to wrap your operations in an interface. The recipes in this chapter will examine various storage interfaces, considering parallel access with things such as connection pools, and look at general tips for integrating a new library, which is often the case when using a new storage technology.

# The database/sql package with MySQL

Relational databases are some of the most well understood and common database options. MySQL and Postgres are two of the most popular open source relational databases. This recipe will demonstrate the `database/sql` package, a package that provides hooks for a number of relational databases and automatically handles connection pooling, connection duration, and gives access to a number of basic database operations.

The future versions of this package will include support for context and timeouts.

## Getting ready

Configure your environment according to these steps:

1. Download and install Go on your operating system from `https://golang.org/doc/install`, and configure your `GOPATH` environment variable.
2. Open a terminal/console application, navigate to your `GOPATH/src` and create a project directory such as `$GOPATH/src/github.com/yourusername/customrepo`.

   All code will be run and modified from this directory.

3. Optionally, install the latest tested version of the code using the `go get github.com/agtorre/go-cookbook/` command.
4. Run the `go get github.com/go-sql-driver/mysql` command.
5. Install and configure MySQL using `https://dev.mysql.com/doc/mysql-getting-started/en/`.
6. Run the `export MYSQLUSERNAME=<your mysql username>` command.
7. Run the `export MYSQLPASSWORD=<your mysql password>` command.

## How to do it...

These steps cover writing and running your application:

1. From your terminal/console application, create and navigate to a the directory `chapter5/database`.
2. Copy tests from `https://github.com/agtorre/go-cookbook/tree/master/chapter5/database` or use this as an exercise to write some of your own code.

3. Create a file called `config.go` with the following contents:

```
package database

import (
    "database/sql"
    "fmt"
    "os"
    "time"

    _ "github.com/go-sql-driver/mysql" //we import supported
    libraries for database/sql
)

// Example hold the results of our queries
type Example struct {
    Name string
    Created *time.Time
}

// Setup configures and returns our database
// connection poold
func Setup() (*sql.DB, error) {
    db, err := sql.Open("mysql",
    fmt.Sprintf("%s:%s@/gocookbook?
    parseTime=true", os.Getenv("MYSQLUSERNAME"),
    os.Getenv("MYSQLPASSWORD")))
    if err != nil {
        return nil, err
    }
    return db, nil
}
```

4. Create a file called `create.go` with the following contents:

```
package database

import (
    "database/sql"

    _ "github.com/go-sql-driver/mysql" //we import supported
    libraries for database/sql
)

// Create makes a table called example
// and populates it
func Create(db *sql.DB) error {
    // create the database
```

```
        if _, err := db.Exec("CREATE TABLE example (name
VARCHAR(20), created DATETIME)"); err != nil {
            return err
        }

        if _, err := db.Exec(`INSERT INTO example (name, created)
values ("Aaron", NOW())`); err != nil {
            return err
        }

        return nil
    }
```

5. Create a file called `query.go` with the following contents:

```
package database

import (
    "database/sql"
    "fmt"

    _ "github.com/go-sql-driver/mysql" //we import supported
    libraries for database/sql
)

// Query grabs a new connection
// creates tables, and later drops them
// and issues some queries
func Query(db *sql.DB) error {
    name := "Aaron"
    rows, err := db.Query("SELECT name, created FROM example
    where name=?", name)
    if err != nil {
        return err
    }
    defer rows.Close()
    for rows.Next() {
        var e Example
        if err := rows.Scan(&e.Name, &e.Created); err != nil {
            return err
        }
        fmt.Printf("Results:\n\tName: %s\n\tCreated: %v\n",
        e.Name, e.Created)
    }
    return rows.Err()
}
```

6. Create a file called `exec.go` with the following contents:

```
package dbinterface

// Exec replaces the Exec from the previous
// recipe
func Exec(db DB) error {

    // uncaught error on cleanup, but we always
    // want to cleanup
    defer db.Exec("DROP TABLE example")

    if err := Create(db); err != nil {
        return err
    }

    if err := Query(db); err != nil {
        return err
    }
    return nil
}
```

7. Create and navigate to the `example` directory.
8. Create a file called `main.go` with the following contents; be sure to modify the `database` import to use the path you set up in step 2:

```
package main

import (
    "github.com/agtorre/go-cookbook/chapter5/database"
    _ "github.com/go-sql-driver/mysql" //we import supported
    libraries for database/sql
)

func main() {
    db, err := database.Setup()
    if err != nil {
        panic(err)
    }

    if err := database.Exec(db); err != nil {
        panic(err)
    }
}
```

9. Run `go run main.go`.

10. You could also run this:

    **go build**
    **./example**

    You should see the following output:

    ```
    $ go run main.go
    Results:
     Name: Aaron
     Created: 2017-02-16 19:02:36 +0000 UTC
    ```

11. If you copied or wrote your own tests, go up one directory and run `go test`. Ensure that all tests pass.

# How it works...

The `_ "github.com/go-sql-driver/mysql"` line of the code is how you connect various database connectors to the `database/sql` package. The commands would be similar if you were to connect to Postgres, SQLite, or any others that implement the `database/sql` interfaces.

Once connected, the package sets up a connection pool that is covered in the *Connection pooling, rate limiting, and timeouts for SQL* recipe, and you can either directly execute SQL on the connection or create transaction objects that can do everything a connection can do with the `commit` and `rollback` commands.

The `mysql` package provides some convenience support for Go time objects when talking to the database. This recipe also retrieves the username and password from the `MYSQLUSERNAME` and `MYSQLPASSWORD` environment variables.

# Executing a database transaction interface

When working with connections to services such as database, it can be difficult to write tests. This is because it's difficult in Go to mock or duck-type things at runtime. Although I recommend using a storage interface when working with databases, it's still useful to mock a database transaction interface inside of this interface. The *Creating storage interfaces for data portability* recipe will cover storage interfaces; this one will focus on an interface to wrap database connections and transaction objects.

To show the use of such an interface, we'll rewrite the create and query files from the previous recipe to use our interface. The final output will be the same, but the create and query operations will all be performed in a transaction.

# Getting ready

Configure your environment according to these steps:

1. Refer to the steps given in the *Getting ready* section of the *The database/sql package with MySQL* recipe.
2. Run the `go get` `https://github.com/agtorre/go-cookbook/tree/master/chapter5/database` command or write your own using the *The database/sql package with MySQL* recipe.

# How to do it...

These steps cover writing and running your application:

1. From your terminal/console application, create and navigate to the `chapter5/dbinterface` directory.
2. Copy tests from `https://github.com/agtorre/go-cookbook/tree/master/chapter5/dbinterface` or use this as an exercise to write some of your own code.
3. Create a file called `transaction.go` with the following contents:

```
package database

import _ "github.com/go-sql-driver/mysql" //we import supported
libraries for database/sql
// Exec grabs a new connection
// creates tables, and later drops them
// and issues some queries
func Exec() error {
    db, err := Setup()
    if err != nil {
        return err
    }
    // uncaught error on cleanup, but we always
    // want to cleanup
    defer db.Exec("DROP TABLE example")
```

```
        if err := Create(db); err != nil {
            return err
        }

        if err := Query(db); err != nil {
            return err
        }
        return nil

    }
```

4. Create a file called create.go with the following contents:

```
package dbinterface

import _ "github.com/go-sql-driver/mysql" //we import supported
libraries for database/sql

// Create makes a table called example
// and populates it
func Create(db DB) error {
    // create the database
    if _, err := db.Exec("CREATE TABLE example (name
    VARCHAR(20), created DATETIME)"); err != nil {
        return err
    }

    if _, err := db.Exec(`INSERT INTO example (name, created)
    values ("Aaron", NOW())`); err != nil {
        return err
    }

    return nil
}
```

5. Create a file called query.go with the following contents:

```
package dbinterface

import (
    "fmt"

    "github.com/agtorre/go-cookbook/chapter5/database"
)

// Query grabs a new connection
// creates tables, and later drops them
// and issues some queries
```

```go
func Query(db DB) error {
    name := "Aaron"
    rows, err := db.Query("SELECT name, created FROM example
    where name=?", name)
    if err != nil {
        return err
    }
    defer rows.Close()
    for rows.Next() {
        var e database.Example
        if err := rows.Scan(&e.Name, &e.Created); err != nil {
            return err
        }
        fmt.Printf("Results:\n\tName: %s\n\tCreated: %v\n",
        e.Name, e.Created)
    }
    return rows.Err()
}
```

6. Create a file called `exec.go` with the following contents:

```go
package dbinterface

// Exec replaces the Exec from the previous
// recipe
func Exec(db DB) error {

    // uncaught error on cleanup, but we always
    // want to cleanup
    defer db.Exec("DROP TABLE example")

    if err := Create(db); err != nil {
        return err
    }

    if err := Query(db); err != nil {
        return err
    }
    return nil
}
```

7. Navigate to `example`.

8. Create a file called `main.go` with the following contents; be sure to modify the `dbinterface` import to use the path you set up in step 2:

```go
package main
```

```
import (
    "github.com/agtorre/go-cookbook/chapter5/database"
    "github.com/agtorre/go-cookbook/chapter5/dbinterface"
    _ "github.com/go-sql-driver/mysql" //we import supported
    libraries for database/sql
)

func main() {
    db, err := database.Setup()
    if err != nil {
        panic(err)
    }

    tx, err := db.Begin()
    if err != nil {
        panic(err)
    }
    // this wont do anything if commit is successful
    defer tx.Rollback()

    if err := dbinterface.Exec(db); err != nil {
        panic(err)
    }
    if err := tx.Commit(); err != nil {
        panic(err)
    }
}
}
```

9. Run `go run main.go`.

10. You could also run this:

   **go build**
   **./example**

   You should see the following output:

   **$ go run main.go**
   **Results:**
   **Name: Aaron**
   **Created: 2017-02-16 20:00:00 +0000 UTC**

11. If you copied or wrote your own tests, go up one directory and run `go test`. Ensure that all tests pass.

## How it works...

This recipe works in a very similar way to the previous one, but demonstrates both using transactions and makes generic database functions that work with both `sql.DB` connections and `sql.Transaction` objects. It's also simple to mock these interfaces, as you'll see in `Chapter 8`, *Testing*.

# Connection pooling, rate limiting, and timeouts for SQL

Although the `database/sql` package provides support for connection pooling, rate limiting, and timeouts, it's often important to tweak the defaults to better accommodate your database configuration. This can become important when you have horizontal scaling on microservices and don't want to hold too many active connections to the database.

## Getting ready

Configure your environment according to these steps:

1. Refer to the steps given in the *Getting ready* section of the *The database/sql package with MySQL* recipe.
2. Run the `go get` `https://github.com/agtorre/go-cookbook/tree/master/chapter5/dat abase` command or write your own using the *The database/sql package with MySQL* recipe.

## How to do it...

These steps cover writing and running your application:

1. From your terminal/console application, create and navigate to the `chapter5/pools` directory.
2. Copy tests from `https://github.com/agtorre/go-cookbook/tree/master/cha pter5/pools`or use this as an exercise to write some of your own code.

3. Create a file called `pools.go` with the following contents:

```go
package pools

import (
    "database/sql"
    "fmt"
    "os"

    _ "github.com/go-sql-driver/mysql" //we import supported
    libraries for database/sql
)

// Setup configures the db along with pools
// number of connections and more
func Setup() (*sql.DB, error) {
    db, err := sql.Open("mysql",
    fmt.Sprintf("%s:%s@/gocookbook?
    parseTime=true", os.Getenv("MYSQLUSERNAME"),
    os.Getenv("MYSQLPASSWORD")))
    if err != nil {
        return nil, err
    }

    // there will only ever be 24 open connections
    db.SetMaxOpenConns(24)

    // MaxIdleConns can never be less than max open
    // SetMaxOpenConns otherwise it'll default to that value
    db.SetMaxIdleConns(24)

    return db, nil
}
```

4. Create a file called `timeout.go` with the following contents:

```go
package pools

import (
    "context"
    "time"
)

// ExecWithTimeout will timeout trying
// to get the current time
func ExecWithTimeout() error {
    db, err := Setup()
    if err != nil {
```

```
            return err
    }

    ctx := context.Background()

    // we want to timeout immediately
    ctx, can := context.WithDeadline(ctx, time.Now())

    // call cancel after we complete
    defer can()

    // our transaction is context aware
    _, err = db.BeginTx(ctx, nil)
    return err
}
```

5.  Navigate to `example`.

6.  Create a file called `main.go` with the following contents; be sure to modify the `pools` import to use the path you set up in step 2:

    ```
    package main

    import "github.com/agtorre/go-cookbook/chapter5/pools"

    func main() {
        if err := pools.ExecWithTimeout(); err != nil {
            panic(err)
        }
    }
    ```

7.  Run `go run main.go`.

8.  You could also run this:

    **go build**
    **./example**

    You should see the following output:

    **$ go run main.go**
    **panic: context deadline exceeded**

    **goroutine 1 [running]:**
    **main.main()**
    **/go/src/github.com/agtorre/go-**
    **cookbook/chapter5/pools/example/main.go:7 +0x4e**
    **exit status 2**

9. If you copied or wrote your own tests, go up one directory and run `go test`. Ensure that all tests pass.

## How it works...

Being able to control the depth of our connection pool is very useful. This will allow us not to overload a database, but it's important to consider what it will mean in the context of timeouts. If you enforce both a set number of connections and strict context-based timeouts, as we did in this recipe, there will be cases where you'll have requests frequently timing out on an overloaded application trying to establish too many connections.

This is because connections will timeout waiting for a connection to become available. The newly added context functionality for `database/sql` makes it much simpler to have a shared timeout for the entire request, including the steps involved with performing the query.

With this and the other recipes, it makes sense to use a global `config` object to pass into the `Setup()` function, although this recipe just uses environment variables.

# Working with Redis

Sometimes you want persistent storage or additional functionality provided by third-party libraries and services. This recipe will explore Redis as a form of non-relational data storage and showcase how a language such as Go can interact with these services.

Since Redis supports key-value storage with a simple interface, it's an excellent candidate for session storage or temporary data that has a duration. The ability to specify timeout on data stored in Redis is extremely valuable. This recipe will explore basic Redis usage from configuration, to querying, to using custom sorting.

# Getting ready

Configure your environment according to these steps:

1. Download and install Go on your operating system from `https://golang.org/doc/install`, and configure your `GOPATH` environment variable.
2. Open a terminal/console application.

3. Navigate to your GOPATH/src and create a project directory such as
   $GOPATH/src/github.com/yourusername/customrepo.

   All code will be run and modified from this directory.

4. Optionally, install the latest tested version of the code using the go get
   github.com/agtorre/go-cookbook/ command.
5. Run the go get gopkg.in/redis.v5 command.
6. Install and configure Redis using https://redis.io/topics/quickstart.

# How to do it...

These steps cover writing and running your application:

1. From your terminal/console application, create and navigate to the
   chapter5/redis directory.
2. Copy tests from https://github.com/agtorre/go-cookbook/tree/master/cha
   pter5/redisor use this as an exercise to write some of your own code.
3. Create a file called config.go with the following contents:

```go
package redis

import (
    "os"

    redis "gopkg.in/redis.v5"
)

// Setup initializes a redis client
func Setup() (*redis.Client, error) {
    client := redis.NewClient(&redis.Options{
        Addr: "localhost:6379",
        Password: os.Getenv("REDISPASSWORD"),
        DB: 0, // use default DB
    })

    _, err := client.Ping().Result()
    return client, err
}
```

4. Create a file called `exec.go` with the following contents:

```go
package redis

import (
    "fmt"
    "time"

    redis "gopkg.in/redis.v5"
)

// Exec performs some redis operations
func Exec() error {
    conn, err := Setup()
    if err != nil {
        return err
    }

    c1 := "value"
    // value is an interface, we can store whatever
    // the last argument is the redis expiration
    conn.Set("key", c1, 5*time.Second)

    var result string
    if err := conn.Get("key").Scan(&result); err != nil {
        switch err {
        // this means the key
        // was not found
        case redis.Nil:
            return nil
        default:
            return err
        }
    }

    fmt.Println("result =", result)

    return nil
}
```

5. Create a file called `sort.go` with the following contents:

```go
package redis

import (
    "fmt"

    redis "gopkg.in/redis.v5"
```

```
)

// Sort performs a sort redis operations
func Sort() error {
    conn, err := Setup()
    if err != nil {
        return err
    }

    if err := conn.LPush("list", 1).Err(); err != nil {
        return err
    }
    if err := conn.LPush("list", 3).Err(); err != nil {
        return err
    }
    if err := conn.LPush("list", 2).Err(); err != nil {
        return err
    }

    res, err := conn.Sort("list", redis.Sort{Order:
    "ASC"}).Result()
    if err != nil {
        return err
    }
    fmt.Println(res)
    conn.Del("list")
    return nil
}
```

6. Navigate to `example`.
7. Create a file called `main.go` with the following contents; be sure to modify the `redis` import to use the path you set up in step 2:

```
package main

import "github.com/agtorre/go-cookbook/chapter5/redis"

func main() {
    if err := redis.Exec(); err != nil {
        panic(err)
    }

    if err := redis.Sort(); err != nil {
        panic(err)
    }
}
```

8. Run `go run main.go`.

9. You could also run this:

```
go build
./example
```

You should see the following output:

```
$ go run main.go
result = value
[1 2 3]
```

10. If you copied or wrote your own tests, go up one directory and run `go test`. Ensure that all tests pass.

## How it works...

Working with Redis in Go is very similar to working with MySQL, although there's not a standard library, a lot of the same conventions are followed with functions such as `Scan()` to read data from Redis into Go types. It can be challenging to pick the best library to use in cases like this and I suggest surveying what's available periodically, as things can rapidly change.

This recipe uses a `redis` package to do basic setting and getting, doing a more complex sort function, and basic configuration. Like `database/sql`, you can set additional configuration in the form of write timeouts, poolsize, and more. Redis itself also provides a lot of additional functionality, including Redis cluster support, Zscore and counter objects, distributed locks, and more.

As in the preceding recipe, I recommend using a `config` object, which stores your Redis settings and configuration details for ease of setup and security.

## Using NoSQL with MongoDB and mgo

You might first think that Go is better suited to relational databases due to Go structs and because Go is a typed language. When working with something like the `mgo` package, Go can nearly arbitrarily store and retrieve struct objects. If you version your objects, your schema can adapt and it can provide a very flexible development environment.

Some libraries do a better job of hiding or elevating these abstractions. The mgo package is an excellent example of a library that does an excellent job of the former. This recipe will create a connection in a similar way to Redis and MySQL, but will store and retrieve an object without even defining a concrete schema.

# Getting ready

Configure your environment according to these steps:

1. Download and install Go on your operating system from `https://golang.org/doc/install`, and configure your `GOPATH` environment variable.
2. Open a terminal/console application.
3. Navigate to your `GOPATH/src` and create a project directory such as `$GOPATH/src/github.com/yourusername/customrepo`.

    All code will be run and modified from this directory.

4. Optionally, install the latest tested version of the code using the `go get github.com/agtorre/go-cookbook/` command.
5. Run the `go get gopkg.in/mgo.v2` command.
6. To run the code, you'll need a working database connection to a MongoDB instance that this book will not cover.
7. The basic setup is `https://docs.mongodb.com/getting-started/shell/`.

# How to do it...

These steps cover writing and running your application:

1. From your terminal/console application, create and navigate to the `chapter5/mongodb` directory.
2. Copy tests from `https://github.com/agtorre/go-cookbook/tree/master/chapter5/mongodb` or use this as an exercise to write some of your own code.
3. Create a file called `config.go` with the following contents:

```
package mongodb

import mgo "gopkg.in/mgo.v2"

// Setup initializes a redis client
```

```go
func Setup() (*mgo.Session, error) {
    session, err := mgo.Dial("localhost")
    if err != nil {
        return nil, err
    }
    return session, nil
}
```

4. Create a file called `exec.go` with the following contents:

```go
package mongodb

import (
    "fmt"

    "gopkg.in/mgo.v2/bson"
)

// State is our data model
type State struct {
    Name string `bson:"name"`
    Population int `bson:"pop"`
}

// Exec creates then queries an Example
func Exec() error {
    db, err := Setup()
    if err != nil {
        return err
    }

    conn := db.DB("gocookbook").C("example")

    // we can inserts many rows at once
    if err := conn.Insert(&State{"Washington", 7062000},
    &State{"Oregon", 3970000}); err != nil {
        return err
    }

    var s State
    if err := conn.Find(bson.M{"name": "Washington"}).One(&s);
    err!= nil {
        return err
    }

    if err := conn.DropCollection(); err != nil {
        return err
    }
```

```
        fmt.Printf("State: %#vn", s)
        return nil
    }
```

5. Navigate to `example`.

6. Create a file called `main.go` with the following contents; be sure to modify the `mongodb` import to use the path you set up in step 2:

```
package main

import "github.com/agtorre/go-cookbook/chapter5/mongodb"

func main() {
    if err := mongodb.Exec(); err != nil {
        panic(err)
    }
}
```

7. Run `go run main.go`.

8. You could also run this:

```
go build
./example
```

You should see the following output:

```
$ go run main.go
State: mongodb.State{Name:"Washington", Population:7062000}
```

9. If you copied or wrote your own tests, go up one directory and run `go test`. Ensure that all tests pass.

## How it works...

The `mgo` package also provides connection pooling, and many ways to tweak and configure your connections to the `mongodb` database. The examples of this recipe are fairly basic, but they illustrate how easy it is to reason about and query a document-based database. The package implements a BSON data type, and marshaling to and from it is very similar to working with JSON.

Consistency guarantees and best practice for `mongodb` are outside the scope of this book-- but it's a pleasure to work with it in the Go language.

# Creating storage interfaces for data portability

When working with external storage interfaces, it can be helpful to abstract your operations behind an interface. This is for ease of mocking, portability in case you change storage backends, and isolation of concerns. The downside to this approach may come if you need to perform multiple operations inside of a transaction. In that case, it makes sense to make composite operations, or to allow it to be passed in via a context object or additional function arguments.

This recipe will implement a very simple interface to working with items in MongoDB. These items will have a name and price and we'll use an interface to persist and retrieve these objects.

## Getting ready

Refer to the steps given in the *Getting ready* section of the *Using NoSQL with MongoDB and mgo* recipe.

## How to do it...

These steps cover writing and running your application:

1. From your terminal/console application, create and navigate to the `chapter5/mongodb` directory.
2. Copy tests from `https://github.com/agtorre/go-cookbook/tree/master/chapter5/mongodb` or use this as an exercise to write some of your own code.
3. Create a file called `storage.go` with the following contents:

```
package storage

import "context"

// Item represents an item at
// a shop
type Item struct {
    Name  string
    Price int64
}
```

```go
// Storage is our storage interface
// We'll implement it with Mongo
// storage
type Storage interface {
    GetByName(context.Context, string) (*Item, error)
    Put(context.Context, *Item) error
}
```

4. Create a file called `mongoconfig.go` with the following contents:

```go
package storage

import mgo "gopkg.in/mgo.v2"

// MongoStorage implements our storage interface
type MongoStorage struct {
    *mgo.Session
    DB string
    Collection string
}

// NewMongoStorage initializes a MongoStorage
func NewMongoStorage(connection, db, collection string)
(*MongoStorage, error) {
    session, err := mgo.Dial("localhost")
    if err != nil {
        return nil, err
    }
    ms := MongoStorage{
        Session: session,
        DB: db,
        Collection: collection,
    }
    return &ms, nil
}
```

5. Create a file called `mongointerface.go` with the following contents:

```go
package storage

import (
    "context"

    "gopkg.in/mgo.v2/bson"
)

// GetByName queries mongodb for an item with
// the correct name
```

```go
func (m *MongoStorage) GetByName(ctx context.Context, name
string) (*Item, error) {
    c := m.Session.DB(m.DB).C(m.Collection)
    var i Item
    if err := c.Find(bson.M{"name": name}).One(&i); err != nil
    {
        return nil, err
    }

    return &i, nil
}

// Put adds an item to our mongo instance
func (m *MongoStorage) Put(ctx context.Context, i *Item) error
{
    c := m.Session.DB(m.DB).C(m.Collection)
    return c.Insert(i)
}
```

6. Create a file called `exec.go` with the following contents:

```go
package storage

import (
    "context"
    "fmt"
)

// Exec initializes storage, then performs operations
// using the storage interface
func Exec() error {
    m, err := NewMongoStorage("localhost", "gocookbook",
    "items")
    if err != nil {
        return err
    }
    if err := PerformOperations(m); err != nil {
        return err
    }

    if err :=
    m.Session.DB(m.DB).C(m.Collection).DropCollection();
    err != nil {
        return err
    }

    return nil
}
```

```go
// PerformOperations creates a candle item
// then gets it
func PerformOperations(s Storage) error {
    ctx := context.Background()
    i := Item{Name: "candles", Price: 100}
    if err := s.Put(ctx, &i); err != nil {
        return err
    }

    candles, err := s.GetByName(ctx, "candles")
    if err != nil {
        return err
    }
    fmt.Printf("Result: %#vn", candles)
        return nil
}
```

7. Navigate to `example`.

8. Create a file called `main.go` with the following contents; be sure to modify the `storage` import to use the path you set up in step 2:

```go
package main

import "github.com/agtorre/go-cookbook/chapter5/storage"

func main() {
    if err := storage.Exec(); err != nil {
        panic(err)
    }
}
```

9. Run `go run main.go`.

10. You could also run this:

**go build**
**./example**

You should see the following output:

**$ go run main.go**
**Result: &storage.Item{Name:"candles", Price:100}**

11. If you copied or wrote your own tests, go up one directory and run `go test`. Ensure that all tests pass.

# How it works...

The most important function for demonstrating this recipe is `PerformOperation`. This function takes an interface to the storage as a parameter. This means we can dynamically replace the underlying storage without even modifying this function. It would be simple, for example, to connect storage to a separate API in order to consume and modify it.

We added a context to these interfaces to add additional flexibility and allow the interface to handle timeout as well. Separating your application logic from the underlying storage provides a variety of benefits, but it can be difficult to pick the right places to draw boundaries, and this will vary widely by application.

# 6
# Web Clients and APIs

In this chapter we will cover the following recipes:

- Initializing, storing, and passing http.Client structs
- Writing a client for a REST API
- Executing parallel and async client requests
- Making use of OAuth2 clients
- Implementing an OAuth2 token storage interface
- Wrapping a client in added functionality and function composition
- Understanding GRPC clients

# Introduction

Working with APIs and writing web clients can be a tricky subject. Different APIs have different types of authorization, authentication, and protocols. We'll explore the http.Client struct object, working with OAuth2 clients and long-term token storage, and finish off with GRPC with an additional REST interface.

By the end of this chapter, you should have an idea of how to interface with third-party or in-house APIs and have some patterns for common operations, such as async requests to APIs.

# Initializing, storing, and passing http.Client structs

The Go `net/http` package exposes a flexible `http.Client` struct for working with HTTP APIs. This struct has separate transport functionality and is relatively simple to short-circuit requests, modify headers for each client operation, and handle any REST operations. Creating clients is a very common operation, and this recipe will start with the basics of working and creating an `http.Client` object.

## Getting ready

Configure your environment according to these steps:

1. Download and install Go on your operating system from `https://golang.org/doc/install`and configure your `GOPATH` environment variable.

2. Open a terminal/console application.

3. Navigate to `GOPATH/src` and create a project directory. For example, `$GOPATH/src/github.com/yourusername/customrepo`.

   All code will be run and modified from this directory.

4. Optionally, install the latest tested version of the code using the `go get` `github.com/agtorre/go-cookbook/` command.

## How to do it...

These steps cover writing and running your application:

1. From your terminal/console application, create the `chapter6/client` directory and navigate to it.

2. Copy tests from `https://github.com/agtorre/go-cookbook/tree/master/chapter6/client`or use this as an exercise to write some of your own code.

3. Create a file called `client.go` with the following content:

```
package client

import (
    "crypto/tls"
    "net/http"
```

```
)

// Setup configures our client and redefines
// the global DefaultClient
func Setup(isSecure, nop bool) *http.Client {
    c := http.DefaultClient

    // Sometimes for testing, we want to
    // turn off SSL verification
    if !isSecure {
        c.Transport = &http.Transport{
        TLSClientConfig: &tls.Config{
            InsecureSkipVerify: false,
        },
    }
}
if nop {
    c.Transport = &NopTransport{}
}
http.DefaultClient = c
return c
}

// NopTransport is a No-Op Transport
type NopTransport struct {
}

// RoundTrip Implements RoundTripper interface
func (n *NopTransport) RoundTrip(*http.Request)
(*http.Response, error) {
    // note this is an unitialized Response
    // if you're looking at headers etc
    return &http.Response{StatusCode: http.StatusTeapot}, nil
}
```

4. Create a file called `exec.go` with the following content:

```
package client

import (
    "fmt"
    "net/http"
)

// DoOps takes a client, then fetches
// google.com
func DoOps(c *http.Client) error {
    resp, err := c.Get("http://www.google.com")
```

```
        if err != nil {
            return err
        }
        fmt.Println("results of DoOps:", resp.StatusCode)

        return nil
    }

    // DefaultGetGolang uses the default client
    // to get golang.org
    func DefaultGetGolang() error {
        resp, err := http.Get("https://www.golang.org")
        if err != nil {
            return err
        }
        fmt.Println("results of DefaultGetGolang:",
        resp.StatusCode)
        return nil
    }
```

5. Create a file called `store.go` with the following content:

```
    package client

    import (
        "fmt"
        "net/http"
    )

    // Controller embeds an http.Client
    // and uses it internally
    type Controller struct {
        *http.Client
    }

    // DoOps with a controller object
    func (c *Controller) DoOps() error {
        resp, err := c.Client.Get("http://www.google.com")
        if err != nil {
            return err
        }
        fmt.Println("results of client.DoOps", resp.StatusCode)
        return nil
    }
```

6. Create a new directory named `example` and navigate to it.

7. Create a file named `main.go` with the following content. Ensure that you modify the `client` import to use the path you set up in step 2:

```
package main

import "github.com/agtorre/go-cookbook/chapter6/client"

func main() {
    // secure and op!
    cli := client.Setup(true, false)

    if err := client.DefaultGetGolang(); err != nil {
        panic(err)
    }

    if err := client.DoOps(cli); err != nil {
        panic(err)
    }

    c := client.Controller{Client: cli}
    if err := c.DoOps(); err != nil {
        panic(err)
    }

    // secure and noop
    // also modifies default
    client.Setup(true, true)

    if err := client.DefaultGetGolang(); err != nil {
        panic(err)
    }
}
```

8. Run `go run main.go`.

9. You may also run the following:

```
go build
./example
```

You should now see the following output:

```
$ go run main.go
results of DefaultGetGolang: 200
results of DoOps: 200
results of client.DoOps 200
results of DefaultGetGolang: 418
```

10. If you copied or wrote your own tests, go up one directory and run `go test`. Ensure that all the tests pass.

## How it works...

The `net/http` package exposes a `DefaultClient` package variable, which is used by the internal operations, `Do`, `GET`, `POST`, and so on. Our `Setup()` function returns a client and sets the default client to be the same. When setting up a client, most of your modifications will take place in the transport, which only needs to implement the `RoundTripper` interface.

This recipe gives an example of a no-op round tripper that always returns a 418 status code. You can imagine how this might be useful for testing. It also demonstrates passing in clients as function arguments, using them as struct parameters, and using the default client to process requests.

# Writing a client for a REST API

Writing a client for a REST API will not only help you better understand the API in question, but also gives you a useful tool for all future applications using that API. This will explore structuring a client and show some strategies that you can immediately take advantage of.

For this client, we'll assume that the authentication is handled by basic auth, but it would also be possible to hit an endpoint to retrieve a token, and so on. For the sake of simplicity, we'll assume our API exposes one endpoint, `GetGoogle()`, which returns that status code returned from doing a `GET` request to `https://www.google.com`.

## Getting ready

Refer to the *Getting ready* section of the *Initializing, storing, and passing http.Client structs* recipe.

# How to do it...

These steps cover writing and running your application:

1. From your terminal/console application, create the `chapter6/rest` directory and navigate to it.
2. Copy tests from `https://github.com/agtorre/go-cookbook/tree/master/chapter6/rest` or use this as an exercise to write some of your own code.
3. Create a file called `client.go` with the following content:

```go
package rest

import "net/http"

// APIClient is our custom client
type APIClient struct {
    *http.Client
}

// NewAPIClient constructor initializes the client with our
// custom Transport
func NewAPIClient(username, password string) *APIClient {
    t := http.Transport{}
    return &APIClient{
        Client: &http.Client{
            Transport: &APITransport{
                Transport: &t,
                username: username,
                password: password,
            },
        },
    }
}

// GetGoogle is an API Call - we abstract away
// the REST aspects
func (c *APIClient) GetGoogle() (int, error) {
    resp, err := c.Get("http://www.google.com")
    if err != nil {
        return 0, err
    }
    return resp.StatusCode, nil
}
```

4. Create a file called `transport.go` with the following content:

```go
package rest

import "net/http"

// APITransport does a SetBasicAuth
// for every request
type APITransport struct {
    *http.Transport
    username, password string
}

// RoundTrip does the basic auth before deferring to the
// default transport
func (t *APITransport) RoundTrip(req *http.Request)
(*http.Response, error) {
    req.SetBasicAuth(t.username, t.password)
    return t.Transport.RoundTrip(req)
}
```

5. Create a file called `exec.go` with the following content:

```go
package rest

import "fmt"

// Exec creates an API Client and uses its
// GetGoogle method, then prints the result
func Exec() error {
    c := NewAPIClient("username", "password")

    StatusCode, err := c.GetGoogle()
    if err != nil {
        return err
    }
    fmt.Println("Result of GetGoogle:", StatusCode)
    return nil
}
```

6. Create a new directory named `example` and navigate to it.

7. Create a file named `main.go` with the following content. Ensure that you modify the `rest` import to use the path you set up in step 2:

```go
package main
```

```
import "github.com/agtorre/go-cookbook/chapter6/rest"

func main() {
    if err := rest.Exec(); err != nil {
        panic(err)
    }
}
```

8. Run `go run main.go`.

9. You may also run the following commands:

   ```
   go build
   ./example
   ```

   You should now see the following output:

   ```
   $ go run main.go
   Result of GetGoogle: 200
   ```

10. If you copied or wrote your own tests, go up one directory and run `go test`. Ensure that all the tests pass.

# How it works...

This code demonstrates how to hide logic such as authentication, token refresh, and more using the `Transport` interface. It also demonstrates exposing an API call via a method. Had we been implementing against something like a user API, we would expect methods like:

```
type API interface{
    GetUsers() (Users, error)
    CreateUser(User) error
    UpdateUser(User) error
    DeleteUser(User)
}
```

If you've read `Chapter 5`, *All about Databases and Storage*, this may look similar to the recipe. This composition through interfaces, especially common interfaces like the `RoundTripper` interface, provide a lot of flexibility for writing APIs. In addition, it may be useful to write a top-level interface as we did earlier and pass the interface around instead of the client directly. We'll explore this more in the next recipe as we explore writing an OAuth2 client.

# Executing parallel and async client requests

Performing client requests in parallel is relatively simple in Go. In the following recipe, we'll use a client to retrieve multiple URLs using Go buffered channels. Responses and errors will both go to a separate channel that is readily accessible by anyone with access to the client.

In the case of this recipe, creation of the client, reading the channels, and handling of responses and errors will all be done in the `main.go` file.

## Getting ready

Refer to the *Getting ready* section of the *Initializing, storing, and passing http.Client structs* recipe in this chapter.

## How to do it...

These steps cover writing and running your application:

1. From your terminal/console application, create the `chapter6/async` directory and navigate to it.
2. Copy tests from `https://github.com/agtorre/go-cookbook/tree/master/chapter6/async` or use this as an exercise to write some of your own code.
3. Create a file called `config.go` with the following content:

```
package async

import "net/http"

// NewClient creates a new client and
// sets its appropriate channels
func NewClient(client *http.Client, bufferSize int) *Client {
    respch := make(chan *http.Response, bufferSize)
    errch := make(chan error, bufferSize)
    return &Client{
        Client: client,
        Resp: respch,
        Err: errch,
    }
}

// Client stores a client and has two channels to aggregate
```

```
// responses and errors
type Client struct {
    *http.Client
    Resp chan *http.Response
    Err chan error
}

// AsyncGet performs a Get then returns
// the resp/error to the appropriate channel
func (c *Client) AsyncGet(url string) {
    resp, err := c.Get(url)
    if err != nil {
        c.Err <- err
        return
    }
    c.Resp <- resp
}
```

4. Create a file called `exec.go` with the following content:

```
package async

// FetchAll grabs a list of urls
func FetchAll(urls []string, c *Client) {
    for _, url := range urls {
        go c.AsyncGet(url)
    }
}
```

5. Create a new directory named `example` and navigate to it.

6. Create a file named `main.go` with the following content. Ensure that you modify the `client` import to use the path you set up in step 2:

```
package main

import (
    "fmt"
    "net/http"

    "github.com/agtorre/go-cookbook/chapter6/async"
)

func main() {
    urls := []string{
        "https://www.google.com",
        "https://golang.org",
        "https://www.github.com",
```

```
        }
        c := async.NewClient(http.DefaultClient, len(urls))
        async.FetchAll(urls, c)

        for i := 0; i < len(urls); i++ {
            select {
                case resp := <-c.Resp:
                fmt.Printf("Status received for %s: %d\n",
                resp.Request.URL, resp.StatusCode)
                case err := <-c.Err:
                fmt.Printf("Error received: %s\n", err)
            }
        }
    }
}
```

7. Run `go run main.go`.

8. You may also run the following commands:

   ```
   go build
   ./example
   ```

   You should see the following output:

   ```
   $ go run main.go
   Status received for https://www.google.com: 200
   Status received for https://golang.org: 200
   Status received for https://github.com/: 200
   ```

9. If you copied or wrote your own tests, go up one directory and run `go test`. Ensure that all the tests pass.

# How it works...

This recipe creates a framework for processing requests in a fan-out async way using a single client. It will attempt to retrieve as many URLs as you specify as quickly as it can. In many cases, you'd want to restrict this further with something like a worker pool. It may also make sense to handle these async Go routines outside of the client and for specific storage or retrieval interfaces.

This recipe also explores using a case statement to switch on multiple channels. We handle the locking problem since we know how many responses we'll receive and we complete only after receiving them all. Another option would be a timeout if we were okay with dropping certain responses.

# Making use of OAuth2 clients

OAuth2 is a relatively common protocol for speaking with APIs. The `golang.org/x/oauth2` package provides a pretty flexible client for working with OAuth2. It has subpackages that specify endpoints for various providers such as Facebook, Google, and GitHub.

This recipe will demonstrate how to create a new GitHub OAuth2 client and some of its basic usage.

# Getting ready

Configure your environment according to these steps:

1. Refer to the *Getting ready* section of the *Initializing, storing, and passing http.Client structs* recipe.
2. Run the `go get golang.org/x/oauth2` command.
3. Configure an OAuth Client at `https://github.com/settings/applications/new`.
4. Set the environment variables with your Client ID and Secret:
    1. `export GITHUB_CLIENT="your_client"`
    2. `export GITHUB_SECRET="your_secret"`
5. Brush up on the GitHub API documentation at `https://developer.github.com/v3/`.

# How to do it...

These steps cover writing and running your application:

1. From your terminal/console application, create and navigate to the `chapter6/client` directory.

2. Copy tests from `https://github.com/agtorre/go-cookbook/tree/master/cha pter6/oauthcli`or use this as an exercise to write some of your own code.

3. Create a file called `config.go` with the following content:

```
package oauthcli

import (
    "context"
    "fmt"
    "os"

    "golang.org/x/oauth2"
    "golang.org/x/oauth2/github"
)

// Setup return an oauth2Config configured to talk
// to github, you need environment variables set
// for your id and secret
func Setup() *oauth2.Config {
    return &oauth2.Config{
        ClientID: os.Getenv("GITHUB_CLIENT"),
        ClientSecret: os.Getenv("GITHUB_SECRET"),
        Scopes: []string{"repo", "user"},
        Endpoint: github.Endpoint,
    }
}

// GetToken retrieves a github oauth2 token
func GetToken(ctx context.Context, conf *oauth2.Config)
(*oauth2.Token, error) {
    url := conf.AuthCodeURL("state")
    fmt.Printf("Type the following url into your browser and
    follow the directions on screen: %v\n", url)
    fmt.Println("Paste the code returned in the redirect URL
    and hit Enter:")

    var code string
    if _, err := fmt.Scan(&code); err != nil {
        return nil, err
    }
    return conf.Exchange(ctx, code)
}
```

4. Create a file called `exec.go` with the following content:

```
package oauthcli
```

```
import (
    "fmt"
    "net/http"
)

// GetUsers uses an initialized oauth2 client to get
// information about a user
func GetUsers(client *http.Client) error {
    url := fmt.Sprintf("https://api.github.com/user")

    resp, err := client.Get(url)
    if err != nil {
        return err
    }
    defer resp.Body.Close()
    fmt.Println("Status Code from", url, ":", resp.StatusCode)
    io.Copy(os.Stdout, resp.Body)
    return nil
}
```

5. Create a new directory named `example` and navigate to it.

6. Create a `main.go` file with the following content. Ensure that you modify the `client` import to use the path you set up in step 2:

```
package main

import (
    "context"

    "github.com/agtorre/go-cookbook/chapter6/oauthcli"
)

func main() {
    ctx := context.Background()
    conf := oauthcli.Setup()

    tok, err := oauthcli.GetToken(ctx, conf)
    if err != nil {
        panic(err)
    }
    client := conf.Client(ctx, tok)

    if err := oauthcli.GetUsers(client); err != nil {
        panic(err)
    }

}
```

7. Run `go run main.go`.

8. You may also run the following:

```
go build
./example
```

You should now see the following output:

```
$ go run main.go
Visit the URL for the auth dialog:
https://github.com/login/oauth/authorize?
access_type=offline&client_id=
<your_id>&response_type=code&scope=repo+user&state=state
Paste the code returned in the redirect URL and hit Enter:
<your_code>
Status Code from https://api.github.com/user: 200
{<json_payload>}
```

9. If you copied or wrote your own tests, go up one directory and run `go test`. Ensure that all the tests pass.

# How it works...

The standard OAuth2 flow is redirect-based and ends with the server redirecting to an endpoint you specify. Your server is then responsible for grabbing the code and exchanging it for a token. This recipe bypasses that requirement by allowing us to use a URL such as `https://localhost` or `https://a-domain-you-own` and manually copying/pasting the code, then hitting enter. Once the token has been exchanged, the client will intelligently refresh the token as needed.

It's important to note that we're not storing the token in any way. If the program crashes, it must re-exchange for the token. It's also important to note that we need to retrieve the token explicitly only once unless the refresh token expires, is lost, or is corrupted. Once the client is configure, it should be able to do all typical HTTP operations for the API which it authorized against and for which it has appropriate scopes.

# Implementing an OAuth2 token storage interface

In the previous recipe, we retrieved a token for our client and performed API requests. The downside of this approach is that we have no long-term storage for our token. In an HTTP server, for example, we'd like to have consistent storage of the token between requests.

This recipe will explore modifying the OAuth2 client to store a token between requests and retrieve them at will using a key. For the sake of simplicity, this key will be a file, but it could also be a database, Redis, and so on.

## Getting ready

Refer to the *Getting ready* section of the *Making use of OAuth2 clients* recipe.

## How to do it...

These steps cover writing and running your application:

1. From your terminal/console application, create and navigate to the `chapter6/client` directory.

2. Copy tests from `https://github.com/agtorre/go-cookbook/tree/master/chapter6/oauthstore`or use this as an exercise to write some of your own code.

3. Create a file called `config.go` with the following content:

```go
package oauthstore

import (
    "context"
    "net/http"

    "golang.org/x/oauth2"
)

// Config wraps the default oauth2.Config
// and adds our storage
type Config struct {
    *oauth2.Config
    Storage
}
```

```
// Exchange stores a token after retrieval
func (c *Config) Exchange(ctx context.Context, code string)
(*oauth2.Token, error) {
    token, err := c.Config.Exchange(ctx, code)
    if err != nil {
        return nil, err
    }
    if err := c.Storage.SetToken(token); err != nil {
        return nil, err
    }
    return token, nil
}
// TokenSource can be passed a token which
// is stored, or when a new one is retrieved,
// that's stored
func (c *Config) TokenSource(ctx context.Context, t
*oauth2.Token) oauth2.TokenSource {
    return StorageTokenSource(ctx, c, t)
}

// Client is attached to our TokenSource
func (c *Config) Client(ctx context.Context, t *oauth2.Token)
*http.Client {
    return oauth2.NewClient(ctx, c.TokenSource(ctx, t))
}
```

4. Create a file called `tokensource.go` with the following content:

```
package oauthstore

import (
    "context"

    "golang.org/x/oauth2"
)

type storageTokenSource struct {
    *Config
    oauth2.TokenSource
}

// Token satisfies the TokenSource interface
func (s *storageTokenSource) Token() (*oauth2.Token, error) {
    if token, err := s.Config.Storage.GetToken(); err == nil &&
    token.Valid() {
        return token, err
    }
    token, err := s.TokenSource.Token()
```

```go
    if err != nil {
        return token, err
    }
    if err := s.Config.Storage.SetToken(token); err != nil {
        return nil, err
    }
    return token, nil
}

// StorageTokenSource will be used by out configs TokenSource
// function
func StorageTokenSource(ctx context.Context, c *Config, t
*oauth2.Token) oauth2.TokenSource {
    if t == nil || !t.Valid() {
        if tok, err := c.Storage.GetToken(); err == nil {
            t = tok
        }
    }
    ts := c.Config.TokenSource(ctx, t)
    return &storageTokenSource{c, ts}
}
```

5. Create a file called `storage.go` with the following content:

```go
package oauthstore

import (
    "context"
    "fmt"

    "golang.org/x/oauth2"
)

// Storage is our generic storage interface
type Storage interface {
    GetToken() (*oauth2.Token, error)
    SetToken(*oauth2.Token) error
}

// GetToken retrieves a github oauth2 token
func GetToken(ctx context.Context, conf Config) (*oauth2.Token,
error) {
    token, err := conf.Storage.GetToken()
    if err == nil && token.Valid() {
        return token, err
    }
    url := conf.AuthCodeURL("state")
    fmt.Printf("Type the following url into your browser and
```

```
        follow the directions on screen: %v\n", url)
        fmt.Println("Paste the code returned in the redirect URL
        and hit Enter:")

        var code string
        if _, err := fmt.Scan(&code); err != nil {
            return nil, err
        }
        return conf.Exchange(ctx, code)
}
```

6. Create a file called `filestorage.go` with the following content:

```
package oauthstore

import (
    "encoding/json"
    "errors"
    "os"
    "sync"

    "golang.org/x/oauth2"
)

// FileStorage satisfies our storage interface
type FileStorage struct {
    Path string
    mu sync.RWMutex
}

// GetToken retrieves a token from a file
func (f *FileStorage) GetToken() (*oauth2.Token, error) {
    f.mu.RLock()
    defer f.mu.RUnlock()
    in, err := os.Open(f.Path)
    if err != nil {
        return nil, err
    }
    defer in.Close()
    var t *oauth2.Token
    data := json.NewDecoder(in)
    return t, data.Decode(&t)
}

// SetToken creates, truncates, then stores a token
// in a file
func (f *FileStorage) SetToken(t *oauth2.Token) error {
    if t == nil || !t.Valid() {
```

```
        return errors.New("bad token")
    }

    f.mu.Lock()
    defer f.mu.Unlock()
    out, err := os.OpenFile(f.Path,
    os.O_RDWR|os.O_CREATE|os.O_TRUNC, 0755)
    if err != nil {
        return err
    }
    defer out.Close()
    data, err := json.Marshal(&t)
    if err != nil {
        return err
    }

    _, err = out.Write(data)
    return err
}
```

7. Create a new directory named `example` and navigate to it.

8. Create a file named `main.go` with the following content. Ensure that you modify the `oauthstore` import to use the path you set up in step 2:

```go
package main

import (
    "context"
    "io"
    "os"
    "github.com/agtorre/go-cookbook/chapter6/oauthstore"

    "golang.org/x/oauth2"
    "golang.org/x/oauth2/github"
)

func main() {
    conf := oauthstore.Config{
        Config: &oauth2.Config{
            ClientID: os.Getenv("GITHUB_CLIENT"),
            ClientSecret: os.Getenv("GITHUB_SECRET"),
            Scopes: []string{"repo", "user"},
            Endpoint: github.Endpoint,
        },
        Storage: &oauthstore.FileStorage{Path: "token.txt"},
    }
    ctx := context.Background()
```

```
                token, err := oauthstore.GetToken(ctx, conf)
                if err != nil {
                    panic(err)
                }

                cli := conf.Client(ctx, token)
                resp, err := cli.Get("https://api.github.com/user")
                if err != nil {
                    panic(err)
                }
                defer resp.Body.Close()
                io.Copy(os.Stdout, resp.Body)
            }
```

9.  Run `go run main.go`.

10. You may also run the following:

    ```
    go build
    ./example
    ```

    You should now see the following output:

    ```
    $ go run main.go
    Visit the URL for the auth dialog:
    https://github.com/login/oauth/authorize?
    access_type=offline&client_id=
    <your_id>&response_type=code&scope=repo+user&state=state
    Paste the code returned in the redirect URL and hit Enter:
    <your_code>
    {<json_payload>}

    $ go run main.go
    {<json_payload>}
    ```

11. If you copied or wrote your own tests, go up one directory and run `go test`.
    Ensure that all the tests pass.

# How it works...

This recipe takes care of storing and retrieving the contents of the token to/from a file. If it's a first run, it must execute the entire code exchange, but the subsequent runs will reuse the access token, and if one is available, it will refresh using the refresh token.

There is currently no way in this code to differentiate between users/tokens, but that could be accomplished with cookies as a key for a filename or a row in the database as well. Let's walk through what this code does:

- The `config.go` file wraps the standard OAuth2 config. For every method that involves retrieving a token, we first check whether we have a valid token in the local storage. If not, we retrieve one using the standard config and then store it.
- The `tokensource.go` file implements our custom `TokenSource` interface that pairs with `Config`. Similar to `Config`, we always first try to retrieve our token from a file and set it with the new token otherwise.
- The `storage.go` file is the `storage` interface used by `Config` and `TokenSource`. It only defines two methods and we also include a helper function to bootstrap the OAuth2 code-based flow similar to what we did in the previous recipe, but if the file with a valid token already exists, it will be used instead.
- The `filestorage.go` file implements the `storage` interface. When we store a new token, we first truncate the file and write a JSON representation of the `token` struct. Otherwise, we decode the file and return `token`.

# Wrapping a client in added functionality and function composition

In 2015, Tomás Senart gave an excellent talk on wrapping an `http.Client` struct with an interface, allowing you to take advantage of middleware and function composition. You can find out more on this at `https://github.com/gophercon/2015-talks`. This recipe takes from his ideas and demonstrates an example of doing the same to the `Transport` interface of the `http.Client` struct similar to our earlier recipe, *Writing a client for a REST API*.

This recipe will implement a logging and basic auth middleware for a standard `http.Client` struct. It also includes a decorate function that can be used when you need to with a large variety of middleware.

## Getting ready

Refer to the *Getting ready* section of the *Initializing, storing, and passing http.Client structs* recipe in this chapter.

# How to do it...

These steps cover writing and running your application:

1. From your terminal/console application, create the `chapter6/decorator` directory and navigate to it.

2. Copy tests from `https://github.com/agtorre/go-cookbook/tree/master/cha pter6/decorator`or use this as an exercise to write some of your own code.

3. Create a file called `config.go` with the following content:

```go
package decorator

import (
    "log"
    "net/http"
    "os"
)

// Setup initializes our ClientInterface
func Setup() *http.Client {
    c := http.Client{}

    t := Decorate(&http.Transport{},
        Logger(log.New(os.Stdout, "", 0)),
        BasicAuth("username", "password"),
    )
    c.Transport = t
    return &c
}
```

4. Create a file called `decorator.go` with the following content:

```go
package decorator

import "net/http"

// TransportFunc implements the RountTripper interface
type TransportFunc func(*http.Request) (*http.Response, error)

// RoundTrip just calls the original function
func (tf TransportFunc) RoundTrip(r *http.Request)
(*http.Response, error) {
    return tf(r)
}

// Decorator is a convenience function to represent our
```

```
// middleware inner function
type Decorator func(http.RoundTripper) http.RoundTripper

// Decorate is a helper to wrap all the middleware
func Decorate(t http.RoundTripper, rts ...Decorator)
http.RoundTripper {
    decorated := t
    for _, rt := range rts {
        decorated = rt(decorated)
    }
    return decorated
}
```

5. Create a file called `middleware.go` with the following content:

```go
package decorator

import (
    "log"
    "net/http"
    "time"
)

// Logger is one of our 'middleware' decorators
func Logger(l *log.Logger) Decorator {
    return func(c http.RoundTripper) http.RoundTripper {
        return TransportFunc(func(r *http.Request)
        (*http.Response, error) {
            start := time.Now()
            l.Printf("started request to %s at %s", r.URL,
            start.Format("2006-01-02 15:04:05"))
            resp, err := c.RoundTrip(r)
            l.Printf("completed request to %s in %s", r.URL,
            time.Since(start))
            return resp, err
        })
    }
}

// BasicAuth is another of our 'middleware' decorators
func BasicAuth(username, password string) Decorator {
    return func(c http.RoundTripper) http.RoundTripper {
        return TransportFunc(func(r *http.Request)
        (*http.Response, error) {
            r.SetBasicAuth(username, password)
            resp, err := c.RoundTrip(r)
            return resp, err
        })
```

```
            }
    }
```

6. Create a file called `exec.go` with the following content:

```
package decorator

import "fmt"

// Exec creates a client, calls google.com
// then prints the response
func Exec() error {
    c := Setup()

    resp, err := c.Get("https://www.google.com")
    if err != nil {
        return err
    }
    fmt.Println("Response code:", resp.StatusCode)
    return nil
}
```

7. Create a new directory named `example` and navigate to it.

8. Create a `main.go` file with the following content. Ensure that you modify the `decorator` import to use the path you set up in step 2:

```
package main

import "github.com/agtorre/go-cookbook/chapter6/decorator"

func main() {
    if err := decorator.Exec(); err != nil {
        panic(err)
    }
}
```

9. Run `go run main.go`.

10. You may also run the following:

```
go build
./example
```

You should now see the following output:

```
$ go run main.go
started request to https://www.google.com at 2017-01-01 13:38:42
completed request to https://www.google.com in 194.013054ms
Response code: 200
```

11. If you copied or wrote your own tests, go up one directory and run `go test`. Ensure that all the tests pass.

# How it works...

This recipe takes advantage of closures as first-class citizens and interfaces. The main trick that allows for this is having a function implement an interface. This allows us to wrap an interface implemented by a structure with an interface implemented by a function.

The `middleware.go` file contains two example client middleware functions. These could be extended to contain additional middleware, such as more sophisticated auth, metrics, and more. This recipe can also be combined with the previous recipe to produce an OAuth2 client that can be extended by additional middleware.

The `Decorator` function is a convenience function that allows the following:

```
Decorate(RoundTripper, Middleware1, Middleware2, etc)

vs

var t RoundTripper
t = Middleware1(t)
t = Middleware2(t)
etc
```

The advantage of this approach compared to wrapping the client is that we can keep the interface sparse. If you want a fully featured client, you'd also need to implement methods such as `GET`, `POST`, and `PostForm`.

# Understanding GRPC clients

GRPC is a high performance RPC framework that is built using protocol buffers (`https://developers.google.com/protocol-buffers`) and HTTP/2 (`https://http2.github.io`). Creating a GRPC client in Go has a lot of the same intricacies as working with Go HTTP clients. In order to demonstrate basic client usage, it's easiest to also implement a server. This recipe will create a `greeter` service, which takes a greeting and a name and returns the sentence `<greeting> <name>!`. In addition, the server can specify whether to exclaim `!` or not `.`.

This recipe won't explore some details about GRPC such as streaming, but will hopefully serve as an introduction to creating a very basic server and client.

## Getting ready

Configure your environment according to these steps:

1. Refer to the *Getting ready* section of the *Initializing, storing, and passing http.Client structs* recipe in this chapter.
2. Install GRPC at `https://github.com/grpc/grpc/blob/master/INSTALL.md`.
3. Run the `go get github.com/golang/protobuf/proto` command.
4. Run the `go get github.com/golang/protobuf/protoc-gen-go` command.

## How to do it...

These steps cover writing and running your application:

1. From your terminal/console application, create and navigate to the `chapter6/grpc` directory.
2. Copy tests from `https://github.com/agtorre/go-cookbook/tree/master/chapter6/grpc` or use this as an exercise to write some of your own code.
3. Create a new directory named `greeter` and navigate to it.
4. Create a file called `greeter.proto` with the following content:

```
syntax = "proto3";

package greeter;

service GreeterService{
```

```
        rpc Greet(GreetRequest) returns (GreetResponse) {}
    }

    message GreetRequest {
        string greeting = 1;
        string name = 2;
    }

    message GreetResponse{
        string response = 1;
    }
```

5. Run the following command:

   **protoc --go_out=plugins=grpc:. greeter.proto**

6. Navigate back up a directory.
7. Create a new directory named `server` and navigate to it.
8. Create a file called `server.go` with the following content. Ensure that you modify the `greeter` import to use the path you set up in step 3:

```
    package main

    import (
        "fmt"
        "net"

        "github.com/agtorre/go-cookbook/chapter6/grpc/greeter"
        "google.golang.org/grpc"
    )

    func main() {
        grpcServer := grpc.NewServer()
        greeter.RegisterGreeterServiceServer(grpcServer,
        &Greeter{Exclaim: true})
        lis, err := net.Listen("tcp", ":4444")
        if err != nil {
            panic(err)
        }
        fmt.Println("Listening on port :4444")
        grpcServer.Serve(lis)
    }
```

9. Create a file called `greeter.go` with the following content. Ensure that you modify the `greeter` import to use the path you set up in step 3:

```go
package main

import (
    "fmt"

    "github.com/agtorre/go-cookbook/chapter6/grpc/greeter"
    "golang.org/x/net/context"
)

// Greeter implements the interface
// generated by protoc
type Greeter struct {
    Exclaim bool
}

// Greet implements grpc Greet
func (g *Greeter) Greet(ctx context.Context, r
*greeter.GreetRequest) (*greeter.GreetResponse, error) {
    msg := fmt.Sprintf("%s %s", r.GetGreeting(), r.GetName())
    if g.Exclaim {
        msg += "!"
    } else {
        msg += "."
    }
    return &greeter.GreetResponse{Response: msg}, nil
}
```

10. Navigate back up a directory.
11. Create a new directory named `client` and navigate to it.
12. Create a file called `client.go` with the following content. Ensure that you modify the `greeter` import to use the path you set up in step 3:

```go
package main

import (
    "context"
    "fmt"

    "github.com/agtorre/go-cookbook/chapter6/grpc/greeter"
    "google.golang.org/grpc"
)

func main() {
```

```
    conn, err := grpc.Dial(":4444", grpc.WithInsecure())
    if err != nil {
        panic(err)
    }
    defer conn.Close()

    client := greeter.NewGreeterServiceClient(conn)

    ctx := context.Background()
    req := greeter.GreetRequest{Greeting: "Hello", Name:
    "Reader"}
    resp, err := client.Greet(ctx, &req)
    if err != nil {
        panic(err)
    }
    fmt.Println(resp)

    req.Greeting = "Goodbye"
    resp, err = client.Greet(ctx, &req)
    if err != nil {
        panic(err)
    }
    fmt.Println(resp)
}
```

13. Navigate back up a directory.

14. Run `go run server/server.go server/greeter.go`, and you will see the following output:

    ```
    $ go run server/server.go server/greeter.go
    Listening on port :4444
    ```

15. In a separate terminal, run `go run client/client.go` from the `grpc` directory, you will see the following output:

    ```
    $ go run client/client.go
    response:"Hello Reader!"
    response:"Goodbye Reader!"
    ```

16. If you copied or wrote your own tests, go up one directory and run `go test`. Ensure that all the tests pass.

# How it works...

The GRPC server is set up to listen on port 4444. Once the client connects, it can send requests and receive responses from the server. The structure of the requests, responses, and supported methods are dictated by the .proto file we created in step 4. In practice, when integrating against GRPC servers, they should provide the .proto file, which can be used to automatically generate a client.

In addition to the client, the protoc command generates the stubs for the server and all that's required is to fill in the implementation details. The generated Go code also has JSON tags and the same structs could be reused for JSON REST services. Our code sets up an insecure client. To handle GRPC securely, you need to use an SSL certificate.

# 7
# Microservices for Applications in Go

In this chapter the following recipes will be covered:

- Working with web handlers, requests, and ResponseWriters
- Using structs and closures for stateful handlers
- Validating input for Go structs and user inputs
- Rendering and content negotiation
- Implementing and using middleware
- Building a reverse proxy application
- Exporting GRPC as a JSON API

## Introduction

Out of the box, Go is an excellent choice for writing web applications. The built-in `net/http` packages combined with packages like `html/template` allow for fully-featured modern web applications out of the box. It's so easy that it encourages spinning up web interfaces for management of even basic long-running applications. Although the standard library is fully featured, there are still a large variety of third-party web packages for everything from routes to full-stack frameworks including these:

- `https://github.com/urfave/negroni`
- `https://github.com/gin-gonic/gin`
- `https://github.com/labstack/echo`
- `http://www.gorillatoolkit.org/`

- `https://github.com/julienschmidt/httprouter`

The recipes in this chapter will focus on basic tasks you might run into when working with handlers, when navigating response and request objects, and in dealing with concepts such as middleware.

# Working with web handlers, requests, and ResponseWriters

Go defines `HandlerFuncs` and a `Handler` interface with the following signatures:

```
// HandlerFunc implements the Handler interface
type HandlerFunc func(http.ResponseWriter, *http.Request)

type Handler interface {
    ServeHTTP(http.ResponseWriter, *http.Request)
}
```

By default, the `net/http` package makes extensive use of these types. For example, a route can be attached to a `Handler` or `HandlerFunc` interface. This recipe will explore creating a `Handler` interface, listening on a local port, and performing some operations on an `http.ResponseWriter` interface after processing `http.Request`. This should be considered the basis for Go web applications and RESTFul APIs.

# Getting ready

Configure your environment according to these steps:

1. Download and install Go on your operating system from `https://golang.org/doc/install`, and configure your `GOPATH` environment variable.

2. Open a terminal/console application.

3. Navigate to your `GOPATH/src` and create a project directory, such as `$GOPATH/src/github.com/yourusername/customrepo`.

   All code will be run and modified from this directory.

4. Optionally, install the latest tested version of the code using the `go get` `github.com/agtorre/go-cookbook/` command.

5. Install the curl command from `https://curl.haxx.se/download.html`.

# How to do it...

These steps cover writing and running your application:

1. From your terminal/console application, create and navigate to the chapter7/handlers directory.

2. Copy tests from https://github.com/agtorre/go-cookbook/tree/master/chapter7/handlersor use this as an exercise to write some of your own code.

3. Create a file called get.go with the following contents:

```go
package handlers

import (
    "fmt"
    "net/http"
)

// HelloHandler takes a GET parameter "name" and responds
// with Hello <name>! in plaintext
func HelloHandler(w http.ResponseWriter, r *http.Request) {
    w.Header().Set("Content-Type", "text/plain")
    if r.Method != http.MethodGet {
        w.WriteHeader(http.StatusMethodNotAllowed)
        return
    }
    name := r.URL.Query().Get("name")

    w.WriteHeader(http.StatusOK)
    w.Write([]byte(fmt.Sprintf("Hello %s!", name)))
}
```

4. Create a file called post.go with the following contents:

```go
package handlers

import (
    "encoding/json"
    "net/http"
)

// GreetingResponse is the JSON Response that
// GreetingHandler returns
type GreetingResponse struct {
    Payload struct {
        Greeting string `json:"greeting,omitempty"`
        Name string `json:"name,omitempty"`
```

```
            Error string `json:"error,omitempty"`
        } `json:"payload"`
        Successful bool `json:"successful"`
    }

    // GreetingHandler returns a GreetingResponse which either has
    // errors or a useful payload
    func GreetingHandler(w http.ResponseWriter, r *http.Request) {
        w.Header().Set("Content-Type", "application/json")
        if r.Method != http.MethodPost {
            w.WriteHeader(http.StatusMethodNotAllowed)
            return
        }
        var gr GreetingResponse
        if err := r.ParseForm(); err != nil {
            gr.Payload.Error = "bad request"
            if payload, err := json.Marshal(gr); err == nil {
                w.Write(payload)
            }
        }
        name := r.FormValue("name")
        greeting := r.FormValue("greeting")

        w.WriteHeader(http.StatusOK)
        gr.Successful = true
        gr.Payload.Name = name
        gr.Payload.Greeting = greeting
        if payload, err := json.Marshal(gr); err == nil {
            w.Write(payload)
        }
    }
```

5. Create a new directory named `example` and navigate to it.

6. Create a file called `main.go` with the following contents; be sure to modify the `handlers` import to use the path you set up in step 2:

```
package main

import (
    "fmt"
    "net/http"

    "github.com/agtorre/go-cookbook/chapter7/handlers"
)

func main() {
    http.HandleFunc("/name", handlers.HelloHandler)
```

```
http.HandleFunc("/greeting", handlers.GreetingHandler)
fmt.Println("Listening on port :3333")
err := http.ListenAndServe(":3333", nil)
panic(err)
}
```

7. Run `go run main.go`.

8. You could also run the following command:

   ```
   go build
   ./example
   ```

   You should see the following output:

   ```
   $ go run main.go
   Listening on port :3333
   ```

9. In a separate terminal, run the following commands:

   ```
   curl "http://localhost:3333/name?name=Reader" -X GET
   curl "http://localhost:3333/greeting" -X POST -d
   'name=Reader;greeting=Goodbye'
   ```

   You will see the following output:

   ```
   $curl "http://localhost:3333/name?name=Reader" -X GET
   Hello Reader!

   $curl "http://localhost:3333/greeting" -X POST -d
   'name=Reader;greeting=Goodbye'
   {"payload":
   {"greeting":"Goodbye","name":"Reader"},"successful":true}
   ```

10. If you copied or wrote your own tests, go up one directory and run `go test`.
    Ensure that all tests pass.

# How it works...

For this recipe, we set up two handlers. The first handler expects a GET request with a GET
parameter called name. When we curl it, it returns the plain text string Hello <name>!

The second handler expects a POST method with PostForm requests. This is what you'd get if you used a standard HTML form without any AJAX calls. Alternatively, we could parse JSON out of the request body instead. This is commonly done with json.Decoder. I recommend trying this as an exercise as well. Lastly, the handler sends a JSON-formatted response and sets all the appropriate headers.

Although all of this was written explicitly, there are a number of methods for making the code less verbose, as follows:

- Using https://github.com/unrolled/render to handle responses
- Using various web frameworks mentioned in the *Working with web handlers, requests, and ResponseWriters* recipe of this chapter to parse route arguments, restrict routes to specific HTTP verbs, handle graceful shutdown, and more

# Using structs and closures for stateful handlers

Due to the sparse signatures of HTTP handler functions, it may seem tricky to add state to a handler. For example, there are a variety of ways to include a database connection. Two approaches to doing this are to pass in the state via closures, which is useful for flexibility on a single handler, or by using a struct.

This recipe will demonstrate both. We'll use a struct controller to store a storage interface and create two routes with a single handler that are modified by an outer function.

## Getting ready

Refer to the steps given in the *Getting ready* section of the *Working with web handlers, requests, and ResponseWriters* recipe.

## How to do it...

These steps cover writing and running your application:

1. From your terminal/console application, create and navigate to the chapter7/rest directory.

2. Copy tests from `https://github.com/agtorre/go-cookbook/tree/master/cha
pter7/controllers`or use this as an exercise to write some of your own.

3. Create a file called `controller.go` with the following contents:

```go
package controllers

// Controller passes state to our handlers
type Controller struct {
    storage Storage
}

// New is a Controller 'constructor'
func New(storage Storage) *Controller {
    return &Controller{
        storage: storage,
    }
}

// Payload is our common response
type Payload struct {
    Value string `json:"value"`
}
```

4. Create a file called `storage.go` with the following contents:

```go
package controllers

// Storage Interface Supports Get and Put
// of a single value
type Storage interface {
    Get() string
    Put(string)
}

// MemStorage implements Storage
type MemStorage struct {
    value string
}

// Get our in-memory value
func (m *MemStorage) Get() string {
    return m.value
}

// Put our in-memory value
func (m *MemStorage) Put(s string) {
    m.value = s
```

```
}
```

5. Create a file called post.go with the following contents:

```go
package controllers

import (
    "encoding/json"
    "net/http"
)

// SetValue modifies the underlying storage of the controller
// object
func (c *Controller) SetValue(w http.ResponseWriter, r
*http.Request) {
    if r.Method != http.MethodPost {
        w.WriteHeader(http.StatusMethodNotAllowed)
        return
    }
    if err := r.ParseForm(); err != nil {
        w.WriteHeader(http.StatusInternalServerError)
        return
    }
    value := r.FormValue("value")
    c.storage.Put(value)
    w.WriteHeader(http.StatusOK)
    p := Payload{Value: value}
    if payload, err := json.Marshal(p); err == nil {
        w.Write(payload)
    }

}
```

6. Create a file called get.go with the following contents:

```go
package controllers

import (
    "encoding/json"
    "net/http"
)

// GetValue is a closure that wraps a HandlerFunc, if
// UseDefault is true value will always be "default" else it'll
// be whatever is stored in storage
func (c *Controller) GetValue(UseDefault bool) http.HandlerFunc
{
    return func(w http.ResponseWriter, r *http.Request) {
```

```
        w.Header().Set("Content-Type", "application/json")
        if r.Method != http.MethodGet {
            w.WriteHeader(http.StatusMethodNotAllowed)
            return
        }
        value := "default"
        if !UseDefault {
            value = c.storage.Get()
        }
        w.WriteHeader(http.StatusOK)
        p := Payload{Value: value}
        if payload, err := json.Marshal(p); err == nil {
            w.Write(payload)
        }
    }
}
```

7. Create a new directory named `example` and navigate to it.

8. Create a file called `main.go` with the following contents; be sure to modify the `controllers` import to use the path you set up in step 2:

```
package main

import (
    "fmt"
    "net/http"

    "github.com/agtorre/go-cookbook/chapter7/controllers"
)

func main() {
    storage := controllers.MemStorage{}
    c := controllers.New(&storage)
    http.HandleFunc("/get", c.GetValue(false))
    http.HandleFunc("/get/default", c.GetValue(true))
    http.HandleFunc("/set", c.SetValue)

    fmt.Println("Listening on port :3333")
    err := http.ListenAndServe(":3333", nil)
    panic(err)
}
```

9. Run `go run main.go`.

10. You could also run:

```
go build
./example
```

You should see the following output:

```
$ go run main.go
Listening on port :3333
```

11. In a separate terminal, run the following commands:

```
curl "http://localhost:3333/set -X POST -d "value=value"
curl "http://localhost:3333/get -X GET
curl "http://localhost:3333/get/default -X GET
```

You will see the following output:

```
$curl "http://localhost:3333/set -X POST -d "value=value"
{"value":"value"}

$curl "http://localhost:3333/get -X GET
{"value":"value"}

$curl "http://localhost:3333/get/default -X GET
{"value":"default"}
```

12. If you copied or wrote your own tests, go up one directory and run `go test`. Ensure that all tests pass.

## How it works...

These strategies work because Go allows methods to satisfy typed functions such as `http.HandlerFunc`. By using a struct, we can inject various pieces in `main.go`, which could include database connections, logging, and more. In this recipe, we inserted a `Storage` interface. All handlers connected to the controller can make use of its methods and attributes.

The `GetValue` method doesn't have an `http.HandlerFunc` signature and instead returns it. This is how we can use a closure to inject state. In `main.go`, we define two routes one with `UseDefault` set to `false` and the other with it set to `true`. This could be used when defining a function that spans multiple routes, or when using a struct where your handlers feel too cumbersome.

# Validating input for Go structs and user inputs

Validation for web can be a difficult problem. This recipe will explore using closures to support easy mocking of validation functions and to allow flexibility in the type of validation performed when initializing a controller struct as described by the previous recipe.

We'll perform this validation on a struct, but not explore how to populate the struct. We can assume that the data will be populated by parsing a JSON payload, populating explicitly from the form input, or other methods.

## Getting ready

Refer to the steps given in the *Getting ready* section of the *Working with web handlers, requests, and ResponseWriters* recipe.

## How to do it...

These steps cover writing and running your application:

1. From your terminal/console application, create and navigate to the `chapter7/validation` directory.
2. Copy tests from `https://github.com/agtorre/go-cookbook/tree/master/chapter7/validation` or use this as an exercise to write some of your own code.
3. Create a file called `controller.go` with the following contents:

```
package validation

// Controller holds our validation functions
type Controller struct {
    ValidatePayload func(p *Payload) error
}

// New initializes a controller with our
// local validation, it can be overwritten
func New() *Controller {
    return &Controller{
        ValidatePayload: ValidatePayload,
    }
}
```

```
}
```

4. Create a file called `validate.go` with the following contents:

```go
package validation

import "errors"

// Verror is an error that occurs
// during validation, we can
// return this to a user
type Verror struct {
    error
}

// Payload is the value we
// process
type Payload struct {
    Name string `json:"name"`
    Age int `json:"age"`
}

// ValidatePayload is 1 implementation of
// the closure in our controller
func ValidatePayload(p *Payload) error {
    if p.Name == "" {
        return Verror{errors.New("name is required")}
    }

    if p.Age <= 0 || p.Age >= 120 {
        return Verror{errors.New("age is required and must be a
        value greater than 0 and less than 120")}
    }
    return nil
}
```

5. Create a file called `process.go` with the following contents:

```go
package validation

import (
    "encoding/json"
    "fmt"
    "net/http"
)

// Process is a handler that validates a post payload
func (c *Controller) Process(w http.ResponseWriter, r
```

```
*http.Request) {
    if r.Method != http.MethodPost {
        w.WriteHeader(http.StatusMethodNotAllowed)
        return
    }

    decoder := json.NewDecoder(r.Body)
    defer r.Body.Close()
    var p Payload

    if err := decoder.Decode(&p); err != nil {
        fmt.Println(err)
        w.WriteHeader(http.StatusBadRequest)
        return
    }

    if err := c.ValidatePayload(&p); err != nil {
        switch err.(type) {
        case Verror:
            w.WriteHeader(http.StatusBadRequest)
            // pass the Verror along
            w.Write([]byte(err.Error()))
            return
        default:
            w.WriteHeader(http.StatusInternalServerError)
            return
        }
    }
}
```

6. Create a new directory named `example` and navigate to it.

7. Create a file called `main.go` with the following contents; be sure to modify the `validation` import to use the path you set up in step 2:

```
package main

import (
    "fmt"
    "net/http"

    "github.com/agtorre/go-cookbook/chapter7/validation"
)

func main() {
    c := validation.New()
    http.HandleFunc("/", c.Process)
    fmt.Println("Listening on port :3333")
```

```
err := http.ListenAndServe(":3333", nil)
panic(err)
}
```

8. Run `go run main.go`.

9. You could also run:

   ```
   go build
   ./example
   ```

   You should see the following output:

   ```
   $ go run main.go
   Listening on port :3333
   ```

10. In a separate terminal run the following commands:

    ```
    curl "http://localhost:3333/-X POST -d '{}'
    curl "http://localhost:3333/-X POST -d '{"name":"test"}'
    curl "http://localhost:3333/-X POST -d '{"name":"test",
    "age": 5}'
    ```

    You should see the following output:

    ```
    $curl "http://localhost:3333/-X POST -d '{}'
    name is required
    ```

    ```
    $curl "http://localhost:3333/-X POST -d '{"name":"test"}'
    age is required and must be a value greater than 0 and
    less than 120
    ```

    ```
    $curl "http://localhost:3333/-X POST -d '{"name":"test",
    "age": 5}' -v
    ```

    ```
    <lots of output, should contain a 200 OK status code>
    ```

11. If you copied or wrote your own tests, go up one directory and run `go test`. Ensure that all tests pass.

# How it works...

We handle validation by passing in a closure to our controller struct. For any input that the controller might need to validate, we'd need one of these closures. The advantage to this approach is that we can mock and replace the validation functions at run time, so testing becomes far simpler. In addition, we're not bound to a single function signature and we can pass in things such as a database connection to our validation functions.

The other thing this recipe demonstrates is returning a typed error called a `Verror`. This type holds validation error messages that can be displayed to users. One shortcoming of this approach is that it doesn't handle multiple validation messages at once. This would be possible by modifying the `Verror` type to allow for more state, for example, by including a map, in order to house a number of validation errors before it returns from our `ValidatePayload` function.

# Rendering and content negotiation

Web handlers can return a variety of content types, for example, they can return JSON, plain text, images, and more. Frequently, when communicating with APIs, it's possible to specify and accept content type to clarify what format you'll pass data in as and what data you want to receive back out.

This recipe will explore using unrolled/render and a custom function to negotiate content type and respond accordingly.

# Getting ready

Configure your environment according to these steps:

1. Refer to the steps in the *Getting ready* section of the *Working with web handlers, requests, and ResponseWriters* recipe.
2. Run the `go get github.com/unrolled/render` command.

# How to do it...

These steps cover writing and running your application:

1. From your terminal/console application, create and navigate to the `chapter7/negotiate` directory.

2. Copy tests from `https://github.com/agtorre/go-cookbook/tree/master/chapter7/negotiate` or use this as an exercise to write some of your own code.

3. Create a file called `negotiate.go` with the following contents:

```go
package negotiate

import (
    "net/http"

    "github.com/unrolled/render"
)

// Negotiator wraps render and does
// some switching on ContentType
type Negotiator struct {
    ContentType string
    *render.Render
}

// GetNegotiator takes a request, and figures
// out the ContentType from the Content-Type header
func GetNegotiator(r *http.Request) *Negotiator {
    contentType := r.Header.Get("Content-Type")

    return &Negotiator{
        ContentType: contentType,
        Render: render.New(),
    }
}
```

4. Create a file called `respond.go` with the following contents:

```go
package negotiate

import "io"
import "github.com/unrolled/render"

// Respond switches on Content Type to determine
// the response
func (n *Negotiator) Respond(w io.Writer, status int, v
```

```
interface{}) {
    switch n.ContentType {
        case render.ContentJSON:
            n.Render.JSON(w, status, v)
        case render.ContentXML:
            n.Render.XML(w, status, v)
        default:
            n.Render.JSON(w, status, v)
    }
}
```

5. Create a file called `handler.go` with the following contents:

```go
package negotiate

import (
    "encoding/xml"
    "net/http"
)

// Payload defines it's layout in xml and json
type Payload struct {
    XMLName xml.Name `xml:"payload" json:"-"`
    Status  string   `xml:"status" json:"status"`
}

// Handler gets a negotiator using the request,
// then renders a Payload
func Handler(w http.ResponseWriter, r *http.Request) {
    n := GetNegotiator(r)

    n.Respond(w, http.StatusOK, &Payload{Status:
    "Successful!"})
}
```

6. Create a new directory named `example` and navigate to it.

7. Create a file called `main.go` with the following contents; be sure to modify the negotiate import to use the path you set up in step 2:

```go
package main

import (
    "fmt"
    "net/http"

    "github.com/agtorre/go-cookbook/chapter7/negotiate"
)
```

```
func main() {
    http.HandleFunc("/", negotiate.Handler)
    fmt.Println("Listening on port :3333")
    err := http.ListenAndServe(":3333", nil)
    panic(err)
}
```

8. Run `go run main.go`.

9. You could also run:

   ```
   go build
   ./example
   ```

   You should see the following output:

   ```
   $ go run main.go
   Listening on port :3333
   ```

10. In a separate terminal run the following:

   ```
   curl "http://localhost:3333 -H "Content-Type: text/xml"
   curl "http://localhost:3333 -H "Content-Type: application/json"
   ```

   You will see the following output:

   ```
   $curl "http://localhost:3333 -H "Content-Type: text/xml"
   <payload><status>Successful!</status></payload>

   $curl "http://localhost:3333 -H "Content-Type: application/json"
   {"status":"Successful!"}
   ```

11. If you copied or wrote your own tests, go up one directory and run `go test`. Ensure that all tests pass.

## How it works...

The `github.com/unrolled/render` package does the heavy lifting for this recipe. There are a huge number of other options you can input if you need to work with HTML templates and more. This recipe can be used to autonegotiate when working through web handlers as is demonstrated here by passing in various content type headers, or directly by manipulating the struct.

A similar pattern can be applied to accept headers, but beware that this header often includes multiple values and your code will have to take that into account.

# Implementing and using middleware

Middleware for handlers in Go is an area that has been widely explored. There are a variety of packages for handling middleware. This recipe will create middleware from scratch and implement an `ApplyMiddleware` function to chain together a bunch of middleware.

It will also explore setting values in the request context object and retrieving them later using middleware. This will all be done with a very basic handler to help demonstrate how to decouple middleware logic from your handlers.

## Getting ready

Refer to the steps given in the *Getting ready* section of the *Working with web handlers, requests, and ResponseWriters* recipe.

## How to do it...

These steps cover writing and running your application:

1. From your terminal/console application, create and navigate to the `chapter7/middleware` directory.

2. Copy tests from `https://github.com/agtorre/go-cookbook/tree/master/chapter7/middleware` or use this as an exercise to write some of your own.

3. Create a file called `middleware.go` with the following contents:

```
package middleware

import (
    "log"
    "net/http"
    "time"
)

// Middleware is what all middleware functions will return
type Middleware func(http.HandlerFunc) http.HandlerFunc

// ApplyMiddleware will apply all middleware, the last
// arguments will be the
// outer wrap for context passing purposes
func ApplyMiddleware(h http.HandlerFunc, middleware
...Middleware) http.HandlerFunc {
    applied := h
```

```
        for _, m := range middleware {
            applied = m(applied)
        }
        return applied
    }

    // Logger logs requests, this will use an id passed in via
    // SetID()
    func Logger(l *log.Logger) Middleware {
        return func(next http.HandlerFunc) http.HandlerFunc {
            return func(w http.ResponseWriter, r *http.Request) {
                start := time.Now()
                l.Printf("started request to %s with id %s", r.URL,
                GetID(r.Context()))
                next(w, r)
                l.Printf("completed request to %s with id %s in
                %s", r.URL, GetID(r.Context()), time.Since(start))
            }
        }
    }
```

4. Create a file called context.go with the following contents:

```
    package middleware

    import (
        "context"
        "net/http"
        "strconv"
    )

    // ContextID is our type to retrieve our context
    // objects
    type ContextID int

    // ID is the only ID we've defined
    const ID ContextID = 0

    // SetID updates context with the id then
    // increments it
    func SetID(start int64) Middleware {
        return func(next http.HandlerFunc) http.HandlerFunc {
            return func(w http.ResponseWriter, r *http.Request) {
                ctx := context.WithValue(r.Context(), ID,
                strconv.FormatInt(start, 10))
                start++
                r = r.WithContext(ctx)
                next(w, r)
```

```
            }
        }
    }

    // GetID grabs an ID from a context if set
    // otherwise it returns an empty string
    func GetID(ctx context.Context) string {
        if val, ok := ctx.Value(ID).(string); ok {
            return val
        }
        return ""
    }
```

5. Create a file called handler.go with the following contents:

```
package middleware

import (
    "net/http"
)

// Handler is very basic
func Handler(w http.ResponseWriter, r *http.Request) {
    w.WriteHeader(http.StatusOK)
    w.Write([]byte("success"))
}
```

6. Create a new directory named example and navigate to it.
7. Create a file called main.go with the following contents; be sure to modify the middleware import to use the path you set up in step 2:

```
package main

import (
    "fmt"
    "log"
    "net/http"
    "os"

    "github.com/agtorre/go-cookbook/chapter7/middleware"
)

func main() {
    // We apply from bottom up
    h := middleware.ApplyMiddleware(
    middleware.Handler,
    middleware.Logger(log.New(os.Stdout, "", 0)),
```

```
                    middleware.SetID(100),
                )
                http.HandleFunc("/", h)
                fmt.Println("Listening on port :3333")
                err := http.ListenAndServe(":3333", nil)
                panic(err)
        }
```

8. Run `go run main.go`.

9. You could also run:

   ```
   go build
   ./example
   ```

   You should see the following output:

   ```
   $ go run main.go
   Listening on port :3333
   ```

10. In a separate terminal, run the following curl command several times:

    ```
    curl "http://localhost:3333
    ```

    You will see the following output:

    ```
    $curl "http://localhost:3333
    success

    $curl "http://localhost:3333
    success

    $curl "http://localhost:3333
    success
    ```

11. In the original `main.go`, you should see the following:

    ```
    Listening on port :3333
    started request to / with id 100
    completed request to / with id 100 in 52.284µs
    started request to / with id 101
    completed request to / with id 101 in 40.273µs
    started request to / with id 102
    ```

12. If you copied or wrote your own tests, go up one directory and run `go test`. Ensure that all tests pass.

# How it works...

Middleware can be used to perform simple operations such as logging, metric collection and analytics. It can also be used to dynamically populate variables on each request. This can be used, for example, to collect an X-Header from the request to set an ID or generate an ID, like we did in this recipe. Another ID strategy might be to generate a UUID for every request--this allows us to easily correlate log messages together and trace your request across different applications if multiple microservices are involved in building the response.

When working with context values, it's important to consider the order of your middleware. Typically, it's better to not make middleware reliant on one another. For example, in this recipe, it would probably be better to generate the UUID in the logging middleware itself. However, this recipe should serve as a guide for layering middleware and initializing them in `main.go`.

# Building a reverse proxy application

In this recipe, we will develop a reverse proxy application. The idea is, by hitting `http://localhost:3333` in a browser, all traffic will be forwarded to a configurable host and the responses will be forwarded to your browser. The end result should be `https://www.golang.org` rendered in a browser through our proxy application.

This can be combined with port forwarding and ssh tunnels in order to securely hit websites through an intermediate server. This recipe will build a reverse proxy from the ground up, but this functionality is also provided by the `net/http/httputil` package. Using this package, the incoming request can be modified by `Director func(*http.Request)` and the outgoing response can be modified by `ModifyResponse func(*http.Response) error`. In addition, there's support for buffering the response.

# Getting ready

Refer to the steps given in the *Getting ready* section of the *Working with web handlers, requests, and ResponseWriters* recipe.

# How to do it...

These steps cover writing and running your application:

1. From your terminal/console application, create and navigate to the `chapter7/proxy` directory.

2. Copy tests from `https://github.com/agtorre/go-cookbook/tree/master/chapter7/proxy`or use this as an exercise to write some of your own code.

3. Create a file called `proxy.go` with the following contents:

```
package proxy

import (
    "log"
    "net/http"
)

// Proxy holds our configured client
// and BaseURL to proxy to
type Proxy struct {
    Client *http.Client
    BaseURL string
}

// ServeHTTP means that proxy implments the Handler interface
// It manipulates the request, forwards it to BaseURL, then
// returns the response
func (p *Proxy) ServeHTTP(w http.ResponseWriter, r
*http.Request) {
    if err := p.ProcessRequest(r); err != nil {
        log.Printf("error occurred during process request: %s",
        err.Error())
        w.WriteHeader(http.StatusBadRequest)
        return
    }

    resp, err := p.Client.Do(r)
    if err != nil {
        log.Printf("error occurred during client operation:
        %s", err.Error())
        w.WriteHeader(http.StatusInternalServerError)
        return
    }
    defer resp.Body.Close()
    CopyResponse(w, resp)
}
```

4. Create a file called `process.go` with the following contents:

```go
package proxy

import (
    "bytes"
    "net/http"
    "net/url"
)

// ProcessRequest modifies the request in accordnance
// with Proxy settings
func (p *Proxy) ProcessRequest(r *http.Request) error {
    proxyURLRaw := p.BaseURL + r.URL.String()

    proxyURL, err := url.Parse(proxyURLRaw)
    if err != nil {
        return err
    }
    r.URL = proxyURL
    r.Host = proxyURL.Host
    r.RequestURI = ""
    return nil
}

// CopyResponse takes the client response and writes everything
// to the ResponseWriter in the original handler
func CopyResponse(w http.ResponseWriter, resp *http.Response) {
    var out bytes.Buffer
    out.ReadFrom(resp.Body)

    for key, values := range resp.Header {
        for _, value := range values {
        w.Header().Add(key, value)
        }
    }

    w.WriteHeader(resp.StatusCode)
    w.Write(out.Bytes())
}
```

5. Create a new directory named `example` and navigate to it.

6. Create a file called `main.go` with the following contents; be sure to modify the `proxy` import to use the path you set up in step 2:

```
package main

import (
    "fmt"
    "net/http"

    "github.com/agtorre/go-cookbook/chapter7/proxy"
)

func main() {
    p := &proxy.Proxy{
        Client: http.DefaultClient,
        BaseURL: "https://www.golang.org",
    }
    http.Handle("/", p)
    fmt.Println("Listening on port :3333")
    err := http.ListenAndServe(":3333", nil)
    panic(err)
}
```

7. Run `go run main.go`.
8. You could also run:

```
go build
./example
```

You should see the following output:

```
$ go run main.go
Listening on port :3333
```

9. Navigate a browser to `localhost:3333/`. You should see the `https://golang.org/` website rendered!
10. If you copied or wrote your own tests, go up one directory and run `go test`. Ensure that all tests pass.

# How it works...

Go request and response objects are largely shareable between clients and handlers. This code takes a request obtained by a `Proxy` struct that satisfies a `Handler` interface. The `main.go` file is using `Handle` instead of `HandleFunc` used elsewhere. Once the request is available, it's modified to prepend `Proxy.BaseURL` for the request which the client then dispatches. Lastly, the response is copied back to the `ResponseWriter` interface. This includes all headers, the body, and the status.

We can also add some additional features such as basic auth for requests, token management, and more if needed. This can be useful for token management where the proxy manages sessions for a JavaScript or other client application.

# Exporting GRPC as a JSON API

In the *Understanding GRPC clients* recipe from `Chapter 6`, *Web Clients and APIs*, we wrote a basic GRPC server and client. This recipe will expand on that idea by putting common RPC functions in a package and wrapping them in both a GRPC server and a standard web handler. This can be useful when your API wants to support both types of client, but you don't want to replicate code for common functionality.

# Getting ready

Configure your environment according to these steps:

1. Refer to the steps given in the *Getting ready* section of the *Working with web handlers, requests, and ResponseWriters* recipe.
2. Install GRPC from `https://github.com/grpc/grpc/blob/master/INSTALL.md`.
3. Run the `go get github.com/golang/protobuf/proto` command.
4. Run the `go get github.com/golang/protobuf/protoc-gen-go` command.

# How to do it...

These steps cover writing and running your application:

1. From your terminal/console application, create and navigate to the `chapter7/grpcjson` directory.

2. Copy tests from `https://github.com/agtorre/go-cookbook/tree/master/cha pter7/grpcjson`or use this as an exercise to write some of your own code.

3. Create a new directory named `keyvalue` and navigate to it.

4. Create a file called `keyvalue.proto` with the following contents:

```
syntax = "proto3";

package keyvalue;

service KeyValue{
    rpc Set(SetKeyValueRequest) returns (KeyValueResponse){}
    rpc Get(GetKeyValueRequest) returns (KeyValueResponse){}
}

message SetKeyValueRequest {
    string key = 1;
    string value = 2;
}

message GetKeyValueRequest{
    string key = 1;
}

message KeyValueResponse{
    string success = 1;
    string value = 2;
}
```

5. Run the following command:

```
protoc --go_out=plugins=grpc:. keyvalue.proto
```

6. Navigate back up a directory.

7. Create a new directory named `internal`.

8. Create a file called `internal/keyvalue.go` with the following contents:

```
package internal

import (
    "golang.org/x/net/context"
    "sync"

    "github.com/agtorre/go-cookbook/chapter7/grpcjson/keyvalue"
    "google.golang.org/grpc"
    "google.golang.org/grpc/codes"
)
```

```go
// KeyValue is a struct that holds a map
type KeyValue struct {
    mutex sync.RWMutex
    m map[string]string
}

// NewKeyValue initializes the map and controller
func NewKeyValue() *KeyValue {
    return &KeyValue{
        m: make(map[string]string),
    }
}

// Set sets a value to a key, then returns the value
func (k *KeyValue) Set(ctx context.Context, r
*keyvalue.SetKeyValueRequest) (*keyvalue.KeyValueResponse,
error) {
    k.mutex.Lock()
    k.m[r.GetKey()] = r.GetValue()
    k.mutex.Unlock()
    return &keyvalue.KeyValueResponse{Value: r.GetValue()}, nil
}

// Get gets a value given a key, or say not found if
// it doesn't exist
func (k *KeyValue) Get(ctx context.Context, r
*keyvalue.GetKeyValueRequest) (*keyvalue.KeyValueResponse,
error) {
    k.mutex.RLock()
    defer k.mutex.RUnlock()
    val, ok := k.m[r.GetKey()]
    if !ok {
        return nil, grpc.Errorf(codes.NotFound, "key not set")
    }
    return &keyvalue.KeyValueResponse{Value: val}, nil
}
```

9. Create a new directory named `grpc`.

10. Create a file called `grpc/main.go` with the following contents:

```go
package main

import (
    "fmt"
    "net"

    "github.com/agtorre/go-cookbook/chapter7/grpcjson/internal"
    "github.com/agtorre/go-cookbook/chapter7/grpcjson/keyvalue"
```

```
        "google.golang.org/grpc"
)

func main() {
    grpcServer := grpc.NewServer()
    keyvalue.RegisterKeyValueServer(grpcServer,
    internal.NewKeyValue())
    lis, err := net.Listen("tcp", ":4444")
    if err != nil {
        panic(err)
    }
    fmt.Println("Listening on port :4444")
    grpcServer.Serve(lis)
}
```

11. Create a new directory named `http`.

12. Create a file called `http/set.go` with the following contents:

```
package main

import (
    "encoding/json"
    "net/http"

    "github.com/agtorre/go-cookbook/chapter7/grpcjson/internal"
    "github.com/agtorre/go-cookbook/chapter7/grpcjson/keyvalue"
    "github.com/apex/log"
)

// Controller holds an internal KeyValueObject
type Controller struct {
    *internal.KeyValue
}

// SetHandler wraps or GRPC Set
func (c *Controller) SetHandler(w http.ResponseWriter, r
*http.Request) {
    var kv keyvalue.SetKeyValueRequest

    decoder := json.NewDecoder(r.Body)
    if err := decoder.Decode(&kv); err != nil {
        log.Errorf("failed to decode: %s", err.Error())
        w.WriteHeader(http.StatusBadRequest)
        return
    }

    gresp, err := c.Set(r.Context(), &kv)
    if err != nil {
```

```
        log.Errorf("failed to set: %s", err.Error())
        w.WriteHeader(http.StatusInternalServerError)
        return
    }

    resp, err := json.Marshal(gresp)
    if err != nil {
        log.Errorf("failed to marshal: %s", err.Error())
        w.WriteHeader(http.StatusInternalServerError)
        return
    }
    w.WriteHeader(http.StatusOK)
    w.Write(resp)
}
```

13. Create a file called `http/get.go` with the following contents:

```
package main

import (
    "encoding/json"
    "net/http"

    "google.golang.org/grpc"
    "google.golang.org/grpc/codes"

    "github.com/agtorre/go-cookbook/chapter7/grpcjson/keyvalue"
    "github.com/apex/log"
)

// GetHandler wraps our RPC Get call
func (c *Controller) GetHandler(w http.ResponseWriter, r
*http.Request) {
    key := r.URL.Query().Get("key")
    kv := keyvalue.GetKeyValueRequest{Key: key}

    gresp, err := c.Get(r.Context(), &kv)
    if err != nil {
        if grpc.Code(err) == codes.NotFound {
            w.WriteHeader(http.StatusNotFound)
            return
        }
        log.Errorf("failed to get: %s", err.Error())
        w.WriteHeader(http.StatusInternalServerError)
        return
    }

    w.WriteHeader(http.StatusOK)
```

```
    resp, err := json.Marshal(gresp)
    if err != nil {
        log.Errorf("failed to marshal: %s", err.Error())
        w.WriteHeader(http.StatusInternalServerError)
        return
    }
    w.Write(resp)
}
```

14. Create a file called `http/main.go` with the following contents:

```
package main

import (
    "fmt"
    "net/http"

    "github.com/agtorre/go-cookbook/chapter7/grpcjson/internal"
)

func main() {
    c := Controller{KeyValue: internal.NewKeyValue()}
    http.HandleFunc("/set", c.SetHandler)
    http.HandleFunc("/get", c.GetHandler)

    fmt.Println("Listening on port :3333")
    err := http.ListenAndServe(":3333", nil)
    panic(err)
}
```

15. Run the `go run http/*.go` command.

    You should see the following output:

    ```
    $ go run http/*.go
    Listening on port :3333
    ```

16. In a separate terminal run the following commands:

    ```
    curl "http://localhost:3333/set" -d '{"key":"test",
    "value":"123"}' -v
    curl "http://localhost:3333/get?key=badtest" -v
    curl "http://localhost:3333/get?key=test" -v
    ```

You should see the following output:

```
$curl "http://localhost:3333/set" -d '{"key":"test",
"value":"123"}' -v
{"value":"123"}

$curl "http://localhost:3333/get?key=badtest" -v
'name=Reader;greeting=Goodbye'
<should return a 404>

$curl "http://localhost:3333/get?key=test" -v
'name=Reader;greeting=Goodbye'
{"value":"123"}
```

17. If you copied or wrote your own tests, go up one directory and run `go test`. Ensure that all tests pass.

# How it works...

Although this recipe omits the client, you could replicate the steps in the *Understanding GRPC clients* recipe from `Chapter 6`, *Web Clients and APIs*, and you should see identical results to what we see with our curls. Both the `http` and `grpc` directories make use of the same internal package. We have to be careful in this package to return appropriate GRPC error codes and to correctly map those error codes to our HTTP response. In this case, we use `codes.NotFound`, which we map to `http.StatusNotFound`. If you have to handle more than a few errors, a `switch` statement may make more sense than an `if...else` statements.

The other thing you may notice is that GRPC signatures are usually very consistent. They take a request and return an optional response and an error. It's possible to create a generic handler shim if your GRPC calls are repetitive enough and it also seems like it lends itself well to code generation, you may eventually see something like that with a package such as `github.com/goadesign/goa`.

# 8
# Testing

In this chapter, we will cover the following recipes:

- Mocking using the standard library
- Using the Mockgen package
- Using table-driven tests to improve coverage
- Using third-party testing tools
- Practical fuzzing
- Behavior testing using Go

## Introduction

This chapter will be different from the previous chapters; this will focus on testing and testing methodologies. Go provides excellent testing support out of the box, however, it can be difficult to understand coming from more dynamic languages where monkey patching and mocking are relatively straightforward.

Go testing encourages a specific structure for your code, in particular, testing and mocking interfaces is very straightforward and well supported. Some types of code can be more difficult to test. For example, it can be difficult to test code that makes use of package-level global variables, places that have not been abstracted into interfaces, and structs that have non-exported variables or methods. This chapter will share some recipes for testing Go code.

# Mocking using the standard library

In Go, mocking typically means implementing an interface with a test version that allows you to control runtime behavior from tests. It may also refer to mocking functions and methods, for which we'll explore another trick in this recipe. This trick uses the `Patch` and `Restore` functions defined at `https://play.golang.org/p/oLF1XnRX3C`.

In general, it's better to compose code so that you can use interfaces frequently and the code is in small testable chunks. Code that contains lots of branching conditions or deeply nested logic can be tricky to test and tests tend to be more brittle at the end. This is because a developer will need to keep track of more mock objects, patches, return values, and states within their tests.

## Getting ready

Configure your environment according to these steps:

1. Download and install Go on your operating system from `https://golang.org/doc/install` and configure your `GOPATH` environment variable.
2. Open a terminal/console application.
3. Navigate to your `GOPATH/src` and create a project directory, for example, `$GOPATH/src/github.com/yourusername/customrepo`.

   All code will be run and modified from this directory.

4. Optionally, install the latest tested version of the code using the `go get github.com/agtorre/go-cookbook/` command.

## How to do it...

These steps cover writing and running your application:

1. From your terminal/console application, create the `chapter8/mocking` directory and navigate to it.
2. Copy tests from `https://github.com/agtorre/go-cookbook/tree/master/chapter8/mocking` or use this as an exercise to write some of your own code.

3. Create a file called `mock.go` with the following content:

```
package mocking

// DoStuffer is a simple interface
type DoStuffer interface {
    DoStuff(input string) error
}
```

4. Create a file called `patch.go` with the following content:

```
package mocking

import "reflect"

// Restorer holds a function that can be used
// to restore some previous state.
type Restorer func()

// Restore restores some previous state.
func (r Restorer) Restore() {
    r()
}

// Patch sets the value pointed to by the given destination to
// the given value, and returns a function to restore it to its
// original value. The value must be assignable to the element
//type of the destination.
func Patch(dest, value interface{}) Restorer {
    destv := reflect.ValueOf(dest).Elem()
    oldv := reflect.New(destv.Type()).Elem()
    oldv.Set(destv)
    valuev := reflect.ValueOf(value)
    if !valuev.IsValid() {
        // This isn't quite right when the destination type is
        // not nilable, but it's better than the complex
        // alternative.
        valuev = reflect.Zero(destv.Type())
    }
    destv.Set(valuev)
    return func() {
        destv.Set(oldv)
    }
}
```

5. Create a file called `exec.go` with the following content:

```
package mocking

import "errors"

var ThrowError = func() error {
    return errors.New("always fails")
}

func DoSomeStuff(d DoStuffer) error {

    if err := d.DoStuff("test"); err != nil {
        return err
    }

    if err := ThrowError(); err != nil {
        return err
    }

    return nil
}
```

6. Create a file called `mock_test.go` with the following content:

```
package mocking

type MockDoStuffer struct {
    // closure to assist with mocking
    MockDoStuff func(input string) error
}

func (m *MockDoStuffer) DoStuff(input string) error {
    if m.MockDoStuff != nil {
        return m.MockDoStuff(input)
    }
    // if we don't mock, return a common case
    return nil
}
```

7. Create a file called `exec_test.go` with the following content:

```
package mocking

import (
    "errors"
    "testing"
)
```

```go
func TestDoSomeStuff(t *testing.T) {
    tests := []struct {
        name       string
        DoStuff    error
        ThrowError error
        wantErr    bool
    }{
        {"base-case", nil, nil, false},
        {"DoStuff error", errors.New("failed"), nil, true},
        {"ThrowError error", nil, errors.New("failed"), true},
    }
    for _, tt := range tests {
        t.Run(tt.name, func(t *testing.T) {
            // An example of mocking an interface
            // with our mock struct
            d := MockDoStuffer{}
            d.MockDoStuff = func(string) error {
            return tt.DoStuff }

            // mocking a function that is declared as a variable
            // will not work for func A(),
            // must be var A = func()
            defer Patch(&ThrowError, func() error { return
            tt.ThrowError }).Restore()

            if err := DoSomeStuff(&d); (err != nil) != tt.wantErr
            {
                t.Errorf("DoSomeStuff() error = %v,
                wantErr %v", err, tt.wantErr)
            }
        })
    }
}
```

8. Fill in tests for the remaining functions, go up one directory and run `go test`. Ensure that all the tests pass:

```
$go test
PASS
ok github.com/agtorre/go-cookbook/chapter8/mocking 0.006s
```

# How it works...

This recipe demonstrates how to mock interfaces as well as functions that have been declared as variables. There are also certain libraries that can mimic this patch/restore directly on declared functions, but they bypass a lot of Go's type safety to accomplish that feat. If you need to patch functions from an external package, you may use the following trick:

```
// whatever package you wanna patch
import "github.com/package"

// this is patchable using the method described in this recipe
var packageDoSomething = package.DoSomething
```

For this recipe, we start by setting up our test and using table-driven tests. There's a lot of literature about this technique, and I recommend exploring it further. Once our tests are set up, we choose outputs for our mocked functions. In order to mock our interface, our mocked objects define closures that can be rewritten at runtime. The patch/restore technique is applied to change our global function and restore it after each loop. This is thanks to t.Run, which sets up a new function for each loop of the test.

# Using the Mockgen package

The previous example used our custom mock objects. When you're working with a lot of interfaces, writing these can become cumbersome and error prone. This is a place where generating code makes a lot of sense. Fortunately, there's a package called github.com/golang/mock/gomock that provides a generation of mock objects and gives us a very useful library to use in conjunction with interface testing.

This recipe will explore some of the functionality of gomock and will cover trade-offs on where, when, and how to work with and generate mock objects.

# Getting ready

Configure your environment according to these steps:

1. Refer to the *Getting ready* section of the *Mocking using the standard library* recipe of this chapter.
2. Run the go get github.com/golang/mock/ command.

# How to do it...

These steps cover writing and running your application:

1. From your terminal/console application, create the `chapter8/mockgen` directory and navigate to it.
2. Copy tests from `https://github.com/agtorre/go-cookbook/tree/master/cha pter8/mockgen`or use this as an exercise to write some of your own.
3. Create a file called `interface.go` with the following content:

```
package mockgen

// GetSetter implements get a set of a
// key value pair
type GetSetter interface {
    Set(key, val string) error
    Get(key string) (string, error)
}
```

4. Create a directory named `internal`.
5. Run the `mockgen -destination internal/mocks.go -package internal github.com/agtorre/go-cookbook/chapter8/mockgen GetSetter` command:
   - Ensure that you replace the package path with your local version.
   - This will create a file named `internal/mocks.go`.
6. Create a file called `exec.go` with the following content:

```
package mockgen

// Controller is a struct demonstrating
// one way to initialize interfaces
type Controller struct {
    GetSetter
}

// GetThenSet checks if a value is set. If not
// it sets it.
func (c *Controller) GetThenSet(key, value string) error {
    val, err := c.Get(key)
    if err != nil {
        return err
    }

    if val != value {
```

```
                return c.Set(key, value)
        }
        return nil
}
```

7. Create a file called `interface_test.go` with the following content:

```go
package mockgen

import (
    "errors"
    "testing"

    "github.com/agtorre/go-cookbook/chapter8/mockgen/internal"
    "github.com/golang/mock/gomock"
)

func TestExample(t *testing.T) {
    ctrl := gomock.NewController(t)
    defer ctrl.Finish()

    mockGetSetter := internal.NewMockGetSetter(ctrl)

    var k string
    mockGetSetter.EXPECT().Get("we can put anything
    here!").Do(func(key string) {
        k = key
    }).Return("", nil)

    customError := errors.New("failed this time")

    mockGetSetter.EXPECT().Get(gomock.Any()).Return("",
    customError)

    if _, err := mockGetSetter.Get("we can put anything
    here!"); err != nil {
        t.Errorf("got %#v; want %#v", err, nil)
    }
    if k != "we can put anything here!" {
        t.Errorf("bad key")
    }

    if _, err := mockGetSetter.Get("key"); err == nil {
        t.Errorf("got %#v; want %#v", err, customError)
    }
}
```

8. Create a file called `exec_test.go` with the following content:

```go
package mockgen

import (
    "errors"
    "testing"

    "github.com/agtorre/go-cookbook/chapter8/mockgen/internal"
    "github.com/golang/mock/gomock"
)

func TestController_Set(t *testing.T) {
    tests := []struct {
        name string
        getReturnVal string
        getReturnErr error
        setReturnErr error
        wantErr bool
    }{
        {"get error", "value", errors.New("failed"), nil,
        true},
        {"value match", "value", nil, nil, false},
        {"no errors", "not set", nil, nil, false},
        {"set error", "not set", nil, errors.New("failed"),
        true},
    }
    for _, tt := range tests {
        t.Run(tt.name, func(t *testing.T) {
            ctrl := gomock.NewController(t)
            defer ctrl.Finish()

            mockGetSetter := internal.NewMockGetSetter(ctrl)
            mockGetSetter.EXPECT().Get("key").AnyTimes()
            .Return(tt.getReturnVal, tt.getReturnErr)
            mockGetSetter.EXPECT().Set("key",
            gomock.Any()).AnyTimes().Return(tt.setReturnErr)

            c := &Controller{
                GetSetter: mockGetSetter,
            }
            if err := c.GetThenSet("key", "value"); (err !=
            nil) != tt.wantErr {
                t.Errorf("Controller.Set() error = %v, wantErr
                %v", err, tt.wantErr)
            }
        })
    }
}
```

```
    }
```

9. Fill in tests for the remaining functions, go up one directory, and run `go test`. Ensure that all the tests pass.

## How it works...

The generated mock objects allow tests to specify what arguments are expected, the number of times a function will be called, and what to return, and they allow us to set additional artifacts, for example, we could write to a channel directly if the original function had a similar workflow. The `interface_test.go` file showcases some examples of using mock objects while calling them in-line. Generally, tests will look more like `exec_test.go` where we'll want intercept interface function calls performed by our actual code and change their behavior at test time.

The `exec_test.go` file also showcases how you might use mocked objects in a table-driven test environment. The `Any()` function means that the mocked function can be called zero or more times, which is great for cases where the code terminates early.

One last trick demonstrated in this recipe is sticking mocked objects into the `internal` package. This is useful when you need to mock functions declared in packages outside your own. This allows those methods to be defined in a `non` `_test.go` file, but doesn't allow to export them to users of your libraries. Generally, it's easier to just stick mocked objects into `_test.go` files using the same package name as the tests you're currently writing.

## Using table-driven tests to improve coverage

This recipe will demonstrate the process to write a table-driven test, collect test coverage, and improve it. It will also make use of the `github.com/cweill/gotests` package to generate tests. If you've been downloading the test code for other chapters, these should look very familiar. Using a combination of this recipe and the previous two, you should be able to achieve 100% test coverage in all cases with some work.

# Getting ready

Configure your environment according to these steps:

1. Refer to the *Getting ready* section of the *Mocking using the standard library* recipe of this chapter.
2. Run the `go get github.com/cweill/gotests/` command.

# How to do it...

These steps cover writing and running your application:

1. From your terminal/console application, create the `chapter8/coverage` directory and navigate to it.
2. Copy tests from `https://github.com/agtorre/go-cookbook/tree/master/chapter8/coverage` or use this as an exercise to write some of your own code.
3. Create a file called `coverage.go` with the following content:

```
package main

import "errors"

// Coverage is a simple function with some branching conditions
func Coverage(condition bool) error {
    if condition {
        return errors.New("condition was set")
    }
    return nil
}
```

4. Run the `gotests -all -w` command.
5. This will generate a file named `coverage_test.go` with the following content:

```
package main

import "testing"

func TestCoverage(t *testing.T) {
    type args struct {
        condition bool
    }
    tests := []struct {
        name string
```

```
                args args
                wantErr bool
        }{
            // TODO: Add test cases.
        }
        for _, tt := range tests {
            t.Run(tt.name, func(t *testing.T) {
                if err := Coverage(tt.args.condition); (err != nil)
                != tt.wantErr {
                    t.Errorf("Coverage() error = %v, wantErr %v",
                    err, tt.wantErr)
                }
            })
        }
    }
```

6. Fill in the TODO section with the following:

    ```
    {"no condition", args{true}, true},
    ```

7. Run the go test -cover command, and you will see the following output:

    ```
    go test -cover
    PASS
    coverage: 66.7% of statements
    ok github.com/agtorre/go-cookbook/chapter8/coverage 0.007s
    ```

8. Add another item to the TODO section:

    ```
    {"condition", args{false}, false},
    ```

9. Run the go test -cover command, and you will see the following output:

    ```
    go test -cover
    PASS
    coverage: 100.0% of statements
    ok github.com/agtorre/go-cookbook/chapter8/coverage 0.007s
    ```

10. Run the following commands:

    ```
    go test -coverprofile=cover.out
    go tool cover -html=cover.out -o coverage.html
    ```

11. Open the coverage.html file in a browser to see a graphical coverage report.

# How it works...

The `go test -cover` command comes with a basic Go installation. It can be used to collect a coverage report of your Go application. In addition, it has the ability to output coverage metrics and an HTML coverage report. This tool is often wrapped by other tools, which will be covered in the next recipe. These table-driven test styles are covered at `https://github.com/golang/go/wiki/TableDrivenTests` and are an excellent way to make clean tests that can handle many cases without writing a bunch of extra code.

This recipe starts by automatically generating test code, then filling in test cases as needed to help create more coverage. The only time this is especially tricky is when you have non-variable functions or methods being invoked. For example, it can be tricky to make `gob.Encode()` return an error to increase test coverage. It can also seem quirky to use the method described in the *Mocking using the standard library* recipe of this chapter and use `var gobEncode = gob.Encode` to allow patching. For this reason, it can be difficult to advocate for 100% test coverage and instead argue for focusing on testing the external interface extensively, that is, testing many variations of input and output, and in some cases, as we'll see in the *Behavior testing using Go* recipe of this chapter, fuzzing can become useful.

# Using third-party testing tools

There are a number of helpful tools for Go testing. Tools that make it easier to get an idea of code coverage at a per-function level, tools to do assertions to reduce testing lines of code, and test runners. This recipe will cover `github.com/axw/gocov` and `github.com/smartystreets/goconvey` packages to demonstrate some of this functionality. There are a number of other notable test frameworks depending on your needs. The `github.com/smartystreets/goconvey` package supports both assertions and is a test runner. It used to be the cleanest way to have labeled subtests prior to Go 1.7.

# Getting ready

Configure your environment according to these steps:

1. Refer to the *Getting ready* section of the *Mocking using the standard library* recipe of this chapter.
2. Run the `go get github.com/axw/gocov` command.
3. Run the `go get github.com/smartystreets/goconvey/` command.

# How to do it...

These steps cover writing and running your application:

1. From your terminal/console application, create the `chapter8/tools` directory and navigate to it.

2. Copy tests from `https://github.com/agtorre/go-cookbook/tree/master/chapter8/tools`or use this as an exercise to write some of your own code.

3. Create a file called `funcs.go` with the following content:

```
package tools

import (
    "fmt"
)

func example() error {
    fmt.Println("in example")
    return nil
}

var example2 = func() int {
    fmt.Println("in example2")
    return 10
}
```

4. Create a file called `structs.go` with the following content:

```
package tools

import (
    "errors"
    "fmt"
)

type c struct {
    Branch bool
}

func (c *c) example3() error {
    fmt.Println("in example3")
    if c.Branch {
        fmt.Println("branching code!")
        return errors.New("bad branch")
    }
    return nil
```

```
    }
```

5. Create a file called `funcs_test.go` with the following content:

```go
package tools

import (
    "testing"

    . "github.com/smartystreets/goconvey/convey"
)

func Test_example(t *testing.T) {
    tests := []struct {
        name string
    }{
        {"base-case"},
    }
    for _, tt := range tests {
        Convey(tt.name, t, func() {
            res := example()
            So(res, ShouldBeNil)
        })
    }
}

func Test_example2(t *testing.T) {
    tests := []struct {
        name string
    }{
        {"base-case"},
    }
    for _, tt := range tests {
        Convey(tt.name, t, func() {
            res := example2()
            So(res, ShouldBeGreaterThanOrEqualTo, 1)
        })
    }
}
```

6. Create a file called `structs_test.go` with the following content:

```go
package tools

import (
    "testing"

    . "github.com/smartystreets/goconvey/convey"
```

```
    )

    func Test_c_example3(t *testing.T) {
        type fields struct {
            Branch bool
        }
        tests := []struct {
            name string
            fields fields
            wantErr bool
        }{
            {"no branch", fields{false}, false},
            {"branch", fields{true}, true},
        }
        for _, tt := range tests {
            Convey(tt.name, t, func() {
                c := &c{
                    Branch: tt.fields.Branch,
                }
                So((c.example3() != nil), ShouldEqual, tt.wantErr)
            })
        }
    }
```

7.  Run the `gocov test | gocov report` command, and you will see the following output:

```
$ gocov test | gocov report
ok github.com/agtorre/go-cookbook/chapter8/tools 0.006s
coverage: 100.0% of statements

github.com/agtorre/go-cookbook/chapter8/tools/struct.go
c.example3 100.00% (5/5)
github.com/agtorre/go-cookbook/chapter8/tools/funcs.go example
100.00% (2/2)
github.com/agtorre/go-cookbook/chapter8/tools/funcs.go @12:16
100.00% (2/2)
github.com/agtorre/go-cookbook/chapter8/tools ----------
100.00% (9/9)

Total Coverage: 100.00% (9/9)
```

8. Run the `goconvey` command, and it will open a browser that should look like this:

9. Ensure that all the tests pass.

# How it works...

This recipe demonstrates how to wire `goconvey` command into your tests. The `Convey` keyword basically replaces `t.Run` and adds additional labels in the `goconvey` web UI, but it behaves slightly differently. If you have nested convey blocks, they're always re-executed in order, that is, as follows:

```
Convey("Outer loop", t, func(){
    a := 1
    Convey("Inner loop", t, func() {
        a = 2
    })
    Convey ("Inner loop2", t, func(){
        fmt.Println(a)
    })
})
```

The preceding code, using `goconvey` command, will print 1. If we would used the built-in `t.Run` instead, it would instead print 2. In other words, Go `t.Run` tests are run sequentially and are never repeated. This behavior can be useful for putting the setup code in outer convey blocks, but it's important to remember this distinction if you have to work with both.

When using convey assertions, there's a check mark on successes in the UI and additional stats. It can also reduce the size of if checks to a single line and it's even possible to create custom assertions.

If you leave up the `goconvey` web interface and turn on notifications, as you save your code, tests will automatically be run and you'll receive notifications on any increase or decrease in coverage as well as when your build fails.

All three tools assertions, the test runner, and the web UI can be used independently or together.

The `gocov` tool can be useful when working toward higher test coverage. It can quickly identify functions that are lacking in coverage and help you deep dive into your coverage report. In addition, `gocov` can be used to generate an alternate HTML report that is shipped with the Go code by using the `github.com/matm/gocov-html` package.

# Practical fuzzing

This recipe will explore fuzzing and how it can be used to help validate functions. In the *Currency conversions and float64 considerations* recipe from `Chapter 3`, *Data Conversion and Composition*, we created a function that takes decimal US currency as a string and returns an int64 version representing cents. We'll modify that function and demonstrate finding a panic with fuzzing.

## Getting ready

Configure your environment according to these steps:

1. Refer to the *Getting ready* section of the *Mocking using the standard library* recipe of this chapter.
2. Run the `go get github.com/dvyukov/go-fuzz/go-fuzz` command.
3. Run the `go get github.com/dvyukov/go-fuzz/go-fuzz-build` command.

# How to do it...

These steps cover writing and running your application:

1. From your terminal/console application, create the `chapter8/fuzz` directory and navigate to it.

2. Copy tests from `https://github.com/agtorre/go-cookbook/tree/master/chapter8/fuzz` or use this as an exercise to write some of your own code.

3. Create a file called `dollars.go` with the following content:

```go
package fuzz

import (
    "errors"
    "strconv"
    "strings"
)

// ConvertStringDollarsToPennies takes a dollar amount
// as a string, i.e. 1.00, 55.12 etc and converts it
// into an int64
func ConvertStringDollarsToPennies(amount string) (int64,
error) {
    // check if amount can convert to a valid float
    val, err := strconv.ParseFloat(amount, 64)
    if err != nil {
        return 0, err
    }

    if val > 1000 && val < 1100 {
        panic("invalid range")
    }

    // split the value on "."
    groups := strings.Split(amount, ".")

    // if there is no . result will still be
    // captured here
    result := groups[0]

    // base string
    r := ""

    // handle the data after the "."
    if len(groups) == 2 {
        if len(groups[1]) != 2 {
```

```
                        return 0, errors.New("invalid cents")
            }
            r = groups[1]
            if len(r) > 2 {
                r = r[:2]
            }
        }

        // pad with 0, this will be
        // 2 0's if there was no .
        for len(r) < 2 {
            r += "0"
        }

        result += r
        // convert it to an int
        return strconv.ParseInt(result, 10, 64)
    }
```

4. Create a file called `fuzz.go` with the following content:

```
package fuzz

// Fuzz is the interface required to use gofuzz
func Fuzz(data []byte) int {
    amount := string(data)

    _, err := ConvertStringDollarsToPennies(amount)
    if err != nil {
        return 0
    }
    return 1
}
```

5. Run the `go-fuzz-build github.com/agtorre/go-cookbook/chapter8/fuzz` command or change the path to match your own code.

6. Run the following commands:

```
mkdir -p output/corpus

echo "0.01" > output/corpus/a
echo "-0.01" > output/corpus/b
echo "0.10" > output/corpus/c
echo "1.00" > output/corpus/d
echo "-1.00" > output/corpus/e
echo "1.11" > output/corpus/f
```

```
echo "1" > output/corpus/g
echo "2" > output/corpus/h
echo "999.99" > output/corpus/i
```

7. Run the `go-fuzz -bin=./fuzz-fuzz.zip -workdir=output` command, and you will see the following output:

```
go-fuzz -bin=./fuzz-fuzz.zip -workdir=output

.
.
.

2017/04/02 10:58:43 slaves: 4, corpus: 91 (11s ago), crashers:
1, restarts: 1/7064, execs: 204856 (13630/sec), cover: 453,
uptime: 15s
2017/04/02 10:58:46 slaves: 4, corpus: 91 (14s ago), crashers:
1, restarts: 1/7244, execs: 253555 (14086/sec), cover: 453,
uptime: 18s
```

8. Exit by pressing *Ctrl + C* after a few iterations have been run.
9. Fill in the tests for the remaining functions, go up one directory, and run the `go test`. Ensure that all the tests pass.

# How it works...

The `github.com/dvyukov/go-fuzz` package uses evolutionary algorithms to build a corpus of inputs in order to test Go code. In our case, we introduced an intentional panic in order to demonstrate the behavior when a crash is found. Fuzzing is a practical way to find unexpected panics, especially when doing programming handling array bounds or arbitrary input.

When fuzzing an application, on of the most difficult parts is writing an appropriate fuzz function. The `go-fuzz` application will adapt based on the responses from this function. If your fuzz function returns 1, it considered a successful input. If -1 is returned, the item will not be included in the corpus, and if 0 is returned, it's given lower priority. We can change the fuzz function in step 4 to return -1 instead of 0 in order to find interesting input that is accepted but that may not have been expected. For example, +1 is a possible input for this function.

We also helped our fuzzer by suggesting some items to the corpus. These items were taken from our unit tests and represent known good values. This is important to help Go fuzz converge on relevant input, for example, if your function takes a range of integers as input, testing non-integer input can take a lot of time.

# Behavior testing using Go

Behavior testing or integration testing is a good method of performing end-to-end black box testing. One popular framework for this type of testing is cucumber (`https://cucumber.io/`), which uses the Gherkin language to describe the steps to a test in English and then implement those steps in code. Go has a cucumber library as well (`github.com/DATA-DOG/godog`). This recipe will explore using `godog` package to write behavior tests.

## Getting ready

Configure your environment according to these steps:

1. Refer to the *Getting ready* section of the *Mocking using the standard library* recipe of this chapter.
2. Run the `go get github.com/DATA-DOG/godog` command.
3. Run the `go get github.com/DATA-DOG/godog/cmd/godog` command.

## How to do it...

These steps cover writing and running your application:

1. From your terminal/console application, create the `chapter8/bdd` directory and navigate to it.
2. Copy tests from `https://github.com/agtorre/go-cookbook/tree/master/chapter8/bdd` or use this as an exercise to write some of your own code.
3. Create a file called `handler.go` with the following content:

```
package bdd

import (
    "encoding/json"
    "fmt"
    "net/http"
```

```
)

// HandlerRequest will be json decoded
// into by Handler
type HandlerRequest struct {
    Name string `json:"name"`
}

// Handler takes a request and renders a response
func Handler(w http.ResponseWriter, r *http.Request) {
    w.Header().Set("Content-Type", "text/plain; charset=utf-8")
    if r.Method != http.MethodPost {
        w.WriteHeader(http.StatusMethodNotAllowed)
        return
    }

    dec := json.NewDecoder(r.Body)
    var req HandlerRequest
    if err := dec.Decode(&req); err != nil {
        w.WriteHeader(http.StatusBadRequest)
        return
    }

    w.WriteHeader(http.StatusOK)
    w.Write([]byte(fmt.Sprintf("BDD testing %s", req.Name)))
}
```

4. Create a new directory called `features`, and create a file called
   `features/handler.go` with the following content:

```
Feature: Bad Method
  Scenario: Good request
  Given we create a HandlerRequest payload with:
      | reader |
      | coder |
      | other |
  And we POST the HandlerRequest to /hello
  Then the response code should be 200
  And the response body should be:
      | BDD testing reader |
      | BDD testing coder |
      | BDD testing other |
```

5. Run the `godog` command, and you will see the following output:

```
$ godog
.
1 scenarios (1 undefined)
4 steps (4 undefined)
89.062µs
.
```

6. This should give you a skeleton to implement the tests that we wrote in our feature file; copy those into `handler_test.go` and implement the first two steps:

```
package bdd

import (
    "bytes"
    "encoding/json"
    "fmt"
    "net/http/httptest"

    "github.com/DATA-DOG/godog"
    "github.com/DATA-DOG/godog/gherkin"
)

var payloads []HandlerRequest
var resps []*httptest.ResponseRecorder

func weCreateAHandlerRequestPayloadWith(arg1
*gherkin.DataTable) error {
    for _, row := range arg1.Rows {
        h := HandlerRequest{
            Name: row.Cells[0].Value,
        }
        payloads = append(payloads, h)
    }
    return nil
}

func wePOSTTheHandlerRequestToHello() error {
    for _, p := range payloads {
        v, err := json.Marshal(p)
        if err != nil {
            return err
        }
        w := httptest.NewRecorder()
        r := httptest.NewRequest("POST", "/hello",
```

```
            bytes.NewBuffer(v))

            Handler(w, r)
            resps = append(resps, w)
        }
        return nil
    }
```

7. Run the `godog` command, and you will see the following output:

```
$ godog
.
1 scenarios (1 pending)
4 steps (2 passed, 1 pending, 1 skipped)
.
```

8. Fill in the remaining two steps:

```
    func theResponseCodeShouldBe(arg1 int) error {
        for _, r := range resps {
            if got, want := r.Code, arg1; got != want {
                return fmt.Errorf("got: %d; want %d", got, want)
            }
        }
        return nil
    }

    func theResponseBodyShouldBe(arg1 *gherkin.DataTable) error {
        for c, row := range arg1.Rows {
            b := bytes.Buffer{}
            b.ReadFrom(resps[c].Body)
            if got, want := b.String(), row.Cells[0].Value;
            got != want
            {
                return fmt.Errorf("got: %s; want %s", got, want)
            }
        }
        return nil
    }

    func FeatureContext(s *godog.Suite) {
        s.Step(`^we create a HandlerRequest payload with:$`,
        weCreateAHandlerRequestPayloadWith)
        s.Step(`^we POST the HandlerRequest to /hello$`,
        wePOSTTheHandlerRequestToHello)
        s.Step(`^the response code should be (d+)$`,
        theResponseCodeShouldBe)
        s.Step(`^the response body should be:$`,
```

```
        theResponseBodyShouldBe)
    }
```

9. Run the `godog` command, and you will see the following output:

```
$ godog
.
1 scenarios (1 passed)
4 steps (4 passed)
552.605µs
.
```

# How it works...

Cucumber frameworks work excellently for pair programming, end-to-end testing, and any sort of testing that is best communicated with written instructions and is understandable for non-technical people. Once a step has been implemented, it's generally possible to reuse it wherever it's needed. If you want to test integrations between services, tests can be written to use actual HTTP clients if you first ensure that your environment is set up to receive HTTP connections.

The datadog implementation of BDD is lacking a few features that you might expect if you've used other Cucumber frameworks, including lack of examples, passing a context between functions, and a number of other key words. However, it's a good start, and by using a few tricks in this recipe, such as globals for tracking state (and ensuring that you clean up those globals between scenarios), it's possible to build a fairly robust set of tests. The datadog testing package also uses a third-party test runner, so it's impossible to put it together with packages such as `gocov` or `go test -cover`.

# 9
# Parallelism and Concurrency

In this chapter, the following recipes will be covered:

- Using channels and the select statement
- Performing async operations with sync.WaitGroup
- Using atomic operations and mutex
- Using the context package
- Executing state management for channels
- Using the worker pool design pattern
- Using workers to create pipelines

## Introduction

This chapter covers worker pools, wait groups for async operations, and the use of the `context` package. Parallelism and concurrency are some of the most advertised and promoted features of the Go language. This chapter will offer a number of useful patterns to get you started and help you understand these features.

Go provides primitives that make parallel applications possible. Goroutines allow any function to become asynchronous and concurrent. Channels allow an application to set up communication with goroutines. One of the famous sayings in Go is *Do not communicate by sharing memory; instead, share memory by communicating* from `https://blog.golang.org/sh are-memory-by-communicating`.

# Using channels and the select statement

Go channels, in combination with goroutines, are first-class citizens for asynchronous communication. Channels become especially powerful when using select statements. These statements allow a goroutine to intelligently handle requests from multiple channels at once.

## Getting ready

Configure your environment according to these steps:

1. Download and install Go on your operating system from `https://golang.org/doc/install` and configure your `GOPATH` environment variable.
2. Open a terminal/console application.
3. Navigate to `GOPATH/src` and create a project directory, such as `$GOPATH/src/github.com/yourusername/customrepo`.

   All code will be run and modified from this directory.

4. Optionally, install the latest tested version of the code using the `go get github.com/agtorre/go-cookbook/` command.

## How to do it...

These steps cover writing and running your application:

1. From your terminal/console application, create the `chapter9/channels` directory and navigate to it.
2. Copy tests from `https://github.com/agtorre/go-cookbook/tree/master/chapter9/channels` or use this as an exercise to write some of your own code.
3. Create a file called `sender.go` with the following content:

   ```
   package channels

   import "time"

   // Sender sends "tick"" on ch until done is
   // written to, then it sends "sender done."
   // and exits
   func Sender(ch chan string, done chan bool) {
   ```

```
        t := time.Tick(100 * time.Millisecond)
        for {
            select {
                case <-done:
                    ch <- "sender done."
                    return
                case <-t:
                    ch <- "tick"
            }
        }
    }
```

4. Create a file called `printer.go` with the following content:

```go
package channels

import (
    "context"
    "fmt"
    "time"
)

// Printer will print anything sent on the ch chan
// and will print tock every 200 milliseconds
// this will repeat forever until a context is
// Done, i.e. timed out or cancelled
func Printer(ctx context.Context, ch chan string) {
    t := time.Tick(200 * time.Millisecond)
    for {
        select {
            case <-ctx.Done():
                fmt.Println("printer done.")
                return
            case res := <-ch:
                fmt.Println(res)
            case <-t:
                fmt.Println("tock")
        }
    }
}
```

5. Create a new directory named `example` and navigate to it.

6. Create a file named `main.go` with the following content and ensure that you modify the `channels` import to use the path you set up in step 2:

```go
package main
```

```
import (
    "context"
    "time"

    "github.com/agtorre/go-cookbook/chapter9/channels"
)

func main() {
    ch := make(chan string)
    done := make(chan bool)

    ctx := context.Background()
    ctx, cancel := context.WithCancel(ctx)
    defer cancel()
    go channels.Printer(ctx, ch)
    go channels.Sender(ch, done)

    time.Sleep(2 * time.Second)
    done <- true
    cancel()
    //sleep a bit extra so channels can clean up
    time.Sleep(1 * time.Second)
}
```

7. Run `go run main.go`.

8. You may also run the following commands:

   **go build**
   **./example**

   You should now see the following output:

   **$ go run main.go**
   **tick**
   **tock**
   **tick**
   **tick**
   **tock**
   **tick**
   **tick**
   **tock**
   **tick**

   **.**

   **.**

   **.**

   **sender done.**
   **printer done.**

9. If you copied or wrote your own tests, go up one directory and run `go test`. Ensure that all the tests pass.

# How it works...

This recipe demonstrates two ways to launch a worker process that either reads or writes to a channel, and may potentially do both. The terminate conditions are a `done` channel, or by using a `context` package. The *Using the context package* recipe will cover the context in more detail.

The `main` package is used to wire together the separate functions; thanks to this, it is possible to set up multiple pairs as long as the channels are not shared. In addition, it's possible to have multiple goroutines listening on the same channel, as we'll explore in the *Using the worker pool design pattern* recipe.

Lastly, due to the asynchronous nature of goroutines, it can be tricky to establish cleanup and terminate conditions; for example, a common mistake is to do the following:

```
select{
    case <-time.Tick(200 * time.Millisecond):
    //this resets whenever any other 'lane' is chosen
}
```

By putting the tick in the `select` statement, it's possible to prevent this case from ever occurring. There's also no simple way to prioritize traffic in a `select` statement.

# Performing async operations with sync.WaitGroup

Sometimes, it is useful to perform a number of operations asynchronously, then wait till they complete before moving on. For example, if an operation requires pulling information from multiple APIs and aggregate that information, it can be helpful to make those client requests asynchronously. This chapter will explore using `sync.WaitGroup` to orchestrate non-dependent tasks in parallel.

# Getting ready

Refer to the *Getting ready* section of the *Using channels and the select statement* recipe in this chapter.

# How to do it...

These steps cover writing and running your application:

1. From your terminal/console application, create the `chapter9/waitgroup` directory and navigate to it.

2. Copy tests from `https://github.com/agtorre/go-cookbook/tree/master/chapter9/waitgroup`or use this as an exercise to write some of your own code.

3. Create a file called `tasks.go` with the following content:

```
package waitgroup

import (
    "fmt"
    "log"
    "net/http"
    "strings"
    "time"
)

// GetURL gets a url, and logs the time it took
func GetURL(url string) (*http.Response, error) {
    start := time.Now()
    log.Printf("getting %s", url)
    resp, err := http.Get(url)
    log.Printf("completed getting %s in %s", url,
    time.Since(start))
    return resp, err
}

// CrawlError is our custom error type
// for aggregating errors
type CrawlError struct {
    Errors []string
}

// Add adds another error
func (c *CrawlError) Add(err error) {
    c.Errors = append(c.Errors, err.Error())
}

// Error implements the error interface
func (c *CrawlError) Error() string {
    return fmt.Sprintf("All Errors: %s", strings.Join(c.Errors,
    ","))
}
```

```
// Valid can be used to determine if
// we should return this
func (c *CrawlError) Valid() bool {
    return len(c.Errors) != 0
}
```

4. Create a file called process.go with the following content:

```go
package waitgroup

import (
    "log"
    "sync"
    "time"
)

// Crawl collects responses from a list of urls
// that are passed in. It waits for all requests
// to complete before returning.
func Crawl(sites []string) ([]int, error) {
    start := time.Now()
    log.Printf("starting crawling")
    wg := &sync.WaitGroup{}

    var resps []int
    cerr := &CrawlError{}
    for _, v := range sites {
        wg.Add(1)
        go func(v string) {
            defer wg.Done()
            resp, err := GetURL(v)
            if err != nil {
                cerr.Add(err)
                return
            }
            resps = append(resps, resp.StatusCode)
        }(v)
    }
    wg.Wait()
    if cerr.Valid() {
        return resps, cerr
    }
    log.Printf("completed crawling in %s", time.Since(start))
    return resps, nil
}
```

5. Create a new directory named example and navigate to it.

6. Create a file named `main.go` with the following content. Ensure that you modify the `waitgroup` import to use the path you set up in step 2:

```
package main

import (
    "fmt"

    "github.com/agtorre/go-cookbook/chapter9/waitgroup"
)

func main() {
    sites := []string{
        "https://golang.org",
        "https://godoc.org",
        "https://www.google.com/search?q=golang",
    }

    resps, err := waitgroup.Crawl(sites)
    if err != nil {
        panic(err)
    }
    fmt.Println("Resps received:", resps)
}
```

7. Run `go run main.go`.

8. You may also run the following commands:

```
go build
./example
```

You should see the following:

```
$ go run main.go
2017/04/05 19:45:07 starting crawling
2017/04/05 19:45:07 getting https://www.google.com/search?
q=golang
2017/04/05 19:45:07 getting https://golang.org
2017/04/05 19:45:07 getting https://godoc.org
2017/04/05 19:45:07 completed getting https://golang.org in
178.22407ms
2017/04/05 19:45:07 completed getting https://godoc.org in
181.400873ms
2017/04/05 19:45:07 completed getting
https://www.google.com/search?q=golang in 238.019327ms
2017/04/05 19:45:07 completed crawling in 238.191791ms
Resps received: [200 200 200]
```

9. If you copied or wrote your own tests, go up one directory and run `go test`. Ensure that all the tests pass.

# How it works...

This recipe shows how to use `waitgroups` as a synchronization mechanism when waiting for work. In essence, `waitgroup.Wait()` will wait until its internal counter has reached 0. The `waitgroup.Add(int)` method will increment the counter by the amount entered, and `waitgroup.Done()` will decrement the counter by 1. Because of this, it is necessary to asynchronously `Wait()` while the various goroutines mark the `waitgroup` as `Done()`.

In this recipe, we increment before dispatching each HTTP request and then call a defer `wg.Done()` method, so that we can decrement whenever the goroutine terminates. We then wait for all goroutines to finish before returning our aggregated results.

In practice, it's better to use channels for passing the error and responses around.

When performing operations asynchronously like this, you should consider thread safety for things such as modifying a shared map. If you keep this in mind, `waitgroups` are a useful feature for waiting on any kind of asynchronous operation.

# Using atomic operations and mutex

In a language like Go, where you have build in asynchronous operations and parallelism, it becomes important to consider things such as thread safety. For example, it is dangerous to access a map from multiple goroutines simultaneously. Go provides a number of helpers in the `sync` and `sync/atomic` packages to make sure that certain events occur only once or that goroutines can serialize on an operation.

This recipe will demonstrate the use of these packages to safely modify a map with various goroutines and to keep a global ordinal value that can be safely accessed by numerous goroutines. It will also showcase the `Once.Do` method, which can be used to ensure that something is only done by a Go application once, such as reading a config or initializing a variable.

# Getting ready

Refer to the *Getting ready* section of the *Using channels and the select statement* recipe in this chapter.

# How to do it...

These steps cover writing and running your application:

1. From your terminal/console application, create the `chapter9/atomic` directory and navigate to it.
2. Copy tests from `https://github.com/agtorre/go-cookbook/tree/master/chapter9/atomic`or use this as an exercise to write some of your own code.
3. Create a file called `map.go` with the following content:

```go
package atomic

import (
    "errors"
    "sync"
)

// SafeMap uses a mutex to allow
// getting and setting in a thread-safe way
type SafeMap struct {
    m map[string]string
    mu *sync.RWMutex
}

// NewSafeMap creates a SafeMap
func NewSafeMap() SafeMap {
    return SafeMap{m: make(map[string]string), mu:
    &sync.RWMutex{}}
}

// Set uses a write lock and sets the value given
// a key
func (t *SafeMap) Set(key, value string) {
    t.mu.Lock()
    defer t.mu.Unlock()

    t.m[key] = value
}

// Get uses a RW lock and gets the value if it exists,
// otherwise an error is returned
func (t *SafeMap) Get(key string) (string, error) {
    t.mu.RLock()
    defer t.mu.RUnlock()

    if v, ok := t.m[key]; ok {
```

```
        return v, nil
    }

    return "", errors.New("key not found")
}
```

4. Create a file called `ordinal.go` with the following content:

```go
package atomic

import (
    "sync"
    "sync/atomic"
)

// Ordinal holds a global a value
// and can only be initialized once
type Ordinal struct {
    ordinal uint64
    once *sync.Once
}

// NewOrdinal returns ordinal with once
// setup
func NewOrdinal() *Ordinal {
    return &Ordinal{once: &sync.Once{}}
}

// Init sets the ordinal value
// can only be done once
func (o *Ordinal) Init(val uint64) {
    o.once.Do(func() {
        atomic.StoreUint64(&o.ordinal, val)
    })
}

// GetOrdinal will return the current
// ordinal
func (o *Ordinal) GetOrdinal() uint64 {
    return atomic.LoadUint64(&o.ordinal)
}

// Increment will increment the current
// ordinal
func (o *Ordinal) Increment() {
    atomic.AddUint64(&o.ordinal, 1)
}
```

5. Create a new directory named `example` and navigate to it.
6. Create a file named `main.go` with the following content and ensure that you modify the `atomic` import to use the path you set up in step 2:

```
package main

import (
    "fmt"
    "sync"

    "github.com/agtorre/go-cookbook/chapter9/atomic"
)

func main() {
    o := atomic.NewOrdinal()
    m := atomic.NewSafeMap()
    o.Init(1123)
    fmt.Println("initial ordinal is:", o.GetOrdinal())
    wg := sync.WaitGroup{}
    for i := 0; i < 10; i++ {
        wg.Add(1)
        go func(i int) {
            defer wg.Done()
            m.Set(fmt.Sprint(i), "success")
            o.Increment()
        }(i)
    }

    wg.Wait()
    for i := 0; i < 10; i++ {
        v, err := m.Get(fmt.Sprint(i))
        if err != nil || v != "success" {
            panic(err)
        }
    }
    fmt.Println("final ordinal is:", o.GetOrdinal())
    fmt.Println("all keys found and marked as: 'success'")
}
```

7. Run `go run main.go`.
8. You may also run the following commands:

```
go build
./example
```

You should now see the following:

```
$ go run main.go

initial ordinal is: 1123
final ordinal is: 1133
all keys found and marked as: 'success'
```

9. If you copied or wrote your own tests, go up one directory and run `go test`. Ensure that all tests pass.

# How it works...

For our map recipe, we used a `ReadWrite` mutex. The idea behind this mutex is that any number of readers can acquire a read lock, but only one writer can acquire a write lock. Additionally, a writer cannot acquire a lock when anyone else (reader or writer) has one. This is useful because reads are very fast and non-blocking when compared to a standard mutex. Whenever we want to set data, we use `Lock()` object and whenever we want to read data we use `RLock()`. It is critical that you use `Unlock()` or `RUnlock()` eventually so that you don't deadlock your application. A defer `Unlock()` object can be useful, but may be slower than calling `Unlock()` manually.

This pattern may not be flexible enough when you want to group additional actions with the locked value. For example, in some cases, you may want to lock, do some additional processing, and only after you've completed this will you unlock. It's important to consider this for your designs.

The `sync/atmoic` package is used by `Ordinal` to get and set values. There are also atomic comparison operations such as `atomic.CompareAndSwapUInt64()`, which are extremely valuable. This recipe allows Init to be called on an `Ordinal` object only once; otherwise, it can only be incremented and does so atomically.

We loop and create 10 goroutines (synchronizing with `sync.Waitgroup`) and show that the ordinal correctly incremented 10 times and that every key in our map was appropriately set.

# Using the context package

Several recipes throughout this book make use of the `context` package. This recipe will explore the basics of creating and managing contexts. A good reference for understanding context is `https://blog.golang.org/context`. Since this blog post was written, context moved from `net/context` to a package called `context`. This still occasionally causes problems when interacting with third-party libraries such as GRPC.

This recipe will explore setting and getting values for contexts, cancelation, and timeouts.

# Getting ready

Refer to the *Getting ready* section of the *Using channels and the select statement* recipe in this chapter.

# How to do it...

These steps cover writing and running your application:

1. From your terminal/console application, create the `chapter9/context` directory and navigate to it.
2. Copy tests from `https://github.com/agtorre/go-cookbook/tree/master/chapter9/context` or use this as an exercise to write some of your own code.
3. Create a file called `values.go` with the following content:

```
package context

import "context"

type key string

const (
    timeoutKey key = "TimeoutKey"
    deadlineKey key = "DeadlineKey"
)

// Setup sets some values
func Setup(ctx context.Context) context.Context {

    ctx = context.WithValue(ctx, timeoutKey,
    "timeout exceeded")
    ctx = context.WithValue(ctx, deadlineKey,
    "deadline exceeded")

    return ctx
}

// GetValue grabs a value given a key and
// returns a string representation of the
// value
func GetValue(ctx context.Context, k key) string {
```

```
        if val, ok := ctx.Value(k).(string); ok {
            return val
        }
        return ""

    }
```

4. Create a file called `exec.go` with the following content:

```go
package context

import (
    "context"
    "fmt"
    "math/rand"
    "time"
)

// Exec sets two random timers and prints
// a different context value for whichever
// fires first
func Exec() {
    // a base context
    ctx := context.Background()
    ctx = Setup(ctx)

    rand.Seed(time.Now().UnixNano())

    timeoutCtx, cancel := context.WithTimeout(ctx,
    (time.Duration(rand.Intn(2)) * time.Millisecond))
    defer cancel()

    deadlineCtx, cancel := context.WithDeadline(ctx,
    time.Now().Add(time.Duration(rand.Intn(2))
    *time.Millisecond))
    defer cancel()

    for {
        select {
            case <-timeoutCtx.Done():
            fmt.Println(GetValue(ctx, timeoutKey))
            return
            case <-deadlineCtx.Done():
                fmt.Println(GetValue(ctx, deadlineKey))
                return
        }
    }
}
```

5. Create a new directory named `example` and navigate to it.

6. Create a file named `main.go` with the following content. Ensure that you modify the `context` import to use the path you set up in step 2:

```
package main

import "github.com/agtorre/go-cookbook/chapter9/context"

func main() {
    context.Exec()
}
```

7. Run `go run main.go`.

8. You may also run the following commands:

```
go build
./example
```

You should now see the following output:

```
$ go run main.go
timeout exceeded
```

**OR**

```
$ go run main.go
deadline exceeded
```

9. If you copied or wrote your own tests, go up one directory and run `go test`. Ensure that all the tests pass.

## How it works...

When working with context values, it's good to create a new type to represent the key. In this case, we created a `key` type, then declared some corresponding `const` values to represent all of our possible keys.

In this case, we initialize all our key/value pairs at the same time using the `Setup()` function. When modifying contexts, functions generally take a `context` argument and return a `context` value. So the signature often looks like this:

```
func ModifyContext(ctx context.Context) context.Context
```

Sometimes, these methods also return an error or `cancel()` function, such as in the cases of `context.WithCancel`, `context.WithTimeout`, and `context.WithDeadline`. All child contexts inherit the attributes of the parent.

In this recipe, we create two child contexts, one with a deadline and one with a timeout. We set these to timeout to be random ranges, then terminate when either is received. Lastly, we extract a value given a set key and print it.

# Executing state management for channels

Channels can be any type in Go. A channel of structs allows you to pass a lot of state with a single message. This recipe will explore using of channels to pass around complex request structs and return their results in complex response structs.

In the next recipe, *Using the worker pool design pattern*, the value of this becomes even more apparent as you can create general purpose workers capable of performing a variety of tasks.

# Getting ready

Refer to the *Getting ready* section of the *Using channels and the select statement* recipe in this chapter.

# How to do it...

These steps cover writing and running your application:

1. From your terminal/console application, create and navigate to the `chapter9/state` directory.

2. Copy tests from `https://github.com/agtorre/go-cookbook/tree/master/chapter9/state` or use this as an exercise to write some of your own code.

3. Create a file called `state.go` with the following content:

```
package state

type op string

const (
    // Add values
    Add op = "add"
    // Subtract values
```

```
        Subtract = "sub"
        // Multiply values
        Multiply = "mult"
        // Divide values
        Divide = "div"
    )

    // WorkRequest perform an op
    // on two values
    type WorkRequest struct {
        Operation op
        Value1 int64
        Value2 int64
    }

    // WorkResponse returns the result
    // and any errors
    type WorkResponse struct {
        Wr *WorkRequest
        Result int64
        Err error
    }
```

4. Create a file called `processor.go` with the following content:

```
    package state

    import "context"

    // Processor routes work to Process
    func Processor(ctx context.Context, in chan *WorkRequest, out
    chan *WorkResponse) {
        for {
            select {
                case <-ctx.Done():
                    return
                case wr := <-in:
                    out <- Process(wr)
            }
        }
    }
```

5. Create a file called `process.go` with the following content:

```go
package state

import "errors"

// Process switches on operation type
// Then does work
func Process(wr *WorkRequest) *WorkResponse {
    resp := WorkResponse{Wr: wr}

    switch wr.Operation {
        case Add:
            resp.Result = wr.Value1 + wr.Value2
        case Subtract:
            resp.Result = wr.Value1 - wr.Value2
        case Multiply:
            resp.Result = wr.Value1 * wr.Value2
        case Divide:
            if wr.Value2 == 0 {
                resp.Err = errors.New("divide by 0")
                break
            }
            resp.Result = wr.Value1 / wr.Value2
        default:
            resp.Err = errors.New("unsupported operation")
    }
    return &resp
}
```

6. Create a new directory named `example` and navigate to it.
7. Create a file named `main.go` with the following content. Ensure that you modify the `state` import to use the path you set up in step 2:

```go
package main

import (
    "context"
    "fmt"

    "github.com/agtorre/go-cookbook/chapter9/state"
)

func main() {
    in := make(chan *state.WorkRequest, 10)
    out := make(chan *state.WorkResponse, 10)
    ctx := context.Background()
```

```
        ctx, cancel := context.WithCancel(ctx)
        defer cancel()

        go state.Processor(ctx, in, out)
        req := state.WorkRequest{state.Add, 3, 4}
        in <- &req

        req2 := state.WorkRequest{state.Subtract, 5, 2}
        in <- &req2

        req3 := state.WorkRequest{state.Multiply, 9, 9}
        in <- &req3

        req4 := state.WorkRequest{state.Divide, 8, 2}
        in <- &req4

        req5 := state.WorkRequest{state.Divide, 8, 0}
        in <- &req5

        for i := 0; i < 5; i++ {
            resp := <-out
            fmt.Printf("Request: %v; Result: %v, Error: %vn",
            resp.Wr, resp.Result, resp.Err)
        }
    }
```

8. Run `go run main.go`.

9. You may also run the following commands:

   ```
   go build
   ./example
   ```

   You should now see the following output:

   ```
   $ go run main.go
   Request: &{add 3 4}; Result: 7, Error: <nil>
   Request: &{sub 5 2}; Result: 3, Error: <nil>
   Request: &{mult 9 9}; Result: 81, Error: <nil>
   Request: &{div 8 2}; Result: 4, Error: <nil>
   Request: &{div 8 0}; Result: 0, Error: divide by 0
   ```

10. If you copied or wrote your own tests, go up one directory and run `go test`. Ensure that all the tests pass.

# How it works...

The Processor() function in this recipe is a function that loops forever until its context is canceled, either through explicit calls to cancel or via timeout. It dispatches all work to Process(), which can handle different functions given various operations. It would also be possible to have each of these cases dispatch another function for even more modular code.

Ultimately, the response is returned to a response channel, and we loop over and print all the results at the very end. We also demonstrate an error case in the divide by 0 example.

# Using the worker pool design pattern

The worker pool design pattern is one where you dispatch long-running goroutines as workers. These workers can process a variety of work either using multiple channels or by using a stateful request struct that specifies the type as described in the preceding recipe. This recipe will create stateful workers and demonstrate how to coordinate and spin up multiple workers all handling requests concurrently on the same channel. These workers will be crypto workers like in a web authentication app. Their purpose will be to hash plain text strings using bcrypt package and compare a text password against a hash.

# Getting ready

Refer to the *Getting ready* section of the *Using channels and the select statement* recipe in this chapter.

# How to do it...

These steps cover writing and running your application:

1. From your terminal/console application, create the chapter9/pool directory and navigate to it.
2. Copy tests from https://github.com/agtorre/go-cookbook/tree/master/chapter9/poolor use this as an exercise to write some of your own code.
3. Create a file called worker.go with the following content:

```
package pool

import (
    "context"
```

```
        "fmt"
)

// Dispatch creates numWorker workers, returns a cancel
// function channels for adding work and responses,
// cancel must be called
func Dispatch(numWorker int) (context.CancelFunc, chan
WorkRequest, chan WorkResponse) {
    ctx := context.Background()
    ctx, cancel := context.WithCancel(ctx)
    in := make(chan WorkRequest, 10)
    out := make(chan WorkResponse, 10)

    for i := 0; i < numWorker; i++ {
        go Worker(ctx, i, in, out)
    }
    return cancel, in, out
}

// Worker loops forever and is part of the worker pool
func Worker(ctx context.Context, id int, in chan WorkRequest,
out chan WorkResponse) {
    for {
        select {
            case <-ctx.Done():
                return
            case wr := <-in:
                fmt.Printf("worker id: %d, performing %s
                workn", id, wr.Op)
                out <- Process(wr)
        }
    }
}
```

4. Create a file called `work.go` with the following content:

```
package pool

import "errors"

type op string

const (
    // Hash is the bcrypt work type
    Hash op = "encrypt"
    // Compare is bcrypt compare work
    Compare = "decrypt"
)
```

```
// WorkRequest is a worker req
type WorkRequest struct {
    Op op
    Text []byte
    Compare []byte // optional
}

// WorkResponse is a worker resp
type WorkResponse struct {
    Wr WorkRequest
    Result []byte
    Matched bool
    Err error
}

// Process dispatches work to the worker pool channel
func Process(wr WorkRequest) WorkResponse {
    switch wr.Op {
    case Hash:
        return hashWork(wr)
    case Compare:
        return compareWork(wr)
    default:
        return WorkResponse{Err: errors.New("unsupported
        operation")}
    }
}
```

5. Create a file called `crypto.go` with the following content:

```
package pool

import "golang.org/x/crypto/bcrypt"

func hashWork(wr WorkRequest) WorkResponse {
    val, err := bcrypt.GenerateFromPassword(wr.Text,
    bcrypt.DefaultCost)
    return WorkResponse{
        Result: val,
        Err: err,
        Wr: wr,
    }
}

func compareWork(wr WorkRequest) WorkResponse {
    var matched bool
    err := bcrypt.CompareHashAndPassword(wr.Compare, wr.Text)
    if err == nil {
```

```
            matched = true
        }
        return WorkResponse{
            Matched: matched,
            Err: err,
            Wr: wr,
        }
    }
}
```

6. Create a new directory named `example` and navigate to it.
7. Create a file named `main.go` with the following content. Ensure that you modify the `state` import to use the path you set up in step 2:

```go
package main

import (
    "fmt"

    "github.com/agtorre/go-cookbook/chapter9/pool"
)

func main() {
    cancel, in, out := pool.Dispatch(10)
    defer cancel()

    for i := 0; i < 10; i++ {
        in <- pool.WorkRequest{Op: pool.Hash, Text:
        []byte(fmt.Sprintf("messages %d", i))}
    }

    for i := 0; i < 10; i++ {
        res := <-out
        if res.Err != nil {
            panic(res.Err)
        }
        in <- pool.WorkRequest{Op: pool.Compare, Text:
        res.Wr.Text, Compare: res.Result}
    }

    for i := 0; i < 10; i++ {
        res := <-out
        if res.Err != nil {
            panic(res.Err)
        }
        fmt.Printf("string: "%s"; matched: %vn",
        string(res.Wr.Text), res.Matched)
    }
```

```
}
```

8. Run `go run main.go`.

9. You may also run the following commands:

```
go build
./example
```

You should now see the following:

```
$ go run main.go
worker id: 9, performing encrypt work
worker id: 5, performing encrypt work
worker id: 2, performing encrypt work
worker id: 8, performing encrypt work
worker id: 6, performing encrypt work
worker id: 1, performing encrypt work
worker id: 0, performing encrypt work
worker id: 4, performing encrypt work
worker id: 3, performing encrypt work
worker id: 7, performing encrypt work
worker id: 2, performing decrypt work
worker id: 6, performing decrypt work
worker id: 8, performing decrypt work
worker id: 1, performing decrypt work
worker id: 0, performing decrypt work
worker id: 9, performing decrypt work
worker id: 3, performing decrypt work
worker id: 4, performing decrypt work
worker id: 7, performing decrypt work
worker id: 5, performing decrypt work
string: "messages 9"; matched: true
string: "messages 3"; matched: true
string: "messages 4"; matched: true
string: "messages 0"; matched: true
string: "messages 1"; matched: true
string: "messages 8"; matched: true
string: "messages 5"; matched: true
string: "messages 7"; matched: true
string: "messages 2"; matched: true
string: "messages 6"; matched: true
```

10. If you copied or wrote your own tests, go up one directory and run `go test`. Ensure that all the tests pass.

# How it works...

This recipe uses the `Dispatch()` method to create a number of workers on a single input channel, output channel, and those attached to a single `cancel()` function. This can be used if you want to make different pools for different purposes. For example, you can create 10 crypto and 20 compare workers by using separate pools. For this recipe, we use a single pool, send hash requests to the workers, retrieve the responses, and then send compare requests to the same pool. Because of this, the worker performing the work will be different each time, but they're all capable of performing either type of work.

The advantage to this approach is that both allow for parallelism and can also control the maximum concurrency. Bounding the maximum number of goroutines can also be important for limiting memory. I chose crypto for this recipe because crypto is a good example of code that can overwhelm your CPU or memory if you spin up a new goroutine for every new request, for example in a web service.

# Using workers to create pipelines

This recipe demonstrates creating groups of worker pools and connecting them together to form a pipeline. For this recipe, we link together two pools, but the pattern can be used for much more complex operations similar to middleware.
Worker pools can be useful to keep workers relatively simple and to also further control concurrency. For example, it may be useful to serialize logging while parallelizing other operations. This may also be useful to have a smaller pool for more expensive operations, so you don't overload machine resources.

# Getting ready

Refer to the *Getting ready* section of the *Using channels and the select statement* recipe in this chapter.

# How to do it...

These steps cover writing and running your application:

1. From your terminal/console application, create the `chapter9/pipeline` directory and navigate to it.

2. Copy tests from `https://github.com/agtorre/go-cookbook/tree/master/cha`
   `pter9/pipeline`or use this as an exercise to write some of your own
   code.

3. Create a file called `worker.go` with the following content:

```go
package pipeline

import "context"

// Worker have one role
// that is determined when
// Work is called
type Worker struct {
    in chan string
    out chan string
}

// Job is a job a worker can do
type Job string

const (
    // Print echo's all input to
    // stdout
    Print Job = "print"
    // Encode base64 encodes input
    Encode Job = "encode"
)

// Work is how to dispatch a worker, they are assigned
// a job here
func (w *Worker) Work(ctx context.Context, j Job) {
    switch j {
        case Print:
            w.Print(ctx)
        case Encode:
            w.Encode(ctx)
        default:
            return
    }
}
```

4. Create a file called `print.go` with the following content:

```go
package pipeline

import (
    "context"
```

```
            "fmt"
    )

    // Print prints w.in and repalys it
    // on w.out
    func (w *Worker) Print(ctx context.Context) {
        for {
            select {
                case <-ctx.Done():
                    return
                case val := <-w.in:
                    fmt.Println(val)
                    w.out <- val
            }
        }
    }
```

5. Create a file called encode.go with the following content:

```
    package pipeline

    import (
        "context"
        "encoding/base64"
        "fmt"
    )

    // Encode takes plain text as int
    // and returns "string => <base64 string encoding>
    // as out
    func (w *Worker) Encode(ctx context.Context) {
        for {
            select {
                case <-ctx.Done():
                    return
                case val := <-w.in:
                    w.out <- fmt.Sprintf("%s => %s", val,
                        base64.StdEncoding.EncodeToString([]byte(val)))
            }
        }
    }
```

6. Create a file called pipeline.go with the following content:

```
    package pipeline

    import "context"
```

```
// NewPipeline initializes the workers and
// connects them, it returns the input of the pipeline
// and the final output
func NewPipeline(ctx context.Context, numEncoders, numPrinters
int) (chan string, chan string) {
    inEncode := make(chan string, numEncoders)
    inPrint := make(chan string, numPrinters)
    outPrint := make(chan string, numPrinters)
    for i := 0; i < numEncoders; i++ {
        w := Worker{
            in: inEncode,
            out: inPrint,
        }
        go w.Work(ctx, Encode)
    }

    for i := 0; i < numPrinters; i++ {
        w := Worker{
            in: inPrint,
            out: outPrint,
        }
        go w.Work(ctx, Print)
    }
    return inEncode, outPrint
}
```

7. Create a new directory named `example` and navigate to it.
8. Create a file named `main.go` with the following content and ensure that you modify the `state` import to use the path you set up in step 2:

```
package main

import (
    "context"
    "fmt"

    "github.com/agtorre/go-cookbook/chapter9/pipeline"
)

func main() {
    ctx := context.Background()
    ctx, cancel := context.WithCancel(ctx)
    defer cancel()

    in, out := pipeline.NewPipeline(ctx, 10, 2)

    go func() {
```

```
        for i := 0; i < 20; i++ {
            in <- fmt.Sprint("Message", i)
        }
    }()

    for i := 0; i < 20; i++ {
        <-out
    }
}
```

9. Run `go run main.go`.

10. You may also run the following commands:

    ```
    go build
    ./example
    ```

    You should now see the following:

    ```
    $ go run main.go
    Message3 => TWVzc2FnZTM=
    Message7 => TWVzc2FnZTc=
    Message8 => TWVzc2FnZTg=
    Message9 => TWVzc2FnZTk=
    Message5 => TWVzc2FnZTU=
    Message11 => TWVzc2FnZTEx
    Message10 => TWVzc2FnZTEw
    Message4 => TWVzc2FnZTQ=
    Message12 => TWVzc2FnZTEy
    Message6 => TWVzc2FnZTY=
    Message14 => TWVzc2FnZTE0
    Message13 => TWVzc2FnZTEz
    Message0 => TWVzc2FnZTA=
    Message15 => TWVzc2FnZTE1
    Message1 => TWVzc2FnZTE=
    Message17 => TWVzc2FnZTE3
    Message16 => TWVzc2FnZTE2
    Message19 => TWVzc2FnZTE5
    Message18 => TWVzc2FnZTE4
    Message2 => TWVzc2FnZTI=
    ```

11. If you copied or wrote your own tests, go up one directory and run `go test`.
    Ensure that all the tests pass.

# How it works...

The `main` package creates a pipeline consisting of 10 encoders and two printers. It enqueues 20 strings on the in channel and waits for 20 responses on the out channel. If messages reach the out channel, it indicates that they've gone through the entire pipeline successfully.

The `NewPipeline` function is used to wire up the pools. It ensures that the channels are created with the proper buffered sizes and that the output channels of some pools are connected to the appropriate input channels of other pools. It's also possible to fan out the pipeline by using an array of in channels and an array of out channels on each worker, multiple named channels, or maps of channels. This would allow for things such as sending messages to a logger at each step.

# 10
# Distributed Systems

In this chapter, we will cover the following recipes:

- Using service discovery with Consul
- Implementing basic consensus using Raft
- Using containerization with Docker
- Orchestration and deployment strategies
- Monitoring applications
- Collecting metrics

## Introduction

Sometimes, application-level parallelism is not enough, and things that seem simple in development can become complex during deployment. Distributed systems provide a number of challenges not found when developing on a single machine. These applications have added complexity for things such as monitoring, writing applications that require strong consistency guarantees, and service discovery. In addition, you must always be mindful of single points of failure, such as a database. Otherwise your distributed applications can fail when this single component fails.

This chapter will explore methods of managing distributed data, orchestration, containerization, metrics, and monitoring. These will become part of your toolbox for writing and maintaining microservices and large distributed applications.

# Using service discovery with Consul

When using the microservice approach to applications, you end up with a lot of servers listening on a variety of IPs, domains, and ports. These IP addresses will vary by environment (staging versus production), and it can be tricky to keep them static for configuration between services. You also want to know when a machine or service is down or unreachable due to a network partition. Consul is a tool that provides a lot of functionality, but we'll explore registering services with Consul and querying them from our other services.

## Getting ready

Configure your environment according to these steps:

1. Download and install Go on your operating system from `https://golang.org/doc/install` and configure your `GOPATH` environment variable.
2. Open a terminal/console application.
3. Navigate to `GOPATH/src` and create a project directory, for example, `$GOPATH/src/github.com/yourusername/customrepo`. All code will be run and modified from this directory.
4. Optionally, install the latest tested version of the code by running the `go get github.com/agtorre/go-cookbook/` command.
5. Install Consul from `https://www.consul.io/intro/getting-started/install.html`.
6. Run the `go get github.com/hashicorp/consul/api` command.

## How to do it...

These steps cover writing and running your application:

1. From your terminal/console application, create the `chapter10/discovery` directory and navigate to it.
2. Copy tests from `https://github.com/agtorre/go-cookbook/tree/master/chapter10/discovery`, or use this as an exercise to write some of your own code.
3. Create a file called `client.go` with the following content:

```
package discovery
```

```
import "github.com/hashicorp/consul/api"

// Client exposes api methods we care
// about
type Client interface {
    Register(tags []string) error
    Service(service, tag string) ([]*api.ServiceEntry,
    *api.QueryMeta, error)
}

type client struct {
    client *api.Client
    address string
    name string
    port int
}

//NewClient iniitalizes a consul client
func NewClient(config *api.Config, address, name string, port
int) (Client, error) {
    c, err := api.NewClient(config)
    if err != nil {
        return nil, err
    }
    cli := &client{
        client: c,
        name: name,
        address: address,
        port: port,
    }
    return cli, nil
}
```

4. Create a file called operations.go with the following content:

```
package discovery

import "github.com/hashicorp/consul/api"

// Register adds our service to consul
func (c *client) Register(tags []string) error {
    reg := &api.AgentServiceRegistration{
        ID: c.name,
        Name: c.name,
        Port: c.port,
        Address: c.address,
        Tags: tags,
    }
```

```
        return c.client.Agent().ServiceRegister(reg)
    }

    // Service return a service
    func (c *client) Service(service, tag string)
    ([]*api.ServiceEntry, *api.QueryMeta, error) {
        return c.client.Health().Service(service, tag, false,
        nil)
    }
```

5. Create a file called `exec.go` with the following content:

```
    package discovery

    import (
        "fmt"

        consul "github.com/hashicorp/consul/api"
    )

    // Exec creates a consul entry then queries it
    func Exec() error {
        config := consul.DefaultConfig()
        config.Address = "localhost:8500"
        name := "discovery"

        // faked name and port for example
        cli, err := NewClient(config, "localhost", name, 8080)
        if err != nil {
            return err
        }

        if err := cli.Register([]string{"Go", "Awesome"}); err !=
        nil {
            return err
        }

        entries, _, err := cli.Service(name, "Go")
        if err != nil {
            return err
        }
        for _, entry := range entries {
            fmt.Printf("%#v\n", entry.Service)
        }

        return nil
    }
```

6. Create a new directory named `example` and navigate to it.
7. Create a file named `main.go` with the following content. Ensure that you modify the `channels` import to use the path you set up in step 2:

```
package main

import "github.com/agtorre/go-cookbook/chapter10/discovery"

func main() {
    if err := discovery.Exec(); err != nil {
        panic(err)
    }
}
```

8. Start Consul in a separate terminal using the `consul agent -dev -node=localhost` command.
9. Run the `go run main.go` command.
10. You may also run:

```
go build
./example
```

You should see the following output:

```
$ go run main.go
&api.AgentService{ID:"discovery", Service:"discovery", Tags:
[]string{"Go", "Awesome"}, Port:8080, Address:"localhost",
EnableTagOverride:false, CreateIndex:0x23, ModifyIndex:0x23}
```

11. If you copied or wrote your own tests, go up one directory and run `go test`. Ensure that all the tests pass.

# How it works...

Consul provides a robust Go API library. It can feel daunting when first starting, but this recipe shows how you might approach wrapping it. Configuring Consul further is beyond the scope of this recipe, but this shows the basic for registering a service and querying for other services given a key and tag.

It would be possible using this to register new microservices at startup time, query for all dependent services, and deregister at shutdown. You might also want to cache this information so that you're not hitting Consul for every request, but this recipe provides the basic tools that you can expand upon. The Consul agent also makes these repeated requests fast and efficient (`https://www.consul.io/intro/getting-started/agent.html`).

# Implementing basic consensus using Raft

Raft is a consensus algorithm that allows distributed systems to keep a shared and managed state (`https://raft.github.io/`). Setting up a Raft system is complex in many ways, for one you need consensus for an election to occur and succeed. This can be difficult to bootstrap when working with multiple nodes and it can be difficult to get started. A basic cluster can be run on a single node/leader, but if you want redundancy, at least three nodes allows for a single node failure.

This recipe implements a basic in-memory Raft cluster, constructs a state machine that can transition between certain allowed states, and connects the distributed state machine to a web handler that can trigger the transition. This can be useful when you're implementing the base finite state machine interface that Raft requires or when testing. This recipe uses `https://github.com/hashicorp/raft` for the base Raft implementation.

## Getting ready

Configure your environment according to these steps:

1. Refer to the *Getting ready* section of the *Using service discovery with Consul* recipe in this chapter.
2. Run the `go get github.com/hashicorp/raft` command.

## How to do it...

These steps cover writing and running your application:

1. From your terminal/console application, create the `chapter10/consensus` directory and navigate to it.
2. Copy tests from `https://github.com/agtorre/go-cookbook/tree/master/chapter10/consensus`, or use this as an exercise to write some of your own code.

3. Create a file called `state.go` with the following content:

```go
package consensus

type state string

const (
    first state = "first"
    second = "second"
    third = "third"
)

var allowedState map[state][]state

func init() {
    // setup valid states
    allowedState = make(map[state][]state)
    allowedState[first] = []state{second, third}
    allowedState[second] = []state{third}
    allowedState[third] = []state{first}
}

// CanTransition checks if a new state is valid
func (s *state) CanTransition(next state) bool {
    for _, n := range allowedState[*s] {
        if n == next {
            return true
        }
    }
    return false
}

// Transition will move a state to the next
// state if able
func (s *state) Transition(next state) {
    if s.CanTransition(next) {
        *s = next
    }
}
```

4. Create a file called `config.go` with the following content:

```go
package consensus

import "github.com/hashicorp/raft"

var rafts map[string]*raft.Raft
```

```
func init() {
    rafts = make(map[string]*raft.Raft)
}

// Config creates num in-memory raft
// nodes and connects them
func Config(num int) {
    conf := raft.DefaultConfig()
    snapshotStore := raft.NewDiscardSnapshotStore()

    addrs := []string{}
    transports := []*raft.InmemTransport{}
    for i := 0; i < num; i++ {
        addr, transport := raft.NewInmemTransport("")
        addrs = append(addrs, addr)
        transports = append(transports, transport)
    }
    peerStore := &raft.StaticPeers{StaticPeers: addrs}
    memstore := raft.NewInmemStore()

    for i := 0; i < num; i++ {
        for j := 0; j < num; j++ {
            if i != j {
                transports[i].Connect(addrs[j], transports[j])
            }
        }

        r, err := raft.NewRaft(conf, NewFSM(), memstore,
        memstore, snapshotStore, peerStore, transports[i])
        if err != nil {
            panic(err)
        }
        r.SetPeers(addrs)
        rafts[addrs[i]] = r
    }
}
```

5. Create a file called fsm.go with the following content:

```
package consensus

import (
    "io"

    "github.com/hashicorp/raft"
)

// FSM implements the raft FSM interface
```

```
// and holds a state
type FSM struct {
    state state
}

// NewFSM creates a new FSM with
// start state of "first"
func NewFSM() *FSM {
    return &FSM{state: first}
}

// Apply updates our FSM
func (f *FSM) Apply(r *raft.Log) interface{} {
    f.state.Transition(state(r.Data))
    return string(f.state)
}

// Snapshot needed to satisfy the raft FSM interface
func (f *FSM) Snapshot() (raft.FSMSnapshot, error) {
    return nil, nil
}

// Restore needed to satisfy the raft FSM interface
func (f *FSM) Restore(io.ReadCloser) error {
    return nil
}
```

6. Create a file called `handler.go` with the following content:

```
package consensus

import (
    "net/http"
    "time"
)

// Handler grabs the get param ?next= and tries
// to transition to the state contained there
func Handler(w http.ResponseWriter, r *http.Request) {
    r.ParseForm()
    for k, rf := range rafts {
        if k == rf.Leader() {
            state := r.FormValue("next")
            result := rf.Apply([]byte(state), 1*time.Second)
            if result.Error() != nil {
                w.WriteHeader(http.StatusBadRequest)
                return
            }
```

```
                        newState, ok := result.Response().(string)
                        if !ok {
                            w.WriteHeader(http.StatusInternalServerError)
                            return
                        }

                        if newState != state {
                            w.WriteHeader(http.StatusBadRequest)
                            w.Write([]byte("invalid transition"))
                            return
                        }
                        w.WriteHeader(http.StatusOK)
                        w.Write([]byte(result.Response().(string)))
                        return
                    }
                }
            }
```

7. Create a new directory named `example` and navigate to it.

8. Create a file named `main.go` with the following content. Ensure that you modify the `channels` import to use the path you set up in step 2:

```
package main

import (
    "net/http"

    "github.com/agtorre/go-cookbook/chapter10/consensus"
)

func main() {
    consensus.Config(3)

    http.HandleFunc("/", consensus.Handler)
    err := http.ListenAndServe(":3333", nil)
    panic(err)
}
```

9. Run the `go run main.go` command. Alternatively, you may also run the following commands:

```
go build
./example
```

You should now see the following output by running the preceding command:

```
$ go run main.go
2017/04/23 16:49:24 [INFO] raft: Node at 95c86c4c-9192-a8a6-
5e38-66c033bb3955 [Follower] entering Follower state (Leader:
"")
2017/04/23 16:49:24 [INFO] raft: Node at 2406e36b-7e3e-0965-
8863-70a5dc1a2e69 [Follower] entering Follower state (Leader:
"")
2017/04/23 16:49:24 [INFO] raft: Node at 2b5367e6-eea6-e195-
df40-1aeebfe8cdc7 [Follower] entering Follower state (Leader:
"")
2017/04/23 16:49:25 [WARN] raft: Heartbeat timeout from ""
reached, starting election
2017/04/23 16:49:25 [INFO] raft: Node at 2406e36b-7e3e-0965-
8863-70a5dc1a2e69 [Candidate] entering Candidate state
2017/04/23 16:49:25 [DEBUG] raft: Votes needed: 2
2017/04/23 16:49:25 [DEBUG] raft: Vote granted from 2406e36b-
7e3e-0965-8863-70a5dc1a2e69. Tally: 1
2017/04/23 16:49:25 [DEBUG] raft: Vote granted from 95c86c4c-
9192-a8a6-5e38-66c033bb3955. Tally: 2
2017/04/23 16:49:25 [INFO] raft: Election won. Tally: 2
2017/04/23 16:49:25 [INFO] raft: Node at 2406e36b-7e3e-0965-
8863-70a5dc1a2e69 [Leader] entering Leader state
2017/04/23 16:49:25 [INFO] raft: pipelining replication to peer
95c86c4c-9192-a8a6-5e38-66c033bb3955
2017/04/23 16:49:25 [INFO] raft: pipelining replication to peer
2b5367e6-eea6-e195-df40-1aeebfe8cdc7
2017/04/23 16:49:25 [DEBUG] raft: Node 2406e36b-7e3e-0965-8863-
70a5dc1a2e69 updated peer set (2): [2406e36b-7e3e-0965-8863-
70a5dc1a2e69 95c86c4c-9192-a8a6-5e38-66c033bb3955 2b5367e6-
eea6-e195-df40-1aeebfe8cdc7]
2017/04/23 16:49:25 [DEBUG] raft: Node 95c86c4c-9192-a8a6-5e38-
66c033bb3955 updated peer set (2): [2406e36b-7e3e-0965-8863-
70a5dc1a2e69 95c86c4c-9192-a8a6-5e38-66c033bb3955 2b5367e6-
eea6-e195-df40-1aeebfe8cdc7]
2017/04/23 16:49:25 [DEBUG] raft: Node 2b5367e6-eea6-e195-df40-
1aeebfe8cdc7 updated peer set (2): [2406e36b-7e3e-0965-8863-
70a5dc1a2e69 95c86c4c-9192-a8a6-5e38-66c033bb3955 2b5367e6-
eea6-e195-df40-1aeebfe8cdc7]
```

10. In a separate terminal, run the following command:

```
$ curl "http://localhost:3333/?next=second"
second

$ curl "http://localhost:3333/?next=third"
third
```

```
$ curl "http://localhost:3333/?next=second"
invalid transition

$ curl "http://localhost:3333/?next=first"
first
```

11. If you copied or wrote your own tests, go up one directory and run `go test`. Ensure that all tests pass.

# How it works...

When the application starts, we initialize multiple Raft objects. These each have their own address and transport. The `InmemTransport{}` function also provides a method to connect the other transports called `Connect()`. Once these connections are established, the Raft cluster holds an election. When communicating to a Raft cluster, clients must communicate with the leader. In our case, one handler can talk to all of the nodes, so the handler is responsible for having the leader `Raft` object call `Apply()`. This in turn runs `apply()` on all of the other nodes.

This recipe does not deal with snapshots and is only concerned with FSM state changes. The `InmemTransport{}` function simplifies the election and bootstrapping process by allowing everything to reside in memory. In practice, this isn't very helpful besides testing and proof of concepts since go routines can freely access shared memory.

# Using containerization with Docker

Docker is a container technology for packaging and shipping applications. Other advantages include portability, a container will run the same way regardless of the host OS. It provides a lot of the advantages of a virtual machine, in a more light-weight container. It's possible to limit resources consumption of individual containers and sandbox your environment. It can be extremely useful for having a common environment for your applications locally and when you ship your code to production. Docker is written in Go and is open source, so it's simple to take advantage of the client and libraries. This recipe will set up a Docker container for a basic Go application, store some version information about the container, and demonstrate hitting a handler from a Docker endpoint.

# Getting ready

Configure your environment according to these steps:

1. Refer to the *Getting ready* section of the *Using service discovery for Consul* recipe of this chapter.
2. Install Docker from `https://store.docker.com/search?type=edition&offering=community`. This will also include Docker compose.

# How to do it...

These steps cover writing and running your application:

1. From your terminal/console application, create the `chapter10/docker` directory and navigate to it.
2. Copy tests from `https://github.com/agtorre/go-cookbook/tree/master/chapter10/docker` or use this as an exercise to write some of your own code.
3. Create a file called `dockerfile` with the following content:

   ```
   FROM alpine

   ADD ./example/example /example
   EXPOSE 8000
   ENTRYPOINT /example
   ```

4. Create a file called `setup.sh` with the following content:

   ```
   #!/usr/bin/env bash

   pushd example
   env GOOS=linux go build -ldflags "-X main.version=1.0 -X
   main.builddate=$(date +%s)"
   popd
   docker build . -t example
   docker run -d -p 8000:8000 example
   ```

5. Create a file called `version.go` with the following content:

```go
package docker

import (
    "encoding/json"
    "net/http"
    "time"
)

// VersionInfo holds artifacts passed in
// at build time
type VersionInfo struct {
    Version string
    BuildDate time.Time
    Uptime time.Duration
}

// VersionHandler writes the latest version info
func VersionHandler(v *VersionInfo) http.HandlerFunc {
    t := time.Now()
    return func(w http.ResponseWriter, r *http.Request) {
        v.Uptime = time.Since(t)
        vers, err := json.Marshal(v)
            if err != nil {
                w.WriteHeader
                (http.StatusInternalServerError)
                return
            }
            w.WriteHeader(http.StatusOK)
            w.Write(vers)
    }
}
```

6. Create a new directory named `example` and navigate to it.

7. Create a file `main.go` with the following content. Ensure that you modify the `channels` import to use the path you set up in step 2:

```go
package main

import (
    "fmt"
    "net/http"
    "strconv"
    "time"

    "github.com/agtorre/go-cookbook/chapter10/docker"
```

```
)

// these are set at build time
var (
    version string
    builddate string
    )

var versioninfo docker.VersionInfo

func init() {
    // parse buildtime variables
    versioninfo.Version = version
    i, err := strconv.ParseInt(builddate, 10, 64)
        if err != nil {
            panic(err)
        }
        tm := time.Unix(i, 0)
        versioninfo.BuildDate = tm
}

func main() {
http.HandleFunc("/version",
docker.VersionHandler(&versioninfo))
fmt.Printf("version %s listening on :8000\n",
versioninfo.Version)
panic(http.ListenAndServe(":8000", nil))
}
```

8. Navigate back to the starting directory.
9. Run the following command:

```
$ bash setup.sh
```

You should now see the following output:

```
$ bash setup.sh
~/go/src/github.com/agtorre/go-
cookbook/chapter10/docker/example
~/go/src/github.com/agtorre/go-cookbook/chapter10/docker
~/go/src/github.com/agtorre/go-cookbook/chapter10/docker
Sending build context to Docker daemon 6.031 MB
Step 1/4 : FROM alpine
 ---> 4a415e366388
Step 2/4 : ADD ./example/example /example
 ---> de34c3c5451e
Removing intermediate container bdcd9c4f4381
Step 3/4 : EXPOSE 8000
```

```
 ---> Running in 188f450d4e7b
 ---> 35d1a2652b43
Removing intermediate container 188f450d4e7b
Step 4/4 : ENTRYPOINT /example
 ---> Running in cf0af4f48c3a
 ---> 3d737fc4e6e2
Removing intermediate container cf0af4f48c3a
Successfully built 3d737fc4e6e2
b390ef429fbd6e7ff87058dc82e15c3e7a8b2e
69a601892700d1d434e9e8e43b
```

10. Run the following commands:

```
$ docker ps
CONTAINER ID IMAGE COMMAND CREATED STATUS PORTS NAMES
b390ef429fbd example "/bin/sh -c /example" 22 seconds ago Up 23
seconds 0.0.0.0:8000->8000/tcp optimistic_wescoff

$ curl localhost:8000/version
{"Version":"1.0","BuildDate":"2017-04-
30T21:55:56Z","Uptime":48132111264}

$docker kill optimistic_wescoff # grab from first output
optimistic_wescoff
```

11. If you copied or wrote your own tests, go up one directory and run `go test`. Ensure that all the tests pass.

# How it works...

This recipe created a script that compiles the Go binary for the Linux architecture and sets a variety of private variables in `main.go`. These variables are used to return version information on a version endpoint. Once the binary is compiled, a Docker container is created that contains the binary. This allows us to use very small container images as the Go runtime is self contained in the binary. We then run the container while exposing the port on which the container is listening for HTTP traffic. Lastly, we curl the port on localhost and see our version information returned.

# Orchestration and deployment strategies

Docker makes orchestration and deployment much more simple. In this recipe, we'll set up a connection to MongoDB, inserting a document and querying it all from Docker containers. This recipe will set up the same environment as the *Using NoSQL with MongoDB and mgo* recipe, in `Chapter 5`, *All about Databases and Storage*, but will run the application and environment inside of containers and will use Docker compose to orchestrate and connect them. This can later be used in conjunction with Docker Swarm, an integrated Docker tool that allows you to manage a cluster, to create and deploy nodes that can be scaled up or down easily, and to manage load balancing (`https://docs.docker.com/engine/swarm/`). Another good example of container orchestration is Kubernetes (`https://kubernetes.io/`), a container orchestration framework written by Google using the Go programming language.

## Getting ready

Configure your environment according to these steps:

1. Refer to the *Getting ready* section of the *Using containerization with Docker* recipe.
2. Run the `go get gopkg.in/mgo.v2` command.
3. Run the `go get github.com/tools/godep` command.

## How to do it...

These steps cover writing and running your application:

1. From your terminal/console application, create the `chapter10/orchestrate` directory and navigate to it.
2. Copy tests from `https://github.com/agtorre/go-cookbook/tree/master/chapter10/orchestrate` or use this as an exercise to write some of your own code.
3. Create a file called `dockerfile` with the following content:

   ```
   FROM golang:alpine

   ENV GOPATH /code/
   ADD . /code/src/github.com/agtorre/go-
   cookbook/chapter10/docker
   WORKDIR /code/src/github.com/agtorre/go-
   cookbook/chapter10/docker/example
   RUN go build
   ```

```
ENTRYPOINT /code/src/github.com/agtorre/go-
cookbook/chapter10/docker/example/example
```

4. Create a file called `docker-compose.yml` with the following content:

```
version: '2'
services:
 app:
 build: .
 mongodb:
 image: "mongo:latest"
```

5. Create a file called `mongo.go` with the following content:

```go
package orchestrate

import (
    "fmt"

    mgo "gopkg.in/mgo.v2"
    "gopkg.in/mgo.v2/bson"
)

// State is our data model
type State struct {
    Name string `bson:"name"`
    Population int `bson:"pop"`
}

// ConnectAndQuery connects, inserts a document, then
// queries it
func ConnectAndQuery(session *mgo.Session) error {
    conn := session.DB("gocookbook").C("example")

    // we can inserts many rows at once
    if err := conn.Insert(&State{"Washington", 7062000},
    &State{"Oregon", 3970000}); err != nil {
        return err
    }

    var s State
    if err := conn.Find(bson.M{"name": "Washington"}).One(&s);
    err!= nil {
        return err
    }
    fmt.Printf("State: %#v\n", s)
    return nil
}
```

6. Create a new directory named `example` and navigate to it.

7. Create a `main.go` file with the following content. Ensure that you modify the `orchestrate` import to use the path you set up in step 2:

```
package main

import (
        "github.com/agtorre/go-cookbook/chapter10/orchestrate"
        mgo "gopkg.in/mgo.v2"
)

func main() {
    session, err := mgo.Dial("mongodb")
    if err != nil {
        panic(err)
    }
    if err := orchestrate.ConnectAndQuery(session); err != nil
    {
        panic(err)
    }
}
```

8. Navigate back to the starting directory.

9. Run the `godep save ./...` command.

10. Run the `docker-compose up -d` command.

11. Run the `docker logs docker_app_1` command.

You should now see the following output:

```
$ docker logs docker_app_1
State: docker.State{Name:"Washington", Population:7062000}
```

12. If you copied or wrote your own tests, go up one directory and run `go test`. Ensure that all the tests pass.

# How it works...

This configuration is good for local development. Once the `docker-compose up` command is run, the local directory is rebuilt, it establishes a connection to a MongoDB instance using the latest version and begins operating against it. This recipe uses godeps for dependency management so that the entire `GOPATH` environment variable doesn't need to be mounted by the `Dockerfile` file.

This can provide a good baseline when starting on apps that require connections to external services, all of the Chapter 5, *All about Databases and Storage,* can make use of this approach rather than creating a local instance of the database. For production, you likely won't want to run your datastorage behind a Docker container, but you'll also generally have static host names for configuration.

# Monitoring applications

There are a variety of ways to monitor Go applications. One of the easiest ways is to set up Prometheus, a monitoring application written in Go (https://prometheus.io). This is an application that polls an endpoint based on your configuration file and collects a lot of information about your app, including the number of goroutines, memory usage, and much more. This app will use the techniques from the previous recipe to set up a Docker environment to host Prometheus and connect to it.

## Getting ready

Configure your environment according to these steps:

1. Refer to the *Getting ready* section of the *Using containerization with Docker* recipe.
2. Run the go get github.com/prometheus/client_golang/prometheus/promhttp command.

## How to do it...

These steps cover writing and running your application:

1. From your terminal/console application, create the chapter10/monitoring directory and navigate to it.
2. Copy tests from https://github.com/agtorre/go-cookbook/tree/master/chapter10/monitoringor use this as an exercise to write some of your own code.
3. Create a file called Dockerfile with the following content:

```
FROM golang:alpine

ENV GOPATH /code/
ADD . /code/src/github.com/agtorre/go-
```

```
cookbook/chapter10/monitoring
WORKDIR /code/src/github.com/agtorre/go-
cookbook/chapter10/monitoring
RUN go build

ENTRYPOINT /code/src/github.com/agtorre/go-
cookbook/chapter10/monitoring/monitoring
```

4. Create a file called `docker-compose.yml` with the following content:

```
version: '2'
services:
 app:
 build: .
 prometheus:
 ports:
 - 9090:9090
 volumes:
 - ./prometheus.yml:/etc/prometheus/prometheus.yml
 image: "prom/prometheus"
```

5. Create a file called `main.go` with the following content:

```
package main

import (
    "net/http"

    "github.com/prometheus/client_golang/prometheus/promhttp"
)

func main() {
    http.Handle("/metrics", promhttp.Handler())
    panic(http.ListenAndServe(":80", nil))
}
```

6. Create a file called `prometheus.yml` with the following content:

```
global:
 scrape_interval: 15s # By default, scrape targets every 15
 seconds.

# A scrape configuration containing exactly one endpoint to
scrape:
# Here it's Prometheus itself.
scrape_configs:
 # The job name is added as a label `job=<job_name>` to any
 timeseries scraped from this config.
```

```
- job_name: 'app'

# Override the global default and scrape targets from this job
every 5 seconds.
scrape_interval: 5s

static_configs:
- targets: ['app:80']
```

7. Run the `godep save ./...` command.

8. Run the `docker-compose up -d` command.

You should now see the following:

```
$ docker-compose up
Creating monitoring_app_1
Creating monitoring_prometheus_1
Attaching to monitoring_app_1, monitoring_prometheus_1
prometheus_1 | time="2017-04-30T02:35:17Z" level=info
msg="Starting prometheus (version=1.6.1, branch=master,
revision=4666df502c0e239ed4aa1d80abbbfb54f61b23c3)"
source="main.go:88"
prometheus_1 | time="2017-04-30T02:35:17Z" level=info msg="Build
context (go=go1.8.1, user=root@7e45fa0366a7, date=20170419-
14:32:22)" source="main.go:89"
prometheus_1 | time="2017-04-30T02:35:17Z" level=info
msg="Loading configuration file /etc/prometheus/prometheus.yml"
source="main.go:251"
prometheus_1 | time="2017-04-30T02:35:17Z" level=info
msg="Loading series map and head chunks..."
source="storage.go:421"
prometheus_1 | time="2017-04-30T02:35:17Z" level=info msg="0
series loaded." source="storage.go:432"
prometheus_1 | time="2017-04-30T02:35:17Z" level=info
msg="Starting target manager..." source="targetmanager.go:61"
prometheus_1 | time="2017-04-30T02:35:17Z" level=info
msg="Listening on :9090" source="web.go:259"
```

9. Navigate your browser to `http://localhost:9090/`. You should see a variety of metrics related to your app!

# How it works...

The Prometheus client handler will return a variety of stats about your application to a Prometheus server. This allows you to point multiple Prometheus servers at an app without the need to reconfigure or deploy the app. Most of these stats are generic and beneficial for things such as detecting memory leaks. A lot of other solutions require you to periodically send information to a server instead. The next recipe, *Collecting metrics*, will demonstrate how to ship custom metrics to the Prometheus server.

# Collecting metrics

In addition to general information about your app, it can be helpful to emit metrics that are app specific. For example, we might want to collect timing data or keep track of the number of times an event occurs.

This recipe will use the `github.com/rcrowley/go-metrics` package to collect metrics and expose them via an endpoint. There are various exporter tools to export metrics to places such as Prometheus and InfluxDB, also written in Go.

# Getting ready

Configure your environment according to these steps:

1.  Refer to the *Getting ready* section of the *Using service discovery with Consul* recipe in this chapter.
2.  Run the `go get github.com/rcrowley/go-metrics` command.

# How to do it...

These steps cover writing and running your application:

1.  From your terminal/console application, create the `chapter10/metrics` directory and navigate to it.
2.  Copy tests from `https://github.com/agtorre/go-cookbook/tree/master/chapter10/metrics`, or use this as an exercise to write some of your own code.

3. Create a file called `handler.go` with the following content:

```go
package metrics

import (
    "net/http"
    "time"

    metrics "github.com/rcrowley/go-metrics"
)

// CounterHandler will update a counter each time it's called
func CounterHandler(w http.ResponseWriter, r *http.Request) {
    c := metrics.GetOrRegisterCounter("counterhandler.counter",
    nil)
    c.Inc(1)

    w.WriteHeader(http.StatusOK)
    w.Write([]byte("success"))
}

// TimerHandler records the duration required to compelete
func TimerHandler(w http.ResponseWriter, r *http.Request) {
    currt := time.Now()
    t := metrics.GetOrRegisterTimer("timerhandler.timer", nil)

    w.WriteHeader(http.StatusOK)
    w.Write([]byte("success"))
    t.UpdateSince(currt)
}
```

4. Create a file called `report.go` with the following content:

```go
package metrics

import (
    "net/http"

    gometrics "github.com/rcrowley/go-metrics"
)

// ReportHandler will emit the current metrics in json format
func ReportHandler(w http.ResponseWriter, r *http.Request) {

    w.WriteHeader(http.StatusOK)

    t := gometrics.GetOrRegisterTimer(
    "reporthandler.writemetrics", nil)
```

```
    t.Time(func() {
        gometrics.WriteJSONOnce(gometrics.DefaultRegistry, w)
    })
}
```

5. Create a new directory named `example` and navigate to it.

6. Create a file named `main.go` with the following content. Ensure that you modify the `channels` import to use the path you set up in step 2:

```
package main

import (
    "net/http"

    "github.com/agtorre/go-cookbook/chapter10/metrics"
)

func main() {
    // handler to populate metrics
    http.HandleFunc("/counter", metrics.CounterHandler)
    http.HandleFunc("/timer", metrics.TimerHandler)
    http.HandleFunc("/report", metrics.ReportHandler)
    fmt.Println("listening on :8080")
    panic(http.ListenAndServe(":8080", nil))
}
```

7. Run `go run main.go`. Alternatively, you may also run the following:

```
go build
./example
```

You should now see the following:

```
$ go run main.go
listening on :8080
```

8. Run the following commands from a separate shell:

```
$ curl localhost:8080/counter
success

$ curl localhost:8080/timer
success

$ curl localhost:8080/report
{"counterhandler.counter":{"count":1},
"reporthandler.writemetrics":        {"15m.rate":0,"1m.rate":0,"5m.
```

```
rate":0,"75%":0,"95%":0,"99%":0,"99.9%":0,"count":0,"max":0,"mean
":0,"mean.rate":0,"median":0,"min":0,"stddev":0},"timerhandler.ti
mer":{"15m.rate":0.0011080303990206543,"1m.rate"
:0.015991117074135343,"5m.rate":0.0033057092356765017,"75%":60485
,"95%":60485,"99%":60485,"99.9%":60485,"count":1,"max":60485,"mea
n":60485,"mean.rate":1.1334543719787356,"median":60485,"min":6048
5,"stddev":0}}
```

9. Try hitting all the endpoints a few more times to see how they change.
10. If you copied or wrote your own tests, go up one directory and run `go test`. Ensure that all the tests pass.

# How it works...

The gometrics keeps all of your metrics in a registry. Once it's set up, you can use any of the metric omit options, such as counter or timer, and it will store this update in the registry. There are multiple exporters that will export metrics to third-party tools. In our case, we set up a handler that omits all the metrics in the JSON format.

We set up three handlers--one that increments a counter, one that records the time to exit the handler, and one that prints a report (while also incrementing an additional counter). The `GetOrRegister` functions are useful for atomically getting or creating a metric emitter if it doesn't currently exist in a thread-safe way. Alternatively, you can register everything once in advance.

# 11
# Reactive Programming and Data Streams

In this chapter, we will cover the following recipes:

- Goflow for dataflow programming
- Reactive programming with RxGo
- Using Kafka with Sarama
- Using async producers with Kafka
- Connecting Kafka to Goflow
- Writing a GraphQL server in Go

# Introduction

This chapter will discuss reactive programming design patterns in Go. Reactive programming is a programming concept that focuses on data streams and the propagation of change (https://en.wikipedia.org/wiki/Reactive_programming). Technologies such as Kafka allow you to quickly produce or consume a stream of data. As a result, these technologies are a natural fit for one another. In the *Connecting Kafka to Goflow* recipe, we'll explore combining a kafka message queue with goflow to show a practical example of using these technologies. This chapter will also explore various ways to connect with Kafka and use it to process messages. Lastly, this chapter will demonstrate how to create a basic graphql server in Go.

# Goflow for dataflow programming

The `github.com/trustmaster/goflow` package is useful for creating dataflow-based applications. It tries to abstract concepts so that you can write components and connect them together using a custom network. This recipe will recreate the application discussed in `Chapter 8`, *Testing*, but it will do so using the `goflow` package.

## Getting ready

Configure your environment according to these steps:

1. Download and install Go on your operating system from `https://golang.org/d oc/install`and configure your `GOPATH` environment variable.
2. Open a terminal/console application.
3. Navigate to your `GOPATH/src` and create a project directory, for example, `$GOPATH/src/github.com/yourusername/customrepo`. All code will be run and modified from this directory.
4. Optionally, install the latest tested version of the code using the `go get github.com/agtorre/go-cookbook/` command.
5. Run the `go get github.com/trustmaster/goflow` command.

## How to do it...

These steps cover writing and running your application:

1. From your terminal/console application, create the `chapter11/goflow` directory and navigate to it.
2. Copy tests from `https://github.com/agtorre/go-cookbook/tree/master/cha pter11/goflow`or use this as an exercise to write some of your own.
3. Create a file called `components.go` with the following content:

```
package goflow

import (
    "encoding/base64"
    "fmt"
    flow "github.com/trustmaster/goflow"
)
```

```go
// Encoder base64 encodes all input
type Encoder struct {
    flow.Component
    Val <-chan string
    Res chan<- string
}

// OnVal does the encoding then pushes the result onto Re
func (e *Encoder) OnVal(val string) {
    encoded := base64.StdEncoding.EncodeToString([]byte(val))
    e.Res <- fmt.Sprintf("%s => %s", val, encoded)
}

// Printer is a component for printing to stdout
type Printer struct {
    flow.Component
    Line <-chan string
}

// OnLine Prints the current line received
func (p *Printer) OnLine(line string) {
    fmt.Println(line)
}
```

4. Create a file called network.go with the following content:

```go
package goflow

import flow "github.com/trustmaster/goflow"

// EncodingApp creates a flow-based
// pipeline to encode and print the
// result
type EncodingApp struct {
    flow.Graph
}

// NewEncodingApp wires together the components
func NewEncodingApp() *EncodingApp {
    e := &EncodingApp{}
    e.InitGraphState()

    // define component types
    e.Add(&Encoder{}, "encoder")
    e.Add(&Printer{}, "printer")

    // connect the components using channels
    e.Connect("encoder", "Res", "printer", "Line")
```

```
        // map the in channel to Val, which is
        // tied to OnVal function
        e.MapInPort("In", "encoder", "Val")

        return e
}
```

5. Create a new directory named `example` and navigate to it.

6. Create a file named `main.go` with the following content. Ensure that you modify the `goflow` import to use the path you set up in step 2:

```
package main

import (
    "fmt"

    "github.com/agtorre/go-cookbook/chapter11/goflow"
    flow "github.com/trustmaster/goflow"
)

func main() {

    net := goflow.NewEncodingApp()

    in := make(chan string)
    net.SetInPort("In", in)

    flow.RunNet(net)

    for i := 0; i < 20; i++ {
        in <- fmt.Sprint("Message", i)
    }

    close(in)
    <-net.Wait()
}
```

7. Run `go run main.go`.

8. You may also run the following commands:

```
go build
./example
```

You should now see the following output:

```
$ go run main.go
Message6 => TWVzc2FnZTY=
Message5 => TWVzc2FnZTU=
Message1 => TWVzc2FnZTE=
Message0 => TWVzc2FnZTA=
Message4 => TWVzc2FnZTQ=
Message8 => TWVzc2FnZTg=
Message2 => TWVzc2FnZTI=
Message3 => TWVzc2FnZTM=
Message7 => TWVzc2FnZTc=
Message10 => TWVzc2FnZTEw
Message9 => TWVzc2FnZTk=
Message12 => TWVzc2FnZTEy
Message11 => TWVzc2FnZTEx
Message14 => TWVzc2FnZTE0
Message13 => TWVzc2FnZTEz
Message16 => TWVzc2FnZTE2
Message15 => TWVzc2FnZTE1
Message18 => TWVzc2FnZTE4
Message17 => TWVzc2FnZTE3
Message19 => TWVzc2FnZTE5
```

9. If you copied or wrote your own tests, go up one directory and run `go test`. Ensure that all the tests pass.

# How it works...

The `github.com/trustmaster/goflow` package works by defining a network/graph, registering some components, and then wiring them together. This can feel a bit error-prone since these are described using strings, but usually this will fail early in runtime until it's set up correctly.

In this recipe, we set up two components, one that base64 encodes an incoming string and one that prints anything passed to it. We connect it to an in channel that is initialized in `main.go`, and anything passed onto that channel will flow through our pipeline.

A lot of the emphasis of this approach is on ignoring the internals of what's going on. We treat everything like a connected black box and let `goflow` do the rest. You can see in this recipe how small the code is to accomplish this pipeline of tasks and that we have fewer knobs to control the number of workers, among other things.

# Reactive programming with RxGo

ReactiveX (`http://reactivex.io/`) is an API for programming with observable streams. RxGo (`github.com/reactivex/rxgo`) is a library to support this pattern in Go. It helps you to think of your application as a big stream of events that responds in different ways when those events occur. This recipe will create an application that uses this approach to process different wines. Ideally, this approach can be tied to wine data or wine APIs and can aggregate information about wine.

# Getting ready

Configure your environment according to these steps:

1. Refer to the *Getting ready* section of the *Goflow for dataflow programming* recipe in this chapter.
2. Run the `go get github.com/reactivex/rxgo` command.

# How to do it...

These steps cover writing and running your application:

1. From your terminal/console application, create the `chapter11/reactive` directory and navigate to it.
2. Copy tests from `https://github.com/agtorre/go-cookbook/tree/master/chapter11/reactive` or use this as an exercise to write some of your own.
3. Create a file called `wine.go` with the following content:

```go
package reactive

// Wine represents a bottle
// of wine and is our
// input stream
type Wine struct {
    Name string
    Age int
    Rating float64 // 1-5
}

// GetWine returns an array of wines,
// ages, and ratings
func GetWine() interface{} {
```

```
    // some example wines
    w := []interface{}{
        Wine{"Merlot", 2011, 3.0},
        Wine{"Cabernet", 2010, 3.0},
        Wine{"Chardonnay", 2010, 4.0},
        Wine{"Pinot Grigio", 2009, 4.5},
    }
    return w
}

// Results holds a list of results by age
type Results map[int]Result

// Result is used for aggregation
type Result struct {
    SumRating float64
    NumSamples int
}
```

4. Create a file called exec.go with the following content:

```
package reactive

import (
    "github.com/reactivex/rxgo/iterable"
    "github.com/reactivex/rxgo/observable"
    "github.com/reactivex/rxgo/observer"
    "github.com/reactivex/rxgo/subscription"
)

// Exec connects rxgo and returns
// our results side-effect + a subscription
// channel to block on at the end
func Exec() (Results, <-chan subscription.Subscription) {
    results := make(Results)
    watcher := observer.Observer{
        NextHandler: func(item interface{}) {
            wine, ok := item.(Wine)
            if ok {
                result := results[wine.Age]
                result.SumRating += wine.Rating
                result.NumSamples++
                results[wine.Age] = result
            }
        },
    }
    wine := GetWine()
    it, _ := iterable.New(wine)
```

```
        source := observable.From(it)
        sub := source.Subscribe(watcher)

        return results, sub
    }
```

5. Create a new directory named `example` and navigate to it.

6. Create a file named `main.go` with the following content. Ensure that you modify the `reactive` import to use the path you set up in step 2:

```
package main

import (
    "fmt"

    "github.com/agtorre/go-cookbook/chapter11/reactive"
)

func main() {
    results, sub := reactive.Exec()

    // wait for the channel to emit a Subscription
    <-sub

    // process results
    for key, val := range results {
        fmt.Printf("Age: %d, Sample Size: %d, Average Rating:
        %.2f\n", key, val.NumSamples,
        val.SumRating/float64(val.NumSamples))
    }
}
```

7. Run `go run main.go`.

8. You may also run the following command:

```
go build
./example
```

You should now see the following:

```
$ go run main.go
Age: 2011, Sample Size: 1, Average Rating: 3.00
Age: 2010, Sample Size: 2, Average Rating: 3.50
Age: 2009, Sample Size: 1, Average Rating: 4.50
```

9. If you copied or wrote your own tests, go up one directory and run `go test`. Ensure that all the tests pass.

## How it works...

RxGo works by abstracting a source stream, which can be an array or a channel, allowing you to aggregate streams, and finally creating observers that handle events. These can handle errors or data. RxGo uses an `interface{}` type for its argument so that you can pass in arbitrary values. As a result, you must use reflection in order to convert incoming data to its correct type. This can be tricky if you need to return errors on your observers. In addition, the added reflection can be costly in terms of performance.

Lastly, you must modify some shared state, either global or within a local closure, which will be used at the end. In our case, we have a `Results` type, which is a map with a key of the year and the value of the aggregate score and number of samples. This allows us to emit averages about each year. If we had used wine names instead of types, we could also aggregate by types. This library is still in its early stages. In many ways, you can achieve the same effect using basic Go channels. It helps to illustrate how some of these ideas may translate to Go.

## Using Kafka with Sarama

Kafka is a popular distributed message queue with a lot of advanced functions for building distributed systems. This recipe will show how to write to a Kafka topic using a synchronous producer and how to consume the same topic using a partition consumer. This recipe will not explore different configurations of Kafka as that is a much wider topic, but I suggest beginning at `https://kafka.apache.org/intro`.

## Getting ready

Configure your environment according to these steps:

1. Refer to the *Getting ready* section of the *Goflow for dataflow programming* recipe in this chapter.
2. Install Kafka using the steps mentioned at `https://www.tutorialspoint.com/apache_kafka/apache_kafka_installation_steps.htm`.
3. Alternatively, you can also access `https://github.com/spotify/docker-kafka`.
4. Run the `go get gopkg.in/Shopify/sarama.v1` command.

# How to do it...

These steps cover writing and running your application:

1. From your terminal/console application, create the `chapter11/synckafka` directory and navigate to it.
2. Copy tests from `https://github.com/agtorre/go-cookbook/tree/master/chapter11/synckafka`or use this as an exercise to write some of your own.
3. Ensure that Kafka is up and running on `localhost:9092`.
4. Create a file called `main.go` in a directory named `consumer` with the following content:

```go
package main

import (
    "log"

    sarama "gopkg.in/Shopify/sarama.v1"
)

func main() {
    consumer, err :=
    sarama.NewConsumer([]string{"localhost:9092"}, nil)
    if err != nil {
        panic(err)
    }
    defer consumer.Close()

    partitionConsumer, err :=
    consumer.ConsumePartition("example", 0,
     sarama.OffsetNewest)
    if err != nil {
        panic(err)
    }
    defer partitionConsumer.Close()

    for {
        msg := <-partitionConsumer.Messages()
        log.Printf("Consumed message: \"%s\" at offset: %d\n",
        msg.Value, msg.Offset)
    }
}
```

5. Create a file called `main.go` in a directory named `producer` with the following content:

```go
package main

import (

    "fmt"
    "log"

    sarama "gopkg.in/Shopify/sarama.v1"
)

func sendMessage(producer sarama.SyncProducer, value string) {
    msg := &sarama.ProducerMessage{Topic: "example", Value:
    sarama.StringEncoder(value)}
    partition, offset, err := producer.SendMessage(msg)
    if err != nil {

        log.Printf("FAILED to send message: %s\n", err)
        return
    }
    log.Printf("> message sent to partition %d at offset %d\n",
    partition, offset)
}

func main() {
    producer, err :=
    sarama.NewSyncProducer([]string{"localhost:9092"}, nil)
    if err != nil {
        panic(err)
    }
    defer producer.Close()

    for i := 0; i < 10; i++ {
        sendMessage(producer, fmt.Sprintf("Message %d", i))
    }
}
```

6. Run `go run consumer/main.go`.

7. In a separate terminal, run `go run producer/main.go`.

8. In the producer terminal, you should see the following:

```
$ go run producer/main.go
2017/05/07 11:50:38 > message sent to partition 0 at offset 0
2017/05/07 11:50:38 > message sent to partition 0 at offset 1
2017/05/07 11:50:38 > message sent to partition 0 at offset 2
```

```
2017/05/07 11:50:38 > message sent to partition 0 at offset 3
2017/05/07 11:50:38 > message sent to partition 0 at offset 4
2017/05/07 11:50:38 > message sent to partition 0 at offset 5
2017/05/07 11:50:38 > message sent to partition 0 at offset 6
2017/05/07 11:50:38 > message sent to partition 0 at offset 7
2017/05/07 11:50:38 > message sent to partition 0 at offset 8
2017/05/07 11:50:38 > message sent to partition 0 at offset 9
```

9. In the consumer terminal, you should see this:

```
$ go run consumer/main.go
2017/05/07 11:50:38 Consumed message: "Message 0" at offset: 0
2017/05/07 11:50:38 Consumed message: "Message 1" at offset: 1
2017/05/07 11:50:38 Consumed message: "Message 2" at offset: 2
2017/05/07 11:50:38 Consumed message: "Message 3" at offset: 3
2017/05/07 11:50:38 Consumed message: "Message 4" at offset: 4
2017/05/07 11:50:38 Consumed message: "Message 5" at offset: 5
2017/05/07 11:50:38 Consumed message: "Message 6" at offset: 6
2017/05/07 11:50:38 Consumed message: "Message 7" at offset: 7
2017/05/07 11:50:38 Consumed message: "Message 8" at offset: 8
2017/05/07 11:50:38 Consumed message: "Message 9" at offset: 9
```

10. If you copied or wrote your own tests, go up one directory and run `go test`. Ensure all tests pass.

# How it works...

This recipe demonstrates passing simple messages via Kafka. More complex methods should use a serialization format such as `json`, `gob`, `protobuf`, or others. The producer can send a message to Kafka synchronously through `sendMessage`. This does not the handle cases well where the Kafka cluster is down and may result in a hung process for these cases. This is important to consider for applications such as web handlers as it may result in timeouts and hard dependencies on the Kafka cluster.

Assuming the message queues correctly, our consumer will observe the Kafka stream and do something with the results. Previous recipes in this chapter might make use of this stream to do some additional processing.

# Using async producers with Kafka

It's often useful to not wait for a Kafka producer to complete before moving on to the next task. In cases like this, you can use an async producer. These producers take Sarama messages on a channel and have methods to return a success/error channel that can be checked separately.

In this recipe, we'll create a go routine that will handle success and failure messages while we allow a handler to queue messages to send regardless of the result.

## Getting ready

Refer to the *Getting ready* section of the *Using Kafka with Sarama* recipe.

## How to do it...

These steps cover writing and running your application:

1. From your terminal/console application, create the `chapter11/asyncsarama` directory and navigate to it.
2. Copy tests from `https://github.com/agtorre/go-cookbook/tree/master/chapter11/asyncsarama`or use this as an exercise to write some of your own.
3. Ensure that Kafka is up and running on `localhost:9092`.
4. Copy the consumer directory from the previous recipe.
5. Create a directory named `producer` and navigate to it.
6. Create a file called `producer.go`:

```go
package main

import (
    "log"

    sarama "gopkg.in/Shopify/sarama.v1"
)

// Process response grabs results and errors from a producer
// asynchronously
func ProcessResponse(producer sarama.AsyncProducer) {
    for {
        select {
            case result := <-producer.Successes():
```

```
                              log.Printf("> message: \"%s\" sent to partition
                              %d at offset %d\n", result.Value,
                              result.Partition, result.Offset)
                              case err := <-producer.Errors():
                              log.Println("Failed to produce message", err)
                }
        }
    }
```

7. Create a file called `handler.go`:

```
package main

import (
    "net/http"

    sarama "gopkg.in/Shopify/sarama.v1"
)

// KafkaController allows us to attach a producer
// to our handlers
type KafkaController struct {
    producer sarama.AsyncProducer
}

// Handler grabs a message from a GET parama and
// send it to the kafka queue asynchronously
func (c *KafkaController) Handler(w http.ResponseWriter, r
*http.Request) {
    if err := r.ParseForm(); err != nil {
        w.WriteHeader(http.StatusBadRequest)
        return
    }

    msg := r.FormValue("msg")
    if msg == "" {
        w.WriteHeader(http.StatusBadRequest)
        w.Write([]byte("msg must be set"))
        return
    }
    c.producer.Input() <- &sarama.ProducerMessage{Topic:
    "example", Key: nil, Value:
    sarama.StringEncoder(r.FormValue("msg"))}
    w.WriteHeader(http.StatusOK)
}
```

8. Create a file called `main.go`:

```
package main

import (
    "fmt"
    "net/http"

    sarama "gopkg.in/Shopify/sarama.v1"
)

func main() {
    config := sarama.NewConfig()
    config.Producer.Return.Successes = true
    config.Producer.Return.Errors = true
    producer, err :=
    sarama.NewAsyncProducer([]string{"localhost:9092"}, config)
    if err != nil {
        panic(err)
    }
    defer producer.AsyncClose()

    go ProcessResponse(producer)

    c := KafkaController{producer}
    http.HandleFunc("/", c.Handler)
    fmt.Println("Listening on port :3333")
    panic(http.ListenAndServe(":3333", nil))
}
```

9. Run the `go build` command.
10. Navigate up a directory.
11. Run `go run consumer/main.go`.
12. In a separate terminal from the same directory, run `./producer/producer`.
13. In a third terminal, run the following commands:

```
$ curl "http://localhost:3333/?msg=this"
$ curl "http://localhost:3333/?msg=is"
$ curl "http://localhost:3333/?msg=an"
$ curl "http://localhost:3333/?msg=example"
```

In the producer terminal, you should see the following:

```
$ ./producer/producer
Listening on port :3333
2017/05/07 13:52:54 > message: "this" sent to partition 0 at
```

```
offset 0
2017/05/07 13:53:25 > message: "is" sent to partition 0 at offset
1
2017/05/07 13:53:27 > message: "an" sent to partition 0 at offset
2
2017/05/07 13:53:29 > message: "example" sent to partition 0 at
offset 3
```

14. In the consumer terminal, you should see this:

```
$ go run consumer/main.go
2017/05/07 13:52:54 Consumed message: "this" at offset: 0
2017/05/07 13:53:25 Consumed message: "is" at offset: 1
2017/05/07 13:53:27 Consumed message: "an" at offset: 2
2017/05/07 13:53:29 Consumed message: "example" at offset: 3
```

15. If you copied or wrote your own tests, go up one directory and run `go test`. Ensure all tests pass.

# How it works...

Our modifications in this chapter were all made to the producer. This time, we created a separate go routine to handle successes and errors. If these are left unhandled, your application will deadlock. Next, we attached our producer to a handler and we emit messages on it whenever a message is received via a `GET` call to the handler.

The handler will immediately return success upon sending the message regardless of its response. If this is not acceptable, a synchronous approach should be used instead. In our case, we're okay with later processing success and errors separately.

Lastly, we curl our endpoint with a few different messages and you can see them flow from the handler to where they're eventually printed by the Kafka consumer we wrote in the previous section.

# Connecting Kafka to Goflow

This recipe will combine a Kafka consumer with a Goflow pipeline. As our consumer receives messages from Kafka, it will run `strings.ToUpper()` on them and then print the results. These naturally pair as Goflow is designed to operate on an incoming stream, which is exactly what Kafka provides us.

# Getting ready

Refer to the *Getting ready* section of the *Using Kafka with Sarama* recipe.

# How to do it...

These steps cover writing and running your application:

1. From your terminal/console application, create the `chapter11/kafkaflow` directory and navigate to it.
2. Copy tests from `https://github.com/agtorre/go-cookbook/tree/master/cha pter11/kafkaflow`or use this as an exercise to write some of your own.
3. Ensure that Kafka is up and running on `localhost:9092`.
4. Create a file called `components.go` with the following content:

```go
package kafkaflow

import (
    "fmt"
    "strings"

    flow "github.com/trustmaster/goflow"
)

// Upper upper cases the incoming
// stream
type Upper struct {
    flow.Component
    Val <-chan string
    Res chan<- string
}

// OnVal does the encoding then pushes the result onto Re
func (e *Upper) OnVal(val string) {
    e.Res <- strings.ToUpper(val)
}

// Printer is a component for printing to stdout
type Printer struct {
    flow.Component
    Line <-chan string
}

// OnLine Prints the current line received
```

```
func (p *Printer) OnLine(line string) {
    fmt.Println(line)
}
```

5. Create a file called `network.go` with the following content:

```
package kafkaflow

import flow "github.com/trustmaster/goflow"

// UpperApp creates a flow-based
// pipeline to upper case and print the
// result
type UpperApp struct {
    flow.Graph
}

// NewUpperApp wires together the compoents
func NewUpperApp() *UpperApp {
    u := &UpperApp{}
    u.InitGraphState()

    u.Add(&Upper{}, "upper")
    u.Add(&Printer{}, "printer")

    u.Connect("upper", "Res", "printer", "Line")
    u.MapInPort("In", "upper", "Val")

    return u
}
```

6. Create a file called `main.go` in a directory named `consumer` with the following content:

```
package main

import (
    "github.com/agtorre/go-cookbook/chapter11/kafkaflow"
    flow "github.com/trustmaster/goflow"
    sarama "gopkg.in/Shopify/sarama.v1"
)

func main() {
    consumer, err :=
    sarama.NewConsumer([]string{"localhost:9092"}, nil)
    if err != nil {
        panic(err)
    }
```

```
    defer consumer.Close()

    partitionConsumer, err :=
    consumer.ConsumePartition("example", 0,
    sarama.OffsetNewest)
    if err != nil {
        panic(err)
    }
    defer partitionConsumer.Close()

    net := kafkaflow.NewUpperApp()

    in := make(chan string)
    net.SetInPort("In", in)

    flow.RunNet(net)
    defer func() {
        close(in)
        <-net.Wait()
    }()

    for {
        msg := <-partitionConsumer.Messages()
        in <- string(msg.Value)
    }
}
```

7. Copy the consumer directory from the *Using Kafka with Saram* recipe.
8. Run `go run consumer/main.go`.
9. In a separate terminal, run `go run producer/main.go`.
10. In the producer terminal, you should now see the following:

```
$ go run producer/main.go
go run producer/main.go !3300
2017/05/07 18:24:12 > message "Message 0" sent to partition 0 at
offset 0
2017/05/07 18:24:12 > message "Message 1" sent to partition 0 at
offset 1
2017/05/07 18:24:12 > message "Message 2" sent to partition 0 at
offset 2
2017/05/07 18:24:12 > message "Message 3" sent to partition 0 at
offset 3
2017/05/07 18:24:12 > message "Message 4" sent to partition 0 at
offset 4
2017/05/07 18:24:12 > message "Message 5" sent to partition 0 at
offset 5
2017/05/07 18:24:12 > message "Message 6" sent to partition 0 at
```

```
offset 6
2017/05/07 18:24:12 > message "Message 7" sent to partition 0 at
offset 7
2017/05/07 18:24:12 > message "Message 8" sent to partition 0 at
offset 8
2017/05/07 18:24:12 > message "Message 9" sent to partition 0 at
offset 9
```

In the consumer terminal, you should see the following:

```
$ go run consumer/main.go
MESSAGE 0
MESSAGE 1
MESSAGE 2
MESSAGE 3
MESSAGE 4
MESSAGE 5
MESSAGE 6
MESSAGE 7
MESSAGE 8
MESSAGE 9
```

11. If you copied or wrote your own tests, go up one directory and run `go test`. Ensure that all the tests pass.

# How it works...

This recipe combines ideas from previous recipes in this chapter. Like previous recipes, we set up a Kafka consumer and producer. This recipe uses the synchronous producer from the *Using Kafka With Sarama* recipe, but could have also used an asynchronous producer instead. Once a message is received, we enqueue it on an in channel just like we did in the *Goflow for dataflow programming* recipe. We modify the components from this recipe to uppercase our incoming string rather than base64 encoding it. We reuse the print components and the resultant network configuration is similar.

The end result is that all messages received through the Kafka consumer are transported into our flow-based work pipeline to be operated on. This allows us to instrument our pipeline components to be modular and reusable, and we can use the same component multiple times in different configurations. Similarly, we'll receive traffic from any producer that writes to Kafka, so we can multiplex producers into a single data stream.

# Writing a GraphQL server in Go

GraphQL is an alternative to REST, created by Facebook (http://graphql.org/). This technology allows a server to implement and publish a schema and the clients then can ask for the information they need rather than understanding and making use of various API endpoints.

For this recipe, we'll create a `Graphql` schema that represents a deck of playing cards. We'll expose one resource card, which can be filtered by suit and value. Alternatively, it can return all the cards in the deck if no arguments are specified.

## Getting ready

Configure your environment according to these steps:

1. Refer to the *Getting ready* section of the *Goflow for dataflow programming* recipe in this chapter.
2. Run the `go get github.com/graphql-go/graphql` command.

## How to do it...

These steps cover writing and running your application:

1. From your terminal/console application, create the `chapter11/graphql` directory and navigate to it.
2. Copy tests from https://github.com/agtorre/go-cookbook/tree/master/chapter11/graphql or use this as an exercise to write some of your own.
3. Create and navigate to the `cards` directory.
4. Create a file called `card.go` with the following content:

```
package cards

// Card represents a standard playing
// card
type Card struct {
    Value string
    Suit string
}

var cards []Card
```

```
func init() {
    cards = []Card{
        {"A", "Spades"}, {"2", "Spades"}, {"3", "Spades"},
        {"4", "Spades"}, {"5", "Spades"}, {"6", "Spades"},
        {"7", "Spades"}, {"8", "Spades"}, {"9", "Spades"},
        {"10", "Spades"}, {"J", "Spades"}, {"Q", "Spades"},
        {"K", "Spades"},
        {"A", "Hearts"}, {"2", "Hearts"}, {"3", "Hearts"},
        {"4", "Hearts"}, {"5", "Hearts"}, {"6", "Hearts"},
        {"7", "Hearts"}, {"8", "Hearts"}, {"9", "Hearts"},
        {"10", "Hearts"}, {"J", "Hearts"}, {"Q", "Hearts"},
        {"K", "Hearts"},
        {"A", "Clubs"}, {"2", "Clubs"}, {"3", "Clubs"},
        {"4", "Clubs"}, {"5", "Clubs"}, {"6", "Clubs"},
        {"7", "Clubs"}, {"8", "Clubs"}, {"9", "Clubs"},
        {"10", "Clubs"}, {"J", "Clubs"}, {"Q", "Clubs"},
        {"K", "Clubs"},
        {"A", "Diamonds"}, {"2", "Diamonds"}, {"3",
        "Diamonds"},
        {"4", "Diamonds"}, {"5", "Diamonds"}, {"6",
        "Diamonds"},
        {"7", "Diamonds"}, {"8", "Diamonds"}, {"9",
        "Diamonds"},
        {"10", "Diamonds"}, {"J", "Diamonds"}, {"Q",
        "Diamonds"},
        {"K", "Diamonds"},
    }
}
```

5. Create a file called `type.go`:

```
package cards

import "github.com/graphql-go/graphql"

// CardType returns our card graphql object
func CardType() *graphql.Object {
    cardType := graphql.NewObject(graphql.ObjectConfig{
        Name: "Card",
        Description: "A Playing Card",
        Fields: graphql.Fields{
            "value": &graphql.Field{
                Type: graphql.String,
                Description: "Ace through King",
                Resolve: func(p graphql.ResolveParams)
                (interface{}, error) {
                    if card, ok := p.Source.(Card); ok {
                        return card.Value, nil
```

```
                }
                return nil, nil
            },
        },
        "suit": &graphql.Field{
            Type: graphql.String,
            Description: "Hearts, Diamonds, Clubs, Spades",
            Resolve: func(p graphql.ResolveParams)
            (interface{}, error) {
                if card, ok := p.Source.(Card); ok {
                    return card.Suit, nil
                }
                return nil, nil
            },
        },
    },
})
    return cardType
}
```

6. Create a file called `resolve.go`:

```
package cards

import (
    "strings"

    "github.com/graphql-go/graphql"
)

// Resolve handles filtering cards
// by suit and value
func Resolve(p graphql.ResolveParams) (interface{}, error) {
    finalCards := []Card{}
    suit, suitOK := p.Args["suit"].(string)
    suit = strings.ToLower(suit)

    value, valueOK := p.Args["value"].(string)
    value = strings.ToLower(value)

    for _, card := range cards {
        if suitOK && suit != strings.ToLower(card.Suit) {
            continue
        }
        if valueOK && value != strings.ToLower(card.Value) {
            continue
        }
```

```
                finalCards = append(finalCards, card)
            }
            return finalCards, nil
        }
```

7. Create a file called `schema.go`:

```
package cards

import "github.com/graphql-go/graphql"

// Setup prepares and returns our card
// schema
func Setup() (graphql.Schema, error) {
    cardType := CardType()

    // Schema
    fields := graphql.Fields{
        "cards": &graphql.Field{
            Type: graphql.NewList(cardType),
            Args: graphql.FieldConfigArgument{
                "suit": &graphql.ArgumentConfig{
                    Description: "Filter cards by card suit
                    (hearts, clubs, diamonds, spades)",
                    Type: graphql.String,
                },
                "value": &graphql.ArgumentConfig{
                    Description: "Filter cards by card
                    value (A-K)",
                    Type: graphql.String,
                },
            },
            Resolve: Resolve,
        },
    }

    rootQuery := graphql.ObjectConfig{Name: "RootQuery",
    Fields: fields}
    schemaConfig := graphql.SchemaConfig{Query:
    graphql.NewObject(rootQuery)}
    schema, err := graphql.NewSchema(schemaConfig)

    return schema, err
}
```

8. Navigate back to the `graphql` directory.

9. Create a new directory named `example` and navigate to it.

10. Create a file named `main.go` with the following content. Ensure that you modify the `cards` import to use the path you set up in step 2:

```
package main

import (
    "encoding/json"
    "fmt"
    "log"

    "github.com/agtorre/go-cookbook/chapter11/graphql/cards"
    "github.com/graphql-go/graphql"
)

func main() {
    // grab our schema
    schema, err := cards.Setup()
    if err != nil {
        panic(err)
    }

    // Query
    query := `
    {
        cards(value: "A"){
            value
            suit
        }
    }
    `

    params := graphql.Params{Schema: schema, RequestString:
    query}
    r := graphql.Do(params)
    if len(r.Errors) > 0 {
        log.Fatalf("failed to execute graphql operation,
        errors: %+v", r.Errors)
    }
    rJSON, err := json.MarshalIndent(r, "", "  ")
    if err != nil {
        panic(err)
    }
    fmt.Printf("%s \n", rJSON)
}
```

11. Run `go run main.go`.

12. You may also run the following command:

```
go build
./example
```

You should see the following output:

```
$ go run main.go
{
    "data": {
        "cards": [
            {
                "suit": "Spades",
                "value": "A"
            },
            {
                "suit": "Hearts",
                "value": "A"
            },
            {
                "suit": "Clubs",
                "value": "A"
            },
            {
                "suit": "Diamonds",
                "value": "A"
            }
        ]
    }
}
```

13. Test some additional queries, such as the following:
    - `cards(suit: "Spades")`
    - `cards(value: "3", suit:"Diamonds")`

14. If you copied or wrote your own tests, go up one directory and run `go test`. Ensure that all the tests pass.

# How it works...

The `cards.go` file defines a `card` object and initializes the base deck in a global variable called cards. This state could also be held in long-term storage such as a database. We then define `CardType` in `types.go` that allows `graphql` to resolve card objects to responses. Next, we jump into `resolve.go`, where we define how to filter cards by value and type. This `Resolve` function will be used by the final schema, which is defined in `schema.go`.

For example, you would modify the `Resolve` function in this recipe in order to retrieve data from a database. Lastly, we load the schema and run a query against it. It's a small modification to mount our schema onto a rest endpoint, but for brevity, this recipe just runs a hardcoded query. For more information about `GraphQL` queries, visit `http://graphql.org/learn/queries/`.

# 12
# Serverless Programming

In this chapter, we will cover the following recipes:

- Go programming on Lambda with Apex
- Apex serverless logging and metrics
- Google App Engine with Go
- Working with Firebase using zabawaba99/firego

## Introduction

This chapter will focus on serverless architectures and using them with the Go language. It will also explore app engine and Firebase, two services to quickly deploy applications and data storage to the web.

All of the recipes in this chapter deal with third-party services that bill for use; ensure that you clean up when you're done using them. Otherwise, think of these recipes as kick-starters for spinning up larger applications on these platforms.

## Go programming on Lambda with Apex

Apex is a tool for building, deploying, and managing AWS Lambda functions. It provides wrappers for Go (using a `Node.js` shim). Currently, there is not a way to run native Go code on Lambda without such a shim. This recipe will explore creating Go Lambda functions and deploying them with Apex.

# Getting ready

Configure your environment according to these steps:

1. Download and install Go on your operating system (`https://golang.org/doc/install`) and configure your `GOPATH` environment variable.
2. Open a terminal/console application.
3. Navigate to your `GOPATH/src` directory and create a project directory, for example, `$GOPATH/src/github.com/yourusername/customrepo`. All code will be run and modified from this directory.
4. Optionally, install the latest tested version of the code using the

   `go get github.com/agtorre/go-cookbook/...` command.
5. Install Apex from `http://apex.run/`.
6. Run the `go get github.com/apex/go-apex` command.

# How to do it...

These steps cover writing and running your application:

1. From your terminal/console application, create the `chapter12/lambda` directory and navigate to it.
2. Create an Amazon account and an IAM role that can edit Lambda functions, which can be done from `https://aws.amazon.com/lambda/`.
3. Create a file called `~/.aws/credentials` with the following content, copying your credentials from what you set up in the Amazon console:

   ```
   [example]
   aws_access_key_id = xxxxxxxx
   aws_secret_access_key = xxxxxxxxxxxxxxxxxxxxxxxx
   ```

4. Create an environment variable to hold your desired region:

   ```
   export AWS_REGION=us-west-2
   ```

5. Run the `apex init` command and follow the onscreen instructions:

   ```
   $ apex init
   ```

```
Enter the name of your project. It should be machine-friendly,
as this is used to prefix your functions in Lambda.

Project name: go-cookbook

Enter an optional description of your project.

Project description: Demonstrating Apex with the Go Cookbook

[+] creating IAM go-cookbook_lambda_function role
[+] creating IAM go-cookbook_lambda_logs policy
[+] attaching policy to lambda_function role.
[+] creating ./project.json
[+] creating ./functions

Setup complete, deploy those functions!

$ apex deploy
```

6. Remove the `lambda/functions/hello` directory.
7. Create a new `lambda/functions/greeter/main.go` file with the following content:

```go
package main

import (
    "encoding/json"
    "fmt"

    "github.com/apex/go-apex"
)

type message struct {
    Name string `json:"name"`
}

func main() {
    apex.HandleFunc(func(event json.RawMessage, ctx
    *apex.Context) (interface{}, error) {
        var m message
        if err := json.Unmarshal(event, &m); err != nil {
            return nil, err
        }

        resp := map[string]string{
            "greeting": fmt.Sprintf("Hello, %s", m.Name),
        }
```

```
        return resp, nil
    })
}
```

8. To test your function, you can run the following:

```
$ echo '{"event":{"name": "test"}}' | go run
functions/greeter1/main.go

{"value":{"greeting":"Hello, test"}}
```

9. Deploy it to your specified region:

```
$apex deploy
• creating function env= function=greeter
• created alias current env= function=greeter version=1
• function created env= function=greeter name=go-
  cookbook_greeter1 version=1
```

10. To invoke it, run the following command:

```
$ echo '{"name": "test"}' | apex invoke greeter
{"greeting":"Hello, test"}
```

11. Now modify lambda/functions/greeter/main.go:

```
package main

import (
    "encoding/json"
    "fmt"

    "github.com/apex/go-apex"
)

type message struct {
    FirstName string `json:"first_name"`
    LastName string `json:"last_name"`
}

func main() {
    apex.HandleFunc(func(event json.RawMessage, ctx
    *apex.Context) (interface{}, error) {
        var m message
        if err := json.Unmarshal(event, &m); err != nil {
            return nil, err
        }
```

```
        resp := map[string]string{
            "greeting": fmt.Sprintf("Hello, %s %s",
            m.FirstName, m.LastName),
        }

        return resp, nil
    })
}
```

12. Redeploy, creating version 2:

```
$ apex deploy
• creating function env= function=greeter
• created alias current env= function=greeter version=2
• function created env= function=greeter name=go-
  cookbook_greeter1 version=2
```

13. Invoke the newly deployed function:

```
$ echo '{"first_name": "Go", "last_name": "Coders"}' | apex
invoke greeter2
{"greeting":"Hello, Go Coders"}
```

14. Take a look at the logs:

```
$ apex logs greeter
apex logs greeter
/aws/lambda/go-cookbook_greeter START RequestId: 7c0f9129-3830-
11e7-8755-75aeb52a51b9 Version: 2
/aws/lambda/go-cookbook_greeter END RequestId: 7c0f9129-3830-
11e7-8755-75aeb52a51b9
/aws/lambda/go-cookbook_greeter REPORT RequestId: 7c0f9129-3830-
11e7-8755-75aeb52a51b9 Duration: 93.84 ms Billed Duration: 100 ms
Memory Size: 128 MB Max Memory Used: 19 MB
```

15. Clean up the deployed services:

```
$ apex delete
The following will be deleted:

- greeter

Are you sure? (yes/no) yes
• deleting env= function=greeter
• function deleted env= function=greeter
```

# How it works...

AWS Lambda makes it easy to run functions on demand without maintaining a server. Apex provides facilities for deploying, versioning, and testing functions as you ship them to Lambda. It also provides a shim that allows us to execute arbitrary Go code. This is accomplished by defining a handler, processing incoming request payloads, and returning a response, which is a very similar flow to a standard web handler.

In this recipe, we initially took a name input and greeted that name. Later, we split the name into a first and last name, taking advantage of versioning. It would also be possible to deploy a separate function instead. It's possible to roll back with `apex rollback greeter` as well.

# Apex serverless logging and metrics

When working with serverless functions such as Lambda, it is valuable to have portable, structured logs. In addition, you can combine earlier recipes dealing with logging to this recipe. The recipes covered in `Chapter 4`, *Error Handling in Go*, are just as relevant. Because we're using Apex to handle our lambda functions, we chose to use the Apex logger for this recipe. We'll also rely on metrics provided by Apex as well as the AWS console. The earlier recipes explored more complex logging and metrics examples, and those still apply--the Apex logger can easily be configured to aggregate logs using something like Amazon Kinesis or Elasticsearch.

# Getting ready

Configure your environment according to these steps:

1. Refer to the *Getting ready* section of the *Go programming on Lambda with Apex* recipe in this chapter.
2. Run the `go get github.com/apex/log` command.

# How to do it...

These steps cover writing and running your application:

1. From your terminal/console application, create the `chapter12/logging` directory and navigate to it.

2. Create an Amazon account and an IAM role that can edit lambda functions, which can be done at https://aws.amazon.com/lambda/.

3. Create a ~/.aws/credentials file with the following content, copying your credentials from what you set up in the Amazon console:

```
[example]
aws_access_key_id = xxxxxxxx
aws_secret_access_key = xxxxxxxxxxxxxxxxxxxxxxxxx
```

4. Create an environment variable to hold your desired region:

```
export AWS_REGION=us-west-2
```

5. Run the apex init command and follow the onscreen instructions:

```
$ apex init

Enter the name of your project. It should be machine-friendly, as
this is used to prefix your functions in Lambda.

Project name: logging

Enter an optional description of your project.

Project description: An example of apex logging and metrics

[+] creating IAM logging_lambda_function role
[+] creating IAM logging_lambda_logs policy
[+] attaching policy to lambda_function role.
[+] creating ./project.json
[+] creating ./functions

Setup complete, deploy those functions!

$ apex deploy
```

6. Remove the lambda/functions/hello directory.

7. Create a new lambda/functions/secret/main.go file with the following content:

```go
package main

import (
    "encoding/json"
    "os"
```

```
        "github.com/apex/go-apex"
        "github.com/apex/log"
        "github.com/apex/log/handlers/text"
    )

    // Input takes in a secret
    type Input struct {
        Secret string `json:"secret"`
    }

    func main() {
        apex.HandleFunc(func(event json.RawMessage, ctx
        *apex.Context) (interface{}, error) {
            log.SetHandler(text.New(os.Stderr))

            var input Input
            if err := json.Unmarshal(event, &input); err != nil {
                log.WithError(err).Error("failed to unmarshal key
                input")
                return nil, err
            }
            log.WithField("secret", input.Secret).Info("secret
            guessed")

            if input.Secret == "klaatu barada nikto" {
                return "secret guessed!", nil
            }
            return "try again", nil
        })
    }
```

8. Deploy it to your specified region:

```
$ apex deploy
• creating function env= function=secret
• created alias current env= function=secret version=1
• function created env= function=secret name=logging_secret
  version=1
```

9. To invoke it, run the following command:

```
$ echo '{"secret": "open sesame"}' | apex invoke secret
"try again"

$ echo '{"secret": "open sesame"}' | apex invoke secret
"secret guessed!"
```

10. Check the logs:

```
$ apex logs secret
/aws/lambda/logging_secret START RequestId: cfa6f655-3834-11e7-
b99d-89998a7f39dd Version: 1
/aws/lambda/logging_secret INFO[0000] secret guessed secret=open
sesame
/aws/lambda/logging_secret END RequestId: cfa6f655-3834-11e7-
b99d-89998a7f39dd
/aws/lambda/logging_secret REPORT RequestId: cfa6f655-3834-11e7-
b99d-89998a7f39dd Duration: 52.23 ms Billed Duration: 100 ms
Memory Size: 128 MB Max Memory Used: 19 MB
/aws/lambda/logging_secret START RequestId: d74ea688-3834-11e7-
aa4e-d592c1fbc35f Version: 1
/aws/lambda/logging_secret INFO[0012] secret guessed
secret=klaatu barada nikto
/aws/lambda/logging_secret END RequestId: d74ea688-3834-11e7-
aa4e-d592c1fbc35f
/aws/lambda/logging_secret REPORT RequestId: d74ea688-3834-11e7-
aa4e-d592c1fbc35f Duration: 7.43 ms Billed Duration: 100 ms
Memory Size: 128 MB Max Memory Used: 19 MB
```

11. Check your metrics:

```
$ apex metrics secret !3445

secret
total cost: $0.00
invocations: 0 ($0.00)
duration: 0s ($0.00)
throttles: 0
errors: 0
memory: 128
```

12. Clean up the deployed services:

```
$ apex delete
Are you sure? (yes/no) yes
• deleting env= function=secret
• function deleted env= function=secret
```

# How it works...

In this recipe, we created a new lambda function, secret, that will respond with whether or not you guessed a secret phrase. The function parses an incoming JSON request, performs some logging using Stderr, and returns a response.

After using the function a few times, we see that our logs are visible using the `apex logs` command. This command can be run on a single lambda function or across all of our managed functions. This is especially useful if you are chaining Apex commands together and want to watch logs across many services.

In addition, we show how to use the apex metrics command to collect general metrics about your application, including cost and invocations. You can also see a lot of this information directly in the AWS console in the Lambda section. Like other recipes, we try and clean up after ourselves at the end.

# Google App Engine with Go

App Engine is a Google service that facilitates the quick deployment of web applications. These applications have access to cloud storage and various other Google APIs. The general idea is that App Engine will scale easily with load and simplify any operations management associated with hosting an app. This recipe will show how to create and optionally deploy a basic App Engine application. This recipe won't get into the details of setting up a Google cloud account, setting up billing, or the specifics on cleaning up your instance. At a minimum, access to Google Cloud Datastore (`https://cloud.google.com/datastore/doc s/concepts/overview`) is required for this recipe to work.

# Getting ready

Configure your environment according to these steps:

1. Download and install Go on your operating system from `https://golang.org/d oc/install` and configure your `GOPATH` environment variable.
2. Open a terminal/console application.
3. Navigate to your `GOPATH/src` and create a project directory, for example, `$GOPATH/src/github.com/yourusername/customrepo`. All code will be run and modified from this directory.
4. Optionally, install the latest tested version of the code using the `go get github.com/agtorre/go-cookbook/...` command.
5. Download the Google Cloud SDK from `https://cloud.google.com/appengine /docs/flexible/go/quickstart`.
6. Create an app that allows for deploying and datastore access and record the app name.
7. Run the `go get cloud.google.com/go/datastore` command.

8. Run the `go get google.golang.org/appengine` command.

# How to do it...

These steps cover writing and running your application:

1. From your terminal/console application, create the `chapter12/appengine` directory and navigate to it.

2. Copy tests from `https://github.com/agtorre/go-cookbook/tree/master/chapter12/appengine` or use this as an exercise to write some of your own.

3. Create a file called `app.yml` with the following content, replacing `go-cookbook` with the name of the app you created in the *Getting ready* section:

```
runtime: go
env: flex

#[START env_variables]
env_variables:
    GCLOUD_DATASET_ID: go-cookbook
#[END env_variables]
```

4. Create a file called `message.go` with the following content:

```
package main

import (
    "context"
    "time"

    "cloud.google.com/go/datastore"
)

// Message is the object we store
type Message struct {
    Timestamp time.Time
    Message string
}

func (c *Controller) storeMessage(ctx context.Context, message string) error {
    m := &Message{
        Timestamp: time.Now(),
        Message: message,
```

```
    }

    k := datastore.IncompleteKey("Message", nil)
    _, err := c.store.Put(ctx, k, m)
    return err
}

func (c *Controller) queryMessages(ctx context.Context, limit
int) ([]*Message, error) {
    q := datastore.NewQuery("Message").
    Order("-Timestamp").
    Limit(limit)

    messages := make([]*Message, 0)
    _, err := c.store.GetAll(ctx, q, &messages)
    return messages, err
}
```

5.  Create a file called `controller.go` with the following content:

```
package main

import (
    "context"
    "fmt"
    "log"
    "net/http"

    "cloud.google.com/go/datastore"
)

// Controller holds our storage and other
// state
type Controller struct {
    store *datastore.Client
}

func (c *Controller) handle(w http.ResponseWriter, r
*http.Request) {
    if r.Method != http.MethodGet {
        http.Error(w, "invalid method",
        http.StatusMethodNotAllowed)
    }

    ctx := context.Background()

    // store the new message
    r.ParseForm()
```

```
if message := r.FormValue("message"); message != "" {
    if err := c.storeMessage(ctx, message); err != nil {
        log.Printf("could not store message: %v", err)
        http.Error(w, fmt.Sprintf("could not store
        message"),
        http.StatusInternalServerError)
        return
    }
}

// get the current messages and display them
fmt.Fprintln(w, "Messages:")
messages, err := c.queryMessages(ctx, 10)
if err != nil {
    log.Printf("could not get messages: %v", err)
    http.Error(w, "could not get messages",
    http.StatusInternalServerError)
    return
}

for _, message := range messages {
    fmt.Fprintln(w, message.Message)
}
}
```

6. Create a file `main.go` with the following content:

```
package main

import (
    "log"
    "net/http"
    "os"

    "cloud.google.com/go/datastore"
    "golang.org/x/net/context"
    "google.golang.org/appengine"
)

func main() {
    ctx := context.Background()
    log.SetOutput(os.Stderr)

    // Set this in app.yaml when running in production.
    projectID := os.Getenv("GCLOUD_DATASET_ID")

    datastoreClient, err := datastore.NewClient(ctx, projectID)
    if err != nil {
```

```
        log.Fatal(err)
    }

    c := Controller{datastoreClient}

    http.HandleFunc("/", c.handle)
    appengine.Main()
}
```

7. Run the `gcloud config set project go-cookbook` command, where `go-cookbook` is the project you created in the *Getting ready* section.
8. Run the `gcloud auth application-default login` command and follow the instructions.
9. Run the `export PORT=8080` command.
10. Run the `export GCLOUD_DATASET_ID=go-cookbook` command, where `go-cookbook` is the project you created in the *Getting ready* section.
11. Run the `go build` command.
12. Run the `./example` command.
13. Navigate to `http://localhost:8080/?message=hello%20there`.
14. Try a few more messages (`?message=other`)
15. Optionally, deploy the app to your instance with `gcloud app deploy`.
16. Navigate to the deployed app with `gcloud app browse`.
17. Clean up your appengine instance and datastore:
    - `https://console.cloud.google.com/datastore`
    - `https://console.cloud.google.com/appengine`
18. If you copied or wrote your own tests, run the `go test` command. Ensure that all the tests pass.

## How it works...

Once the cloud SDK is configured to point at your application and has been authenticated, the GCloud tool allows quick deployment and configuration, allowing local applications to access Google services.

After authenticating and setting the port, we run the application on localhost, and we can begin working with code. The application defines a message object that can be stored and retrieved from the datastore. This demonstrates how you might isolate this sort of code. You might also use a storage/database interface, as shown in earlier chapters.

Next, we set up a handler that attempts to insert a message into the datastore, then retrieves all messages, displaying them in a browser. This creates something resembling a basic guestbook. You may notice that the message does not always appear immediately. If you navigate without a message parameter or send another message, it should appear on a reload.

Lastly, ensure that you clean up instances if you're no longer using them.

# Working with Firebase using zabawaba99/firego

Firebase is another Google cloud service that creates a scalable, easy-to-manage database that can support authentication and works especially well with mobile applications. The service provides significantly more than what will be covered in this recipe, but we will look at storing data, reading it, modifying it, and restoring it. We'll also look into how to set up authentication for your application and wrap the Firebase client with our own custom client.

# Getting ready

Configure your environment according to these steps:

1. Download and install Go on your operating system from `https://golang.org/doc/install`and and configure your `GOPATH` environment variable.
2. Open a terminal/console application.
3. Navigate to your `GOPATH/src` and create a project directory, for example, `$GOPATH/src/github.com/yourusername/customrepo`. All code will be run and modified from this directory.
4. Optionally, install the latest tested version of the code using the `go get github.com/agtorre/go-cookbook/...` command.
5. Create an account and database at `https://console.firebase.google.com/`.
6. Generate a service admin token from `https://console.firebase.google.com/project/go-cookbook/settings/serviceaccounts/adminsdk`.
7. Move the downloaded token to `/tmp/service_account.json`.

# How to do it...

These steps cover writing and running your application:

1. From your terminal/console application, create the `chapter12/firebase` directory and navigate to it.

2. Copy tests from `https://github.com/agtorre/go-cookbook/tree/master/chapter12/firebase`or use this as an exercise to write some of your own.

3. Create a file called `client.go` with the following content:

```go
package firebase

import (
    "log"

    "gopkg.in/zabawaba99/firego.v1"
)

// Client Interface for mocking
type Client interface {
    Get() (map[string]interface{}, error)
    Set(key string, value interface{}) error
}
type firebaseClient struct {
    *firego.Firebase
}

func (f *firebaseClient) Get() (map[string]interface{}, error)
{
    var v2 map[string]interface{}
    if err := f.Value(&v2); err != nil {
        log.Fatalf("error getting")
    }
    return v2, nil
}

func (f *firebaseClient) Set(key string, value interface{})
error {
    v := map[string]interface{}{key: value}
    if err := f.Firebase.Set(v); err != nil {
        return err
    }
    return nil
}
```

4. Create a file called `auth.go` with the following contents. Tweak `https://go-coo kbook.firebaseio.com`to match whatever your apps, name is:

```go
package firebase

import (
    "io/ioutil"

    "golang.org/x/oauth2"
    "golang.org/x/oauth2/google"
    "gopkg.in/zabawaba99/firego.v1"
)

// Authenticate grabs oauth scopes using a generated
// service_account.json file from
// https://console.firebase.google.com/project/go-
cookbook/settings/serviceaccounts/adminsdk
func Authenticate() (Client, error) {
    d, err := ioutil.ReadFile("/tmp/service_account.json")
    if err != nil {
        return nil, err
    }

    conf, err := google.JWTConfigFromJSON(d,
    "https://www.googleapis.com/auth/userinfo.email",
    "https://www.googleapis.com/auth/firebase.database")
    if err != nil {
        return nil, err
    }
    f := firego.New("https://go-cookbook.firebaseio.com",
    conf.Client(oauth2.NoContext))
    return &firebaseClient{f}, err
}
```

5. Create a new directory named `example` and navigate to it.

6. Create a file named `main.go` with the following content. Ensure that you modify the `channels` import to use the path you set up in step 2:

```go
package main

import (
    "fmt"
    "log"

    "github.com/agtorre/go-cookbook/chapter12/firebase"
)
```

```
func main() {
    f, err := firebase.Authenticate()
    if err != nil {
        log.Fatalf("error authenticating")
    }
    f.Set("key", []string{"val1", "val2"})
    res, _ := f.Get()
    fmt.Println(res)

    vals := res["key"].([]interface{})
    vals = append(vals, map[string][]string{"key2":
    []string{"val3"}})
    f.Set("key", vals)
    res, _ = f.Get()
    fmt.Println(res)
}
```

7. Run `go run main.go`.

8. You may also run `go build ./example`.

You should now see the following output:

```
$ go run main.go
map[key:[val1 val2]]
map[key:[val1 val2 map[key2:[val3]]]]
```

9. If you copied or wrote your own tests, go up one directory and run `go test`. Ensure that all the tests pass.

# How it works...

Firebase uses OAuth2 for authentication. In this case, we downloaded a credentials file that can be used, along with a request for appropriate scopes, to return a token that may work with the Firebase database. We can store any sort of structured map-like object. In this case, we store `map[string]interface{}`.

The client code wraps all operations in an interface for ease of testing. This is a common pattern when writing client code and is also used in other recipes.

# 13
# Performance Improvements, Tips, and Tricks

In this chapter, we will cover the following recipes:

- Speeding up compilation and testing cycles
- Using the pprof tool
- Benchmarking and finding bottlenecks
- Memory allocation and heap management
- Vendoring and project layout
- Using fasthttprouter and fasthttp

## Introduction

This chapter will focus on optimizing an application, discovering bottlenecks, and vendoring dependencies. These are some tips and tricks that can be used immediately by existing applications. Many of these recipes are necessary if you or your organization require fully reproducible builds. They're also useful when you want to benchmark an applications' performance. The final recipe focuses on increasing the speed of HTTP, however, it's always important to remember that the web world moves quickly, and it's important to refresh yourself on best practices. For example, if you require HTTP/2, it is now available using the built-in Go `net/http` package since version 1.6.

# Speeding up compilation and testing cycles

There are a few reasons why an application might be slow to compile, and by extension, run tests against. Usually, this is a combination requiring the application to compile from scratch every time (no intermediate builds), large code bases, and many dependencies. This recipe will explore some tools that can be used to look at the current dependency lists and to speed up compilation.

## Getting ready

Configure your environment by performing the following steps:

1. Download and install Go on your operating system from `https://golang.org/doc/install` and configure your `GOPATH` environment variable.

2. Open a terminal/console application.

3. Navigate to your `GOPATH/src` directory and create a project directory, for example, `$GOPATH/src/github.com/yourusername/customrepo`.

   All code will be run and modified from this directory.

4. Optionally, install the latest tested version of the code using the `go get github.com/agtorre/go-cookbook/` command.

## How to do it...

These steps cover writing and running your application:

1. To demonstrate how go build performance can degrade, either remove your `pkg` directory by running the `rm -rf $GOPATH/pkg/` command or set up a new `GOPATH` for this recipe. Ensure that `$GOPATH` is set.

2. Build the `github.com/agtorre/go-cookbook/chapter6/grpc/server` package by running the `cd $GOPATH/src/github.com/agtorre/go-cookbook/chapter6/grpc/server` command.

3. Run the `time go build` command:

```
$ time go build .
go build 4.10s user 0.59s system 181% cpu 2.580 total
```

4. Test the `github.com/agtorre/go-cookbook/chapter6/grpc/server` package using the following command:

```
$ time go test
PASS
ok github.com/agtorre/go-cookbook/chapter6/grpc/server 0.014s
go test 4.01s user 0.60s system 176% cpu 2.608 total
```

5. Explore what's causing the 4-second builds; it doesn't appear to be the size of our project:

```
$ wc -l *.go
25 greeter.go
44 greeter_test.go
20 server.go
89 total
```

6. List all imports:

```
$ go list -f '{{ join .Imports "\n"}}'
fmt
github.com/agtorre/go-cookbook/chapter6/grpc/greeter
golang.org/x/net/context
google.golang.org/grpc
net

$go list -f '{{ join .Imports "\n"}}' github.com/agtorre/go-
cookbook/chapter6/grpc/greeter
fmt
github.com/golang/protobuf/proto
golang.org/x/net/context
google.golang.org/grpc
math
```

7. List dependencies instead; check the number. Note the difference when compared to an empty `main.go` file:

```
$ go list -f '{{ join .Deps "\n"}}' .
.
.
.
google.golang.org/grpc
google.golang.org/grpc/codes
google.golang.org/grpc/credentials
google.golang.org/grpc/grpclog
google.golang.org/grpc/internal
google.golang.org/grpc/metadata
```

```
google.golang.org/grpc/naming
google.golang.org/grpc/peer
google.golang.org/grpc/stats
google.golang.org/grpc/tap
google.golang.org/grpc/transport
.
.
.

$ go list -f '{{ join .Deps "\n"}}' . | wc -l
111

$ go list -f '{{ join .Deps "\n"}}' /path/to/empty/main/package |
wc -l
4
```

8. Speed it up:

```
$ cd $GOPATH/src/github.com/agtorre/go-
cookbook/chapter6/grpc/server
$ go install ./...
$ go test -i ./...
```

9. Try running the following commands again:

```
$ time go build .
go build . 0.65s user 0.15s system 117% cpu 0.683 total

$ time go test .
ok github.com/agtorre/go-cookbook/chapter6/grpc/server 0.015s
go test . 0.63s user 0.17s system 118% cpu 0.669 total
```

# How it works...

If you're experiencing slow Go compilation speed, there are a few things to consider. Firstly, Go 1.5 was the first Go compile written entirely in Go. This came with a large increase in compilation times, and every release since has improved this. If you're working with Go 1.5 or later, your first step should be upgrading to the latest version of Go.

Next, some analysis of dependencies can be critical. Some go packages have large dependency changes, and you may unknowingly be adding hundreds of thousands of lines of code with a single import. It's worthwhile analyzing your dependencies. This is possible with the Go list tool, but there are also third-party tools, including the new dep (`https://github.com/golang/dep`), godep (`https://github.com/tools/godep`), and glide (`https://github.com/Masterminds/glide`), and most vendor repositories will place all dependencies in the vendor directory.

Lastly, saving intermediate builds of libraries can often give a significant boost. This is accomplished with the `go install ./...` and `go test -i ./...` commands, which will create artifacts in the `pkg` directory. The `install` command does this for imported packages, and `go test -i` does the same for test packages. This can be useful if you're using a framework such as `goconvey`.

# Using the pprof tool

The pprof tools allows Go applications to collect and export runtime profiling data. It also provides web hooks to access the tool from a web interface. This recipe will create a basic application that verifies a bcrypt hashed password against a plaintext one, then it will profile the application.

You might expect the pprof tool to be in the `Chapter 10`, *Distributed Systems,*with other metrics and monitoring recipes. It was instead put in this chapter because it will be used to analyze and improve a program much in the same way benchmarking can be used. As a result, this recipe will largely focus on pprof for analyzing and improving the memory usage of an application.

# Getting ready

Configure your environment by performing these steps:

1. Refer to the *Getting ready* section of the *Speeding up compilation and testing cycles* recipe in this chapter.
2. Optionally, install Graphviz from `http://www.graphviz.org/Home.php`.

# How to do it...

These steps cover writing and running your application:

1. From your terminal/console application, create and navigate to the chapter13/pprof directory.

2. Copy tests from https://github.com/agtorre/go-cookbook/tree/master/chapter13/pprof
   or use this as an exercise to write some of your own code.

3. Create a directory named crypto and navigate to it.

4. Create a file called handler.go with the following content:

```go
package crypto

import (
    "net/http"

    "golang.org/x/crypto/bcrypt"
)

// GuessHandler checks if ?message=password
func GuessHandler(w http.ResponseWriter, r *http.Request) {
    r.ParseForm()

    msg := r.FormValue("message")

    // "password"
    real :=
    []byte("$2a$10$2ovnPWuIjMx2SOHvCxP/mutzdsGhyt8rq/
JqnJg/6OyC3B0APMG1K")

    if err := bcrypt.CompareHashAndPassword(real, []byte(msg));
    err != nil {
        w.WriteHeader(http.StatusBadRequest)
        w.Write([]byte("try again"))
        return
    }

    w.WriteHeader(http.StatusOK)
    w.Write([]byte("you got it"))
    return
}
```

5. Navigate up a directory.

6. Create a new directory named `example` and navigate to it.

7. Create a `main.go` file with the following content. Ensure that you modify the `crypto` import to use the path you set up in step 2:

```
package main

import (
    "fmt"
    "log"
    "net/http"
    _ "net/http/pprof"

    "github.com/agtorre/go-cookbook/chapter13/pprof/crypto"
)

func main() {

    http.HandleFunc("/guess", crypto.GuessHandler)
    fmt.Println("server started at localhost:8080")
    log.Panic(http.ListenAndServe("localhost:8080", nil))
}
```

8. Run `go run main.go`.

9. You may also run the following command:

```
go build
./example
```

You should now see the following output:

```
$ go run main.go
server started at localhost:8080
```

10. In a separate terminal, run the following:

```
$ go tool pprof http://localhost:8080/debug/pprof/profile
```

11. This will start a 30 second timer.

12. Run several curls while `pprof` runs:

```
$ curl "http://localhost:8080/guess?message=test"
try again

$curl "http://localhost:8080/guess?message=password"
you got it

  .
  .
  .
  .

$curl "http://localhost:8080/guess?message=password"
you got it
```

13. Return to the `pprof` command and wait for it to complete.

14. Run the `top10` command from the `pprof` command:

```
(pprof) top 10
930ms of 930ms total ( 100%)
Showing top 10 nodes out of 15 (cum >= 930ms)
flat flat% sum% cum cum%
870ms 93.55% 93.55% 870ms 93.55%
golang.org/x/crypto/blowfish.encryptBlock
30ms 3.23% 96.77% 900ms 96.77%
golang.org/x/crypto/blowfish.ExpandKey
30ms 3.23% 100% 30ms 3.23% runtime.memclrNoHeapPointers
0 0% 100% 930ms 100% github.com/agtorre/go-
cookbook/chapter13/pprof/crypto.GuessHandler
0 0% 100% 930ms 100%
golang.org/x/crypto/bcrypt.CompareHashAndPassword
0 0% 100% 30ms 3.23% golang.org/x/crypto/bcrypt.base64Encode
0 0% 100% 930ms 100% golang.org/x/crypto/bcrypt.bcrypt
0 0% 100% 900ms 96.77%
golang.org/x/crypto/bcrypt.expensiveBlowfishSetup
0 0% 100% 930ms 100% net/http.(*ServeMux).ServeHTTP
0 0% 100% 930ms 100% net/http.(*conn).serve
```

15. If you installed Graphviz, run the `pprof web` command. You should see something like this:

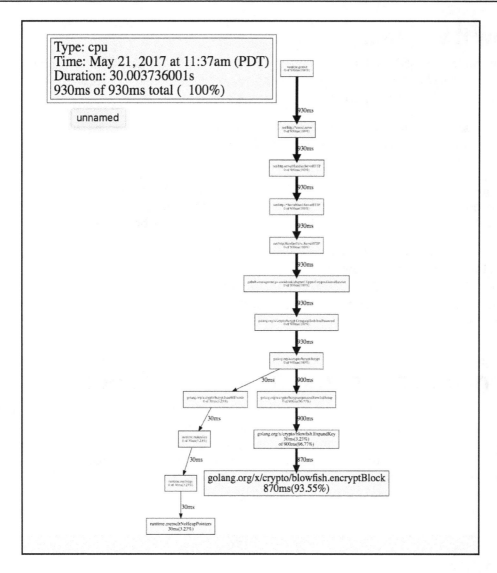

16. If you copied or wrote your own tests, go up one directory and run `go test`.
    Ensure that all the tests pass.

# How it works...

The pprof tool provides a lot of runtime information about your application. Using the `net/pprof` package is usually the most simple to configure--all that's required is listening on a port and doing an import.

In our case, we wrote a handler that uses a very compute-heavy applications (bcrypt) so that we can demonstrate how they pop up when profiling with pprof. This will quickly isolate chunks of code that are creating bottlenecks in your application.

We chose to collect a general profile that causes pprof to poll our application endpoint for 30 seconds. We then generated traffic against the endpoint to help produce results. This can be helpful when you're attempting to check a single handler or branch of code.

Lastly, we looked at the top 10 functions in terms of CPU utilization. It's also possible to look at memory/heap management with the `pprof` `http://localhost:8080/debug/pprof/heap` command. The `pprof web` command can be used to look at a visualization of your CPU/memory profile and helps highlight more active code.

# Benchmarking and finding bottlenecks

Another method for determining slow parts of code is to use benchmarks. Benchmarks can be used to test functions for average performance and can also run benchmarks in parallel. This can be useful when comparing functions or doing micro-optimizations for certain code, especially to see how a function implementation might perform when using it concurrently. For this recipe, we'll create two structs that both implement an atomic counter. The first will use the `sync` package, and the other will use `sync/atomic`. We'll then benchmark both the solutions.

# Getting ready

Refer to the *Getting ready* section of the *Speeding up compilation and testing cycles* recipe in this chapter.

# How to do it...

These steps cover writing and running your application:

1. From your terminal/console application, create the `chapter13/bench` directory and navigate to it.

2. Copy tests from `https://github.com/agtorre/go-cookbook/tree/master/chapter13/bench`or use this as an exercise to write some of your own code.

 Note that copied tests also include benchmarks written later in this recipe.

3. Create a file called `lock.go` with the following content:

```go
package bench

import "sync"

// Counter uses a sync.RWMutex to safely
// modify a value
type Counter struct {
    value int64
    mu *sync.RWMutex
}

// Add increments the counter
func (c *Counter) Add(amount int64) {
    c.mu.Lock()
    c.value += amount
    c.mu.Unlock()
}

// Read returns the current counter amount
func (c *Counter) Read() int64 {
    c.mu.RLock()
    defer c.mu.RUnlock()
    return c.value
}
```

4. Create a file called `atomic.go` with the following content:

```go
package bench

import "sync/atomic"
```

```
// AtomicCounter implements an atmoic lock
// using the atomic package
type AtomicCounter struct {
    value int64
}

// Add increments the counter
func (c *AtomicCounter) Add(amount int64) {
    atomic.AddInt64(&c.value, amount)
}

// Read returns the current counter amount
func (c *AtomicCounter) Read() int64 {
    var result int64
    result = atomic.LoadInt64(&c.value)
    return result
}
```

5. Create a file called `lock_test.go` with the following content:

```
package bench

import "testing"

func BenchmarkCounterAdd(b *testing.B) {
    c := Counter{0, &sync.RWMutex{}}
    for n := 0; n < b.N; n++ {
        c.Add(1)
    }
}

func BenchmarkCounterRead(b *testing.B) {
    c := Counter{0, &sync.RWMutex{}}
    for n := 0; n < b.N; n++ {
        c.Read()
    }
}

func BenchmarkCounterAddRead(b *testing.B) {
    c := Counter{0, &sync.RWMutex{}}
    b.RunParallel(func(pb *testing.PB) {
        for pb.Next() {
            c.Add(1)
            c.Read()
        }
    })
}
```

6. Create a file called `atomic_test.go` with the following content:

```
package bench

import "testing"

func BenchmarkAtomicCounterAdd(b *testing.B) {
    c := AtomicCounter{0}
    for n := 0; n < b.N; n++ {
        c.Add(1)
    }
}

func BenchmarkAtomicCounterRead(b *testing.B) {
    c := AtomicCounter{0}
    for n := 0; n < b.N; n++ {
        c.Read()
    }
}

func BenchmarkAtomicCounterAddRead(b *testing.B) {
    c := AtomicCounter{0}
    b.RunParallel(func(pb *testing.PB) {
        for pb.Next() {
            c.Add(1)
            c.Read()
        }
    })
}
```

7. Run the `go test -bench1` command, and you will see the following output:

```
$ go test -bench .
BenchmarkAtomicCounterAdd-4 200000000 8.38 ns/op
BenchmarkAtomicCounterRead-4 1000000000 2.09 ns/op
BenchmarkAtomicCounterAddRead-4 50000000 24.5 ns/op
BenchmarkCounterAdd-4 50000000 34.8 ns/op
BenchmarkCounterRead-4 20000000 66.0 ns/op
BenchmarkCounterAddRead-4 10000000 146 ns/op
PASS
ok github.com/agtorre/go-cookbook/chapter13/bench 10.919s
```

8. If you copied or wrote your own tests, go up one directory and run `go test`. Ensure that all the tests pass.

# How it works...

This recipe is an example of comparing a critical path of code. For example, sometimes your application must execute certain functionality often, maybe every call. In this case, we've written an atomic counter that can add or read values from multiple go routines.

The first solution uses `RWMutex` and `Lock` or `RLock` objects to write and read, respectively. The second uses the atomic package that provides the same functionality out of the box. We make the signatures of our functions the same, so benchmarks can be reused with minor modifications and so that either can satisfy the same atomic integer interface.

Lastly, we write standard benchmarks for adding values and reading them. Then, we write a parallel benchmark that calls the add and read functions. The parallel benchmark will create lot of lock contention, so we expect a slowdown. Perhaps unexpectedly, the atomic package significantly outperforms `RWMutex`.

# Memory allocation and heap management

Some applications can benefit a lot from optimization. Consider routers, for example, which we'll look at in a later recipe. Fortunately, the tool benchmark suite provides flags to collect a number of memory allocations as well as memory allocation size. It can be helpful to tune certain critical code paths to minimize these two attributes.

This recipe will show two approaches to writing a function that glues together strings with a space, similar to `strings.Join("a", "b", "c")`. One approach will use concatenation, while the other will use the `strings` package. We'll then compare performance and memory allocations between the two.

# Getting ready

Refer to the *Getting ready* section of the *Speeding up compilation and testing cycles* recipe in this chapter.

# How to do it...

These steps cover writing and running your application:

1. From your terminal/console application, create the `chapter13/tuning` directory and navigate to it.

2. Copy tests from `https://github.com/agtorre/go-cookbook/tree/master/cha pter13/tuning`or use this as an exercise to write some of your own code.

Note that copied tests also include benchmarks written later in this recipe.

3. Create a file called `concat.go` with the following content:

```
package tuning

func concat(vals ...string) string {
    finalVal := ""
    for i := 0; i < len(vals); i++ {
        finalVal += vals[i]
        if i != len(vals)-1 {
            finalVal += " "
        }
    }
    return finalVal
}
```

4. Create a file called `join.go` with the following content:

```
package tuning

import "strings"

func join(vals ...string) string {
    c := strings.Join(vals, " ")
    return c
}
```

5. Create a file called `concat_test.go` with the following content:

```
package tuning

import "testing"

func Benchmark_concat(b *testing.B) {
    b.Run("one", func(b *testing.B) {
        one := []string{"1"}
        for i := 0; i < b.N; i++ {
            concat(one...)
        }
    })
```

```
        b.Run("five", func(b *testing.B) {
            five := []string{"1", "2", "3", "4", "5"}
            for i := 0; i < b.N; i++ {
                concat(five...)
            }
        })

        b.Run("ten", func(b *testing.B) {
            ten := []string{"1", "2", "3", "4", "5",
            "6", "7", "8", "9", "10"}
            for i := 0; i < b.N; i++ {
                concat(ten...)
            }
        })
    }
```

6. Create a file called `join_test.go` with the following content:

```
package tuning

import "testing"

func Benchmark_join(b *testing.B) {
    b.Run("one", func(b *testing.B) {
        one := []string{"1"}
        for i := 0; i < b.N; i++ {
            join(one...)
        }
    })
    b.Run("five", func(b *testing.B) {
        five := []string{"1", "2", "3", "4", "5"}
        for i := 0; i < b.N; i++ {
            join(five...)
        }
    })

    b.Run("ten", func(b *testing.B) {
        ten := []string{"1", "2", "3", "4", "5",
        "6", "7", "8", "9", "10"}
        for i := 0; i < b.N; i++ {
            join(ten...)
        }
    })
}
```

7. Run the `GOMAXPROCS=1 go test -bench=. -benchmem -benchtime=1s` command and you will see the following output:

```
$ GOMAXPROCS=1 go test -bench=. -benchmem -benchtime=1s
Benchmark_concat/one 100000000 13.6 ns/op 0 B/op 0 allocs/op
Benchmark_concat/five 5000000 386 ns/op 48 B/op 8 allocs/op
Benchmark_concat/ten 2000000 992 ns/op 256 B/op 18 allocs/op
Benchmark_join/one 200000000 6.30 ns/op 0 B/op 0 allocs/op
Benchmark_join/five 10000000 124 ns/op 32 B/op 2 allocs/op
Benchmark_join/ten 10000000 183 ns/op 64 B/op 2 allocs/op
PASS
ok github.com/agtorre/go-cookbook/chapter13/tuning 12.003s
```

8. If you copied or wrote your own tests, go up one directory and run `go test`. Ensure that all the tests pass.

# How it works...

Benchmarking helps us tune applications and do certain micro-optimizations for things such as memory allocations. When benchmarking allocations for applications with input, it's important to try a variety of input sizes to determine if it affects allocations. We wrote two functions, `concat` and `join`. Both join together a `variadic` string parameter with spaces, so the arguments (*a, b, c*) will return the string *a b c*.

The `concat` approach accomplishes this solely through string concatenation. We create a string and append the strings in the list and spaces in a `for` loop. We omit adding a space on the last loop. The `join` function uses the internal `Strings.Join` function to accomplish this far more efficiently in most cases. It can be helpful to benchmark standard library compared to your own functions to help better understand tradeoffs in performance, simplicity, and functionality.

We used sub-benchmarks to test all of our parameters, which also work excellently with table-driven benchmarks. We can see how the `concat` approach results in a lot more allocations than join, at least for single length inputs. A good exercise would be to try this with variable length input strings as well as number of arguments.

# Vendoring and project layout

Vendoring Go applications is still a largely unresolved issue. There are discussions and plans to produce an official vendoring solution (`https://github.com/golang/dep`), but it's very early days and things are far from complete. For now, there are a number of alternative solutions. By default, you can place packages into a local vendor directory to use them instead of those in your `GOPATH` environment variable. This allows packages to pin on the version in their vendor directory and allows for reproducible builds without having to commit your entire `GOPATH` into version control. Most package managers take advantage of this. For this recipe, we'll explore the layout for a web application and how to manage its vendor dependencies with `godep github.com/tools/godep`, a popular tool for managing dependencies.

# Getting ready

Configure your environment by performing these steps:

1. Refer to the *Getting ready* section of the *Speeding up compilation and testing cycles* recipe in this chapter.
2. Run the `go get github.com/tools/godep` command.
3. Run the `go get github.com/sirupsen/logrus` command.

# How to do it...

These steps cover writing and running your application:

1. From your terminal/console application, create the `chapter13/vendoring` directory and navigate to it.
2. Copy tests from `https://github.com/agtorre/go-cookbook/tree/master/chapter13/vendoring`
   or use this as an exercise to write some of your own code.
3. Create a directory named `models` and navigate to it.

4. Create a file called `models.go` with the following content:

```go
package models

import "sync/atomic"

// DB Interface is our storage
// layer
type DB interface {
    GetScore() (int64, error)
    SetScore(int64) error
}

// NewDB returns our db struct that
// satisfies DB interface
func NewDB() DB {
    return &db{0}
}

type db struct {
    score int64
}

// GetScore returns the score atomically
func (d *db) GetScore() (int64, error) {
    return atomic.LoadInt64(&d.score), nil
}

// SetScore stores a new value atomically
func (d *db) SetScore(score int64) error {
    atomic.StoreInt64(&d.score, score)
    return nil
}
```

5. Navigate back up a directory.
6. Create a directory named `handlers` and navigate to it.
7. Create a file called `controller.go` with the following content:

```go
package handlers

import "github.com/agtorre/go-
cookbook/chapter13/vendoring/models"

type Controller struct {
    db models.DB
}
```

```
func NewController(db models.DB) *Controller {
    return &Controller{db: db}
}

type resp struct {
    Status string `json:"status"`
    Value int64 `json:"value"`
}
```

8. Create a file called get.go with the following content:

```
package handlers

import (
    "encoding/json"
    "net/http"

    "github.com/sirupsen/logrus"
)

// GetHandler returns the current score in a resp object
func (c *Controller) GetHandler(w http.ResponseWriter, r
*http.Request) {
    enc := json.NewEncoder(w)
    payload := resp{Status: "error"}
    oldScore, err := c.db.GetScore()
    if err != nil {
        logrus.WithField("error", err).Error("failed to get the
        score")
        w.WriteHeader(http.StatusInternalServerError)
        enc.Encode(&payload)
        return
    }
    w.WriteHeader(http.StatusOK)
    payload.Value = oldScore
    payload.Status = "ok"
    enc.Encode(&payload)
}
```

9. Create a file called set.go with the following content:

```
package handlers

import (
    "encoding/json"
    "net/http"
    "strconv"
```

```
    "github.com/sirupsen/logrus"
)

// SetHandler Sets the value, and returns it in a resp
func (c *Controller) SetHandler(w http.ResponseWriter, r
*http.Request) {
    enc := json.NewEncoder(w)
    payload := resp{Status: "error"}
    r.ParseForm()
    val := r.FormValue("score")
    score, err := strconv.ParseInt(val, 10, 64)
    if err != nil {
        logrus.WithField("error", err).Error("failed to parse
        input")
        w.WriteHeader(http.StatusBadRequest)
        enc.Encode(&payload)
        return
    }

    if err := c.db.SetScore(score); err != nil {
        logrus.WithField("error", err).Error("failed to set the
        score")
        w.WriteHeader(http.StatusInternalServerError)
        enc.Encode(&payload)
        return
    }
    w.WriteHeader(http.StatusOK)
    payload.Value = score
    payload.Status = "ok"
    enc.Encode(&payload)
}
```

10. Vendor your dependencies:

```
$ godep save ./...
$ cat Godeps/Godeps.json
{
"ImportPath": "github.com/agtorre/go-
cookbook/chapter13/vendoring",
"GoVersion": "go1.8",
"GodepVersion": "v79",
"Packages": [
"./..."
],
"Deps": [
{
"ImportPath": "github.com/sirupsen/logrus",
"Comment": "v0.11.2-1-g3f603f4",
```

```
"Rev": "3f603f494d61c73457fb234161d8982b9f0f0b71"
},
{
"ImportPath": "golang.org/x/sys/unix",
"Rev": "dbc2be9168a660ef302e04b6ff6406de6f967473"
}
]
}
```

11. Navigate up one directory.

12. Create a file called `main.go` with the following content:

```
package main

import (
    "net/http"

    "github.com/agtorre/go-
    cookbook/chapter13/vendoring/handlers"
    "github.com/agtorre/go-cookbook/chapter13/vendoring/models"
    "github.com/sirupsen/logrus"
)

func main() {
    c := handlers.NewController(models.NewDB())

    logrus.SetFormatter(&logrus.JSONFormatter{})

    http.HandleFunc("/get", c.GetHandler)
    http.HandleFunc("/set", c.SetHandler)
    fmt.Println("server started at localhost:8080")
    panic(http.ListenAndServe("localhost:8080", nil))
}
```

13. Run `go run main.go`.

14. You may also run the following command:

```
go build
./vendoring
```

You should see the following output:

```
$ go run main.go
server started at localhost:8080
```

15. In a separate terminal, run some curls:

```
$ curl "http://localhost:8080/set?score=24"
{"status":"ok","value":24}

$ curl "http://localhost:8080/get"
{"status":"ok","value":24}

$ curl "http://localhost:8080/set?score=abc"
{"status":"error","value":0}
```

16. Look at the server logs:

```
{"error":"strconv.ParseInt: parsing \"abc\": invalid
syntax","level":"error","msg":"failed to parse
input","time":"2017-05-26T20:49:47-07:00"}
```

17. If you copied or wrote your own tests, run `go test`. Ensure that all the tests pass.

# How it works...

This recipe shows how to separate basic concerns in an applications. For resources such as models or clients, it's good to first create an interface for what actions it will perform, then satisfy that interface and provide convenient setup functions. Model/client code will also frequently produce custom error types.

Next, we create our controller and handlers, which isolate all client requests to the server. The `Controller` object uses the storage interface, making it easy to swap storage solutions without modifying application code. Lastly, `main.go` is used to set up routes, initialize controllers, and configure things such as logging. We use a package-level global logger so that any of our methods can freely log if needed. We still try to log only when we're dealing with an error rather than whenever we encounter and quickly return one.

We used logrus as our logging system, which introduced a dependency that we'd like to vendor for ease of reproducible builds. We used the Godep tool to store a local copy of logrus in our vendor directory. Checkouts of this project will use the pinned version in vendors for future builds and it can be upgraded when ready.

# Using fasthttprouter and fasthttp

Although the Go standard library provides everything you would need to run an HTTP server, sometimes you need to further optimize for things such as routing and request time. This recipe will explore a library that speeds up request handling called `fasthttp` (`https://github.com/valyala/fasthttp`) and a router, that dramatically speeds up routing performance called `fasthttprouter` (`https://github.com/buaazp/fasthttprouter`). Although fasthttp is quick, it's important to note that it doesn't support HTTP/2 (`https://github.com/valyala/fasthttp/issues/45`).

# Getting ready

Configure your environment by performing these steps:

1. Refer to the *Getting ready* section of the *Speeding up compilation and testing cycles* recipe in this chapter.
2. Run the `go get github.com/buaazp/fasthttprouter` command.
3. Run the `go get github.com/valyala/fasthttp` command.

# How to do it...

These steps cover writing and running your application:

1. From your terminal/console application, create the `chapter13/fastweb` directory and navigate to it.
2. Copy tests from `https://github.com/agtorre/go-cookbook/tree/master/chapter13/fastweb`or use this as an exercise to write some of your own code.
3. Create a file called `items.go` with the following content:

```go
package main

import (
    "sync"
)

var items []string
var mu *sync.RWMutex

func init() {
    mu = &sync.RWMutex{}
```

```
}

// AddItem adds an item to our list
// in a thread-safe way
func AddItem(item string) {
    mu.Lock()
    items = append(items, item)
    mu.Unlock()
}

// ReadItems returns our list of items
// in a thread-safe way
func ReadItems() []string {
    mu.RLock()
    defer mu.RUnlock()
    return items
}
```

4. Create a file called `handlers.go` with the following content:

```
package main

import (
    "encoding/json"

    "github.com/valyala/fasthttp"
)

// GetItems will return our items object
func GetItems(ctx *fasthttp.RequestCtx) {
    enc := json.NewEncoder(ctx)
    items := ReadItems()
    enc.Encode(&items)
    ctx.SetStatusCode(fasthttp.StatusOK)
}

// AddItems modifies our array
func AddItems(ctx *fasthttp.RequestCtx) {
    item, ok := ctx.UserValue("item").(string)
    if !ok {
        ctx.SetStatusCode(fasthttp.StatusBadRequest)
    }

    AddItem(item)
    ctx.SetStatusCode(fasthttp.StatusOK)
}
```

5. Create a file called `main.go` with the following content:

```go
package main

import (
    "fmt"
    "log"

    "github.com/buaazp/fasthttprouter"
    "github.com/valyala/fasthttp"
)

func main() {
    router := fasthttprouter.New()
    router.GET("/item", GetItems)
    router.POST("/item/:item", AddItems)

    fmt.Println("server starting on localhost:8080")
    log.Fatal(fasthttp.ListenAndServe("localhost:8080",
    router.Handler))
}
```

6. Run the `go build` command.
7. Run the `./fastweb` command:

```
$ ./fastweb
server starting on localhost:8080
```

8. From a separate terminal, test it our with some curls:

```
$ curl "http://localhost:8080/item/hi" -X POST

$ curl "http://localhost:8080/item/how" -X POST

$ curl "http://localhost:8080/item/are" -X POST

$ curl "http://localhost:8080/item/you" -X POST

$ curl "http://localhost:8080/item" -X GET
["hi","how", "are", "you"]
```

9. If you copied or wrote your own tests, run `go test`. Ensure that all the tests pass.

# How it works...

The `fasthttp` and `fasthttprouter` packages can do a lot to speed up the life cycle of a web request. Both packages do a lot of optimization on the hot path of code, but with the unfortunate caveat of rewriting your handlers to use a new context object rather than traditional requests and response writer.

There are a number of frameworks that have taken a similar approach to routing, and some have directly incorporated `fasthttp`. These projects keep up-to-date information in their README files.

Our recipe implemented a simple list object that we can append to with one endpoint and that will be returned by the other. The primary purpose of this recipe is to demonstrate working with parameters, setting up a router that now explicitly defines the supported methods instead of the generic `Handle` and `HandleFunc`, and to show how similar it is to standard handlers, but with many other benefits.

# Index